~The~
FORGOTTEN
HISTORY of
AMERICA

~ The ~
FORGOTTEN
HISTORY of
AMERICA

Little-Known Conflicts of Lasting Importance from the Earliest Colonists to the Eve of the Revolution

CORMAC O'BRIEN

CRESTLINE

This edition published in 2013 by
CRESTLINE
a division of BOOK SALES, INC.
276 Fifth Avenue Suite 206
New York, New York 10001
USA

This edition published by arrangement with Fair Winds Press.

First published in the USA in 2008 by
Fair Winds Press, a member of
Quayside Publishing Group
100 Cummings Center
Suite 406-L
Beverly, MA 01915-6101
www.fairwindspress.com

10 9 8 7 6 5 4 3 2

Library of Congress Cataloging-in-Publication Data
O'Brien, Cormac, 1967-
    The forgotten history of America / Cormac O'Brien.
        p.   cm.
    Includes bibliographical references and index.
    ISBN: 978-0-7858-3058-0
    1. United States--History--Colonial period, ca. 1600-1775. I. Title.
  E188.O37 2008
  973.3--dc22

                        2008008138

Cover and book design: Peter Long
Book layout: doublemranch.com

Cover: The Pilgrims depicted in this seventeenth-century English woodcut escape religious persecution
in Europe by departing for the New World, as symbolized by a man being burned atop a funeral pyre,
at left, and the Mayflower, at right. Religious, ethnic, and cultural differences would greet them as
they clashed with native peoples and other Europeans for control of the vast, untamed wildness of
North America.

Printed and bound in China

For Berit—May yours be a more peaceful time.

Contents

Introduction

The American Revolution did more than forge a nation. It also, by its formative nature, created a watershed that seemed to co-opt the significance of all that preceded it. The result, unfortunately, is a kind of temporal inversion: If 1776 marks a beginning, it is also seen as a portal in reverse, where the look backward into America's "before time" begins.

But colonial history hardly needed the Declaration of Independence to give it meaning. The complex two and a half centuries that preceded that document's germination in Thomas Jefferson's head comprised a tumultuous American epic in its own right that, it should be remembered, could easily have turned out very differently.

This book takes a look back at that "before time" on its own terms, capturing important clashes in early American history that have been left behind in the popular imagination. These are moments of conflict that show America as it once was—a raw, indomitable wilderness where divergent worlds struggled to coexist and where empires, both European and Native American, were built and toppled for causes that today seem both exotic and familiar, by turns.

The meeting of the Old and New Worlds began ominously. Indeed, the first North Americans had cause to dread the coming of Europeans to their shores before the latter even arrived. In the south, beginning with Hernán Cortés's 1519 adventure, Spain began expanding her empire from the Caribbean into Mexico, while in the north, fishermen from all over Europe had been filling their nets off the Grand Banks since the time of Columbus's first voyage in 1492, making occasional visits to the Canadian coast.

From these directions, Old World diseases like smallpox crept furtively into North America and then swept like wildfire up and down the continent throughout the sixteenth century. With no genetic resistance to these new afflictions, native populations from Canada to Texas reeled before the invisible onslaught. Most scholars maintain that more than 50 percent of North America's Indian population—and perhaps as much as 90 percent—died during these devastating years, all from microscopic killers whose original hosts had yet to appear in any significant numbers.

When the Europeans themselves arrived, in the sixteenth and early seventeenth centuries, they came to a ravaged land. Disease had profoundly shaped the events to come: Whether in the Gulf of Mexico, the Chesapeake, or New England, these fair-skinned newcomers embarked upon their new epoch alongside indigenous nations that were but a shadow of their former selves. Nevertheless, Amerindian cultures endured-though having suffered epidemics, the people of North America were as vital as ever.

And disease wasn't all that Europeans had brought with them. Armed, self-righteous, bigoted, and acquisitive, they also brought their wars. Catholics fought with Protestants, Spanish with French, English with Dutch, and French with English. As Europe had been for so many generations, so the American wilderness would become: a battleground between implacable factions.

But the Amerindians, of course, had their own implacable factions—and though the issues over which they fought were as esoteric as anything that drove their new Christian neighbors to kill, these original Americans had the added concern of standing their ground before an advancing, swelling tide of strangers from lands they found difficult to imagine. The scene was set for a saga of unusual complexity, on a stage of arresting beauty, awesome size, and daunting extremes. And the stakes could not have been higher: possession of a continent's fate.

If there was any possibility that this meeting of worlds could have turned out peacefully, it vanished with the burgeoning of that same impulse that drew white men to America's shores in the first place: greed.

Both of English America's legendary founding settlements, Jamestown and Plymouth, established their initial footholds—in 1607 and 1620, respectively—with the aid of native peoples who chose, at least at first, to accept their new neighbors rather than simply drive them outright into the sea. But in both regions, differences of perception and culture that proved too large to bridge produced violence and enduring enmity, not least because the English could not reconcile their expansionist nature with the alliances they were creating to ensure their own survival.

For their part, the Indians, ever on the lookout for opportunities they could control, found nothing but confusing extremes in the Europeans they wished to exploit as allies, compelling them to act out of concern for the future. In both Jamestown and

Plymouth, divisions rent the European and Indian camps; in both cases, fear and war ultimately triumphed.

This is the theme of *The Forgotten History of America*. Across the river valleys and mountain passes that we now know as much of the United States, conflict was as regular as the first winter snow, as if the causes that drew people to accept America's challenge took on a fury as great as the wilderness itself.

In the 1530s Álvar Núñez Cabeza de Vaca and three companions walked from the Texas coast through the Great Plains to the Pacific coast of Mexico, sustained by native populations who saw them as healers, only to return to a Spanish empire in which there was no room for such trust between Europeans and Indians. Their story, the first in this book, would play out again and again over the ages.

The Puritans and Indians of New England would exchange a tenuous peace for a long cycle of wars; Dutch New Amsterdam and its English neighbors, once allies in the cause of Protestantism, would slide into a commercial rivalry from which only one could emerge; the French, English, and Indian dominions of North America would find an escalation of hostilities far more attractive than the effort to accommodate each other.

Pushed to the margins of our collective memory by the march of time, the stories here are snapshots of a long-ago reality—one that could not have been more different from the unifying political experiment that followed it. Though not as familiar as many of history's other tales of strife, they are just as important, and often more fascinating. And they help us understand the world that gave birth to our own.

chapter one

Four Castaways Become the First Men of the Old World to Span the New

1528-1536

As far as the eye could see, in every direction stretched a wilderness of green water and rotting tree trunks. Encumbered by armor and gear, the men sloshed and clambered noisily in the chest-high water, eyes shifting nervously to the left and right.

The column, some three hundred strong and heavily armed, looked out of place in these primeval surroundings. Its members were far from home, though one—conspicuous for his nudity, his massive size, and the iron collar about his neck—was an Indian who had been impressed as an unwilling guide. Clumsy and tense, the party staggered through the engulfing swamp, heedless of the predators that stalked their every move.

And then the arrows came hissing at them from seemingly everywhere. Horses reared and screeched in the chaos, soldiers fumbled with their weapons, and the water churned red. Like spirits of the wood, dark shapes moved lithely in the middle distance from log to stump, loosing streams of singing missiles. The Spaniards in their steel carapaces ducked beneath the fusillade, desperate to find an advantage in this alien world, but virtually helpless.

Rage soon overcame them, and the column lurched toward what looked like firm ground. But the Indians were waiting for them there, and a hot fight ensued. Hacking and slashing their way onto terra firma, the Spanish forced their enemies back, and the Indians—as was their custom—scattered into the trees. The conquistadores gathered their wits and saw to the wounded.

Pánfilo de Narváez and his men, shown here staring out at the Gulf of Mexico, were the first Europeans to encounter the native peoples of Texas, and possibly New Mexico and Arizona as well.

IN TOO DEEP

The man who had led them into this ghastly situation was one of the unluckiest conquistadores in the history of Spain's New World adventures. Pánfilo de Narváez had landed with several hundred men on the western coast of Florida, near what is today Tampa Bay, the previous April, in 1528. There, he had instructed the ships to meet him farther up the coast while he and his soldiers struck inland in search of treasure, especially silver or gold. It was now the end of July, and treasure was nowhere in sight.

His little army had gotten as far north as the land of the Apalachee, a nation of unusually tall warriors who employed tremendous bows with deadly accuracy. After rudely occupying a local village and depriving it of much of its food, Narváez decided that it was time to head back toward the sea in the hopes of linking up with his naval contingent. Now, having been led into an Apalachee ambush by their captive guide (who had managed to give his captors the slip during the melee), these wet and hungry warriors of Spain were wondering whether the whole expedition had been a terrible idea.

For God and Gold

The rough handling by Indians in the Florida swamps was merely the latest in a long line of hardships that had plagued the Narváez expedition from its outset. Narváez, a Spaniard who now made his home on the island of Cuba, hoped to join the ranks of Spain's most illustrious conquistadores—men like Hernán Cortés, who, just a few years before, had conquered the mighty Aztec empire with its dazzling capital at Tenochtitlán.

It was an age of immense possibilities for those willing to take equally immense risks. Since Christopher Columbus had stumbled into what increasingly seemed like a whole New World, men of Spain—mostly *hidalgos*, or those of minor nobility, hoping to increase their fortunes—had been making the trip across the Atlantic to settle new lands and discover others that had yet to be seen by European eyes.

There were many ways for such men to make a fortune, including the ruthless enslavement of the indigenous peoples for free labor—an enterprise that became harder with time as Old World diseases, to which the Indians had no immunity, gradually claimed whole populations of natives. Such brutal realities, along with the impulse to conquer "unknown" kingdoms, drove adventurers into missions of discovery, expanding the borders of Spain's empire.

Narváez was typical of these men. In 1526 he appealed to his sovereign, Charles V, for a license to settle the recently discovered Gulf Coast. Such arrangements were typical: Individual ambition drove the expansion of the Spanish empire. The crown, eager to benefit from the exploits of its subjects and increase its growing realm, sanctioned but rarely initiated these expeditions.

By issuing licenses and grants to his enterprising subjects, the king could control the process and ensure his cut of the profits (a tax that would come to be known, rather notoriously, as the "royal fifth"). The contract bound Narváez to a list of requirements, including the creation of fortifications and the settlement of towns. Nevertheless, this was essentially a private enterprise: The cost of the operation would be born by Narváez, who called in old debts and got creditors to share the risk.

And there was more than enough risk to go around, as Narváez soon discovered. By the time he had made landfall in April 1528, he had lost more than a hundred men to desertion and another sixty to a hurricane (along with two ships and numerous horses), been laid up on some shoals off Cuba for three weeks, and been blown off course in the Gulf.

Incredibly, things would only get worse.

Overleaf: The colonization of the great Aztec city of Tenochtitlán by Spanish explorer Hernán Cortés is shown here. More than a decade later, Cortes would joyfully receive Cabeza de Vaca at his table in Tenochtitlan following de Vaca's discovery of America's southwest.

In fact, things were going to get much worse for this doomed group of gold-seekers. The Narváez mission would disintegrate into a tragic disaster. But it would spawn one of the most astounding episodes of the sixteenth century: Set adrift in a vast and hostile land, four of the expedition's survivors would undertake an incredible journey for survival that, in the process, would mark the very first encounter between Europeans (and one African) and the Amerindian peoples of what is now Texas, and possibly New Mexico and Arizona, as well.

Though all but forgotten today, the journey of Cabeza de Vaca and his three companions was the true "first contact" of southern North America—and, sadly, an experience whose message of tolerance was drowned in a much wider tableau of violence and exploitation.

BEYOND THE ISLAND OF MISFORTUNE

The figure emerged out of the vast Texas plain with the deliberate gait of a veteran wanderer. Slung with pouches and draped in rags, he stared ahead and listened more intently with every measured step. The ocean could not be much farther.

His name was Álvar Núñez Cabeza de Vaca, and the year was 1533—five years since he and the others had first landed in Florida with delusions of grandeur. His extraordinary name, which meant "cow's head," owed its origins to the medieval reconquest of Moorish Spain by Christian forces. When King Sancho of Navarre was seeking a way to outflank his Muslim opponents in the thirteenth century, a humble shepherd offered to show him the way by marking the crucial pass in question with a cow's skull. Sancho was victorious, and he rewarded the shepherd with noble status and the title of Cabeza de Vaca. Álvar Núñez was a direct descendent.

But that was a long time ago, and his colorful name was good for nothing in these hostile wastes. Narváez was long dead, as were so many that had tied their fates to his hazardous dream. Hired as treasurer for the expedition, Cabeza de Vaca now plied a very different trade—that of itinerant peddler.

CABEZA DE VACA'S REPUTATION PRECEDED HIM. HE HAD BEEN PEDDLING FOR FOUR YEARS NOW, STAYING ALIVE BY FILLING A CRUCIAL NEED AMONG THE TEXAS TRIBES, AND BECOMING A LEGEND IN THE PROCESS.

Cabeza de Vaca and his companions trade beads with Amerindians, who viewed the Spaniards as shamans.

Ignoring the dust in his throat as he scanned the horizon for signs of the sea, he recalled the saga of horrors that had brought him to this point—the 1528 expedition that had begun with such promise. It now seemed so long ago . . .

Narváez had calculated badly back in 1528; having separated from his ships along a coast whose awesome length was entirely unknown, he had merely ensured that he would never see them again. He and his soldiers were castaways. After escaping the predations of the Apalachee and making it back to the Gulf, the army fashioned boats from the meager materials at hand and set itself adrift in the Gulf of Mexico, hoping to row west toward Mexico and civilization.

Esteban the Black was the first African to cross North America. Despite eight years of relative freedom traveling with Cabeza de Vaca, he was later sold to the governor of New Galicia.

Storms and currents savaged the little fleet, scattering it to the four winds. By the time Cabeza de Vaca guided his particular boat onto an island that is now largely thought to be Galveston, most of his shipmates lingered close to death. Due to starvation and other privations, this stretch of the barrier along the Texas coast would come to be known in the coming weeks as the Island of Misfortune. Death hung about the stranded Spaniards like a curse.

Not for want of help from the locals. In fact, the Indians of "Malhado," as the island was known, were welcoming and generous to the beleaguered conquistadores. But they themselves soon succumbed to a mortal sickness, perhaps brought from the Europeans. Malhado had become a death trap.

Just as ominously, the locals changed their tune and began to treat Cabeza de Vaca with scorn and cruelty. Escaping their control and leaving the island, he remained as determined as ever to return to New Spain, which he knew waited in Mexico. In time he met up with a people known as the Charucco, who took him on as a traveling salesman;

isolated from neighboring peoples by their own warlike habits, the Charucco were look-ing for someone to barter goods on their behalf. And so the lost Spaniard found his new vocation.

He could smell the ocean now, and strained to quicken his pace. About him hung the wares he expected to trade to the coastal Indians: flints for hunting and skinning, ocher for smearing on the face, and sturdy canes to be fashioned into the shafts of arrows. He expected to get plenty of shells and shark teeth in exchange for these valu-ables, as well as some smoked fish. Cabeza de Vaca's reputation preceded him. He had been doing this for four years now, staying alive by filling a crucial need among the Texas tribes, and becoming a legend in the process. But wherever his trading took him, he had never stopped thinking of making it to Mexico.

It lay west and south, across hundreds of miles of unknown territory—a trip he could not make alone. All his hopes had been pinned on Lope de Oviedo, a fellow cast-away who had remained on Malhado. Every year Cabeza de Vaca returned to the island and tried to convince Oviedo to attempt the journey with him. And every year Oviedo had refused, convinced that virtual slavery among a heathen people was preferable to death in a strange and hostile land.

Now, as the blue expanse of the ocean came into view, Cabeza de Vaca dared to hope yet again. Soon he would be on Malhado—and, perhaps this year, Oviedo would relent.

ESCAPE TO THE WILDERNESS

Oviedo was convinced, but not thoroughly enough. He eventually turned back to Malhado, where he stayed. There he would live like the natives, satisfied to live without the trappings of the empire that he had once taken for granted.

The intrepid Cabeza de Vaca, having fallen in with a people known as the Quevenes, decided to go on alone, fortified with a rumor that other shipwrecked survivors of the expedition were living in captivity to the south. The Quevenes beat and degraded him for sport, happy to keep him in a state of frightened servitude. Biding his time, he even-tually encountered Indians who bore news of three Spaniards living nearby. And so he fled the Quevenes, hoping desperately that the news was true.

It was. Andrés Dorantes, Alonso del Castillo, and Esteban the Black—a native of Africa, probably from Morocco, and a slave of Dorantes—lived a brutal and uncertain life among the Mariames and Yguases, nomadic peoples who gathered every year for the pecan harvest around the Guadalupe River. Allowing himself to become a captive of the Indians, Cabeza de Vaca hoped to arrange an escape with the others—a dangerous and challenging prospect, given the fact that the four men were divided among various Indian groups that met only once a year for the harvest.

At last, in September 1534, the Spaniards' plan finally came off after more than a year of anticipation. Fleeing into the wilderness from a slavery that had sustained them even as it had demeaned and abused them, the four men—the last of Narváez's three-hundred-odd adventurers—now relied on each other to take them to a distant place that lay beyond a hundred leagues of unknowable hazards.

The day of running was long, and not only because of the exertion; knowing that the Mariames and Yguases eagerly hunted those who'd escaped their captivity, the four men kept up the pace under the Texas sun like their lives depended on it. And then, late in the afternoon, they spotted a familiar sight: a smoke column on the horizon.

These were the Avavares, who eagerly welcomed the tattered and exotic newcomers into their village. And it was with them that Cabeza de Vaca and his comrades were forced to embrace a new and extraordinary destiny.

A HIGHER CALLING

As darkness deepened in the confines of their crude tent of animal skins, Cabeza da Vaca and Castillo thanked God for their good fortune. But what did the Avavares intend to do with them?

Dorantes and Esteban had been led to another tent, and the four were once again separated. Having dwelt in this land for so long now, all of the Spaniards had picked up enough of the tongue of their former owners, the Mariames and Yguases, to speak halt-ingly, and the Avavares—nomadic traders in the local bow-and-arrow market—were multilingual. Nevertheless, no information had yet been conveyed as to their fate.

Up to now, the travelers had been subjected to a bewildering range of generosity and casual, sadistic violence. Anything could happen, they knew all too well. Then the tent was opened and three of the village men came in, explaining that they were suffer-ing from head pain. Could Castillo heal them?

Things were coming together now. Apparently, the two tents to which the four men had been led were reserved for healers—the Spaniards had become known in these parts as powerful physicians, long before they even encountered the Avavares. Long ago, on Malhado Island, they had helped cure the sick on several occasions, instructed in the arts of the local healers and encouraged to practice in exchange for their meals. Tales of the strangers' abilities must have spread throughout the countryside.

Castillo obliged, making the sign of the cross over the three Indians and mumbling a prayer to his Lord, perhaps a Paternoster. Smiling with relief, they remarked that their headaches had gone completely, and they left the tent in a flurry of excitement. Castillo raised an eyebrow at Cabeza de Vaca, and the two began to speculate silently to themselves.

Presently they heard voices and laughter, and the tent was opened once again. In stepped the erstwhile headache sufferers, their arms laden with prickly pears—the

Pathogenic Holocaust

The discovery by Christopher Columbus of what we now call the Bahamas was, without a doubt, one of the most important moments in all of human history. For the first time since the evolution of modern humans, the two hemispheres had made a distinct, documented, exploitable contact—1492 was the genesis of globalization.

Columbus, a Genoese mariner of middling talent whose calculations of the Earth's size were way off, managed to convince the court of Ferdinand of Aragon and Isabella of Castile, joint monarchs of an inchoate Spain, that he could find a way to the Indies by sailing west instead of east.

Fortunately for Columbus, geography wasn't Ferdinand and Isabella's strong suit, allowing the Genoese entrepreneur to sell them on the idea that the world was a lot smaller than it actually was. According to Columbus's diminutive vision of Earth, he could sail west and, after 2,400 miles of ocean, hit the fabulously rich markets of China and India by a more direct route than anything that had hitherto been tried by the Portuguese, who preferred to sail east around Africa.

His calculations were incorrect by a margin that can justifiably be called gargantuan. Rather than 2,400 miles, Columbus faced a voyage of more than 11,000 miles to get to Asia via a western route. He held to this course until his men were on the verge of mutiny. And then he got lucky.

Spotting land (although which specific island is still debated today), Columbus and his crew were spared the horror of slow death on a boundless sea. And, though they erroneously thought that they had made landfall in India, they would in time come to understand—along with the rest of Europe—that they had uncovered a previously unknown land.

Plight Unseen

This "New World" was already very well known by its original inhabitants, all of whom would soon learn the price of coming into Europe's orbit. But of all the evils that would soon be delivered upon the "Indians" of the Americas— slavery, war, landlessness—none would cost them as dearly as the invisible invaders who came west over the ocean.

Smallpox, influenza, measles, typhus, malaria, bubonic and pneumonic plague, and yellow fever—this was the rogue's gallery that fell so hard upon the Amerindians, brought unwittingly from Eurasia by Christian adventurers who had no reason to suspect that their own germs could wreak such havoc. In the ancient population centers of Africa, Europe, and Asia, these deadly diseases had existed for countless generations, refined and circulated by communities

who lived in such close proximity to a wide variety of domesticated animals. Constant contact between the three continents had not only ensured the spread of these germs, but also the immunity that eventually resulted.

The Americas, by contrast, did not have the diversity of population, the variety of domesticated animals, or the busy trade routes over enormous distances to create the propagation of pathogens on the level of the Old World. And when Columbus and those who followed him arrived, the genetic isolation of Native Americans ended catastrophically.

The meeting of the hemispheres was occasioned by death on a massive scale. Up to 90 percent of the population of the Americas died within two generations of 1492, the diseases racing from one village to the next, running wild among populations with no defense whatsoever against them. In much of North America, this fate befell peoples for whom white-skinned travelers from afar were still the stuff of rumors.

Grisly Verdict

In southern areas like Florida, Alabama, Mississippi, and Texas, the germ-carriers arrived in person, early in the sixteenth century, as Spaniards moved to expand their burgeoning empire in the Caribbean, Mexico, and South America.

One of the most infamous was Hernando de Soto, whose expedition is emblematic of the impact that small groups of Europeans could have on Native Americans. From 1539 to 1543, during a 4,000-mile trek that took them from Florida to the Carolinas to the Mississippi River, de Soto and his 550 men went from village to village on a fruitless quest for gold. The aggressive de Soto—who, along with nearly half of his men, would not survive the odyssey—became infamous for resorting to violence during his mission, but it was the contagious diseases that he and his men were spreading that ended up denuding the country through which they marched.

As intimidated by the Spaniards' churlish behavior as they were mystified by their obsession with precious metals, Indian headmen happily got the travelers to leave their village by fabricating rumors of gold in the next settlement, constantly perpetuating the Spaniards' wild goose chase. But each village probably started succumbing to sickness within days—perhaps hours—of seeing the Europeans off, infected with alien pathogens of which de Soto and his force were chillingly oblivious.

A late sixteenth-century engraving depicts Amerindians fighting disease—much of it brought over by the first Europeans to the Americas—with trepanning and fumigation. Up to 90 percent of population of the Americas died from disease within two generations of 1492.

For Indians, seeing the strange, bearded warriors enter their community was a death sentence: The Europeans had become itinerant reapers in a hapless land of the doomed.

Fortunately, de Soto took notes on the peoples he encountered, most of whom were inheritors of the ancient Mississippian culture that went back centuries, thriving in the heartland of what is now the United States. He and his men were the first Europeans to encounter this civilization at its height, and they would also be the last. De Soto was literally capturing for posterity portraits of a people whom he was driving to near extinction by his mere presence.

Epidemics would continue to break out throughout North America, often without a European in sight, the germs sweeping through the country like an ill wind. In the 1590s, measles killed thousands of Iroquois in what is now central New York State. Plague ravaged the inhabitants of Massachusetts in the years just before the Pilgrims landed at Plymouth Rock; among the first things reported by the English was a plethora of bone yards on the coast. The Huron in what is now Ontario, Canada, died in droves from an outbreak of small pox in 1630, while scarlet fever spread quickly from New England a few years later, infecting settlements throughout the Great Lakes who had yet to meet more than a few fur traders.

And so it went. As it was in the Caribbean and Mesoamerica, so it was in North America, all of which were struck by a holocaust—one of the worst demographic disasters of all time.

✧

juicy, beloved cactus fruit that formed the basis of so many meals in Texas—and something that neither Spaniard had seen or smelled in quite some time: venison. For the last six years, the conquistadores had eaten plenty of prickly pears, as well as spiders, snails, roots, and often nothing at all. But fresh meat was a luxury of the first order. Laying the fragrant gifts at Castillo's feet, the obliging Avavares thanked him and spoke of others who needed his attention, as well.

And so there were—many, in fact. They filed expectantly into the tent, presented themselves to Castillo, received the sign of the cross, listened vacantly to his strange Latin gibberish, and exhibited signs of instant renewal. And all of them left venison.

Clearly, the Spaniards had found sanctuary. After hearing that the foraging would be difficult with the coming winter, the four decided to play it safe and stay with these gentle and munificent nomads who believed them to be men of power. Besides, they were headed in the same direction: south and west. Perhaps they could reach Mexico next year.

Perhaps.

PROMOTED TO SHAMANS

On a fine April morning, Cabeza de Vaca and Esteban walked briskly in search of Spaniards. Before them stretched a trail in the dirt that could only have been left by a large party of horsemen accompanied by an even larger number of people on foot. For three days the two men, in the company of eleven Indians, had been following this trail, taking them farther and farther south toward New Spain. The year was 1536—a year and a half since they'd taken up with the Avavares as healers. And what a year and a half it had been.

The Avavares had been just the first to appreciate the "healers" and their extraordinary gifts. Cabeza de Vaca himself had had an epiphany in the wilderness: Separated from the rest and assumed dead from a snake bite, he had stayed alive in the cold nights, we are told, with the help of a burning bush. After returning to his companions and the Avavares, he had acquired a greater belief in his own abilities. Clearly God's purpose was at work.

The four refugees slipped away from the Avavares and took up with another people. And then another, and another. In each village they found a dramatically different scenario than the one that had defined their experience months ago. They were welcomed, anticipated, as traveling medicine men that could do the amazing.

Then, not long after crossing the Rio Grande, they made an incredible decision. Abandoning the impulse to head south, toward the Spanish settlements of Pánuco that bordered the Gulf of Mexico, they turned inland—west and north, toward regions they had heard were full of maize and villages. Galvanized by their success as men of the people, and always with a crowd of supporters in tow, the conquistadores decided to resume the role of discoverers.

They ascended the eastern slope of the Sierra Madre mountains, recrossed the Rio Grande into buffalo country, and then crossed the Rio Grande once again to its southern bank, following the long gradual descent to the Pacific Coast beyond the western slope of the Sierra Madres. The whole way, they depended on the largesse of local villages to sustain them, each of which anticipated their noisy, crowd-ridden approach. Cabeza de Vaca and his companions threw themselves into the curing of the local sick, nearly all of whom—if we are to believe the sources—benefited from the practitioners' arts.

THE END OF AN ODYSSEY

By the spring of 1536, eight years since they had landed in Florida as creatures of a very different purpose, the four men and the truly huge throng of earnest followers they had acquired along the way reached the valley of the Sinaloa River in what is now western Mexico.

The local inhabitants, however, gave the four shamans a very different reception from the one to which they'd become accustomed. Here, on the frontier with New Spain, the Indians had abandoned their rich farmland for the foothills further inland, leaving in their wake an unkempt landscape of empty houses and smoldering cook fires. Fear stalked the land.

Leaving Dorantes and Castillo behind with hundreds of followers in a place of safety, Cabeza de Vaca and Esteban took eleven Indians and followed the trail of what looked like a party of slavers on horseback. And now, having followed the signs for several days, they confronted the reason why the people of these parts dared not show themselves—a sight that Cabeza de Vaca had once thought he may never see again. There, at the end of the trail, four Spaniards sat on their horses like emissaries from a distant memory. Silent and intimidating on their mounts, with the hot Mexican sun glinting off their helmets and belt buckles, the riders stared at their exotic trackers in palpable disbelief.

The emotions running through Esteban and Cabeza de Vaca must have been intense, to say the least. Their eight-year odyssey was over—they had come out of the wilderness, against all odds, and returned to civilization.

When the tense silence finally broke, Cabeza de Vaca, wild in his animal skins, approached and discovered that the horsemen were indeed slavers whose camp was nearby. He and Esteban agreed to go there with their Indian companions, and were soon standing face to face with the expedition's leader, Diego de Alcaraz. Nearby sat a cluster of chained captives, quiet and sullen.

Alcaraz was all business. Cabeza de Vaca had one hell of a tale to tell, but the slaver had more immediate concerns on his mind. He had come north to capture Indians, and the countryside for leagues in every direction, denuded and desolate, had yielded precious few. Now, like some prophet of old, this Spaniard and his African servant had walked—*walked!*—out of the north desert with smiling Indians in tow. As far as Alcaraz was concerned, there was more here than met the eye. And damn if he wasn't going to profit from it somehow.

The captain of slavers put it to his strange and filthy new associate: Did he know where he could find more Indians like these? Of course, came the reply. After all, fellow shamans Dorantes and Castillo were hiding with hundreds of them just three days from here. Cabeza de Vaca sent Esteban off to fetch them, and he returned five days later with Dorantes, Castillo, and six hundred men, women, and children. Messengers were then sent into the mountains to gather more, and hundreds soon appeared, bringing the total of Indians to more than a thousand.

Alcaraz then dropped his bomb: He intended to enslave as many of these fine people as he could. Rather incredibly, Cabeza de Vaca and his three fellow medicine men expressed shock at this development. They turned to their charges and implored them to disperse back into the hills, commencing a scene of confusion and chaos. Alcaraz attempted to convey to the frightened masses that their patriarchs were nothing special at all, but very much like himself—Spaniards, plain and simple, and just as dangerous as any slaver. They had stupidly put their trust in the wrong leaders.

The crowd was incredulous. How could their beloved shamans be the same people as these despicable, violent traders in flesh? It wasn't easy, but Cabeza de Vaca and his comrades convinced the throngs to return to their settlements and to secure their homes and sow their fields. As for the shamans themselves, they would travel south with the slavers, back to New Spain, and appeal to the Christian authorities on the Indians' behalf.

The strange standoff served to place the four refugees and their uniquely tortuous situation in high relief. All they had prayed for during the previous eight years was to return safely to civilization. But having done so, it was frighteningly clear that "civilization" immediately threatened the safety of those who had sustained Cabeza de Vaca and his comrades through months of hardship. Rage, humiliation, and regret all fought for supremacy in the four men as they tried to negotiate this confusing no-man's-land between cultures.

ALCARAZ THEN DROPPED HIS BOMB: HE INTENDED TO ENSLAVE AS MANY OF THESE FINE PEOPLE AS HE COULD.

Alcaraz had been thwarted for the moment, though he promised to return to these parts with more men after this whole bizarre episode had passed. And, like it or not, he was now the authority figure in whose care the four survivors' passage back to New Spain was entrusted.

And what a grim passage it turned out to be. Alcaraz was determined not to let his four charges see how thoroughly the slave trade had turned once-thriving territories into a depopulated war zone, so took a circuitous route south through badlands devoid of water. In an irony of ironies, Cabeza de Vaca and his friends came closer to death now, at the moment of deliverance, than they did in years of wandering in exile through the wilderness.

It was their final trial, however. By June they had arrived in Compostela, capital of the province of New Galicia. And they were received like living legends.

The King of Spain honored conquistador Hernán Cortés, shown here, for his conquest of Tenochtitlán by making him a Marquis.

WORLDS APART

In New Spain, the only survivors of the Narváez expedition found themselves at the center of a flurry of attention that must have borne a strange resemblance to their experience of just weeks earlier under very different circumstances. The great Cortés himself, illustrious conqueror of the Aztecs, invited them to dine at his table in Tenochtitlán.

Some things could not be altered by heroic deeds, however. Esteban, the first man of African descent to step foot in what is today the United States, was as black now as he'd been when he landed with Dorantes, his legal master, in Florida back in 1528. The freedom that he had experienced during his eight-year adventure—eight years during which he had acted as the group's front man when encountering new tribes, partly because of his gift for foreign languages—was now proven to be a delusion. Dorantes sold Esteban to Nuño de Guzmán, governor of New Galicia.

The immediate effect of the journey from *La Florida* to Mexico was to inspire others to venture north in search of wealth and glory, especially Francisco Vásquez de Coronado, whose name would go down in history as an explorer of America's southwest. But there was a broader, more significant consequence of the experience: From the eastern end of the Gulf of Mexico to the plains of central Texas to the western shore of Mexico, emissaries from one hemisphere had encountered those of another—and had done so on equal terms, based on the exchange of goods, ideas, and language.

The accomplishment of Cabeza de Vaca and his comrades, however accidental, was to find an avenue of contact that didn't involve the subjugation of one people by another, which was defining much of the New World even as the four of them struggled to survive on their astounding adventure. When they finally came south out of the vast, mysterious continent that had threatened to swallow them, they did so as ambassadors of good will to the myriad peoples who embraced them. This message was lost in the scramble for advantage that shaped the European imperial experience.

The One-Eyed Conquistador

Pánfilo de Narváez has been called one of the most unfortunate conquistadores in history, and not just because of the Florida debacle that cost him his life. In 1520, he sailed for Mexico from Cuba with a formidable little army. His mission, however, was not to subdue local Amerindians or to carve out a new realm for himself—it was to defeat and capture a fellow Spaniard. By the time Hernán Cortés had landed in Mexico and started heading toward his historic rendezvous with the Aztec empire, he was operating outside of the law. Diego Velázquez de Cuéllar, governor of Cuba, believed that the headstrong Cortés had exceeded his authority and was undergoing the expedition without the governor's approval. Velázquez dispatched Narváez to arrest him.

Considering the facts, Narváez had every reason to be confident. His force outnumbered that of Cortés, and he had the backing of the king's surrogate in New Spain. In fact, he was downright cocky. Cortés, however, was no amateur; indeed, he soon proved himself to be a singularly capable and ruthless opponent against all comers, Aztecs and Spanish both. After hearing of the arrival of Narváez on the Mexican coast, Cortés raced to meet him with his inferior force, launched a surprise attack, and defeated his would-be jailer. Narváez lost an eye in the battle and was chained by Cortés like a common criminal. Even worse, however, was the fate of his men: Most of them joined Cortés and went on to greater glory.

Cortés ultimately conquered Tenochtitlán, the capital of the Aztecs, and so impressed the King of Spain that all charges against him were dropped, and he was made a Marquis. As for Narváez, he died somewhere in the Gulf of Mexico—emaciated, one-eyed, and broken.

✢

PEDRO MENENDEZ DE AVILES.

Natural de Avilés en Asturias, Comendador
de la orden de Santiago, Conquistador de la Flo-
rida, nombrado Grâl. de la Armada contra Inglaterra.
Murió en Santander Aº. 1574. á los 55. de edad.

chapter two

Spain Plants the First Permanent European Settlement in North America

1565

P edro Menéndez de Avilés anxiously paced the deck of his flagship, *San Pelayo*. Two days earlier, off the coast of Florida, he had gone ashore and met with Indians who offered valuable information about the prey he was desperately seeking. Now, confident of success, he led his five vessels northward along the coastline, scanning the beaches for any sign of European settlement. The day was September 4, 1565, and Menéndez was hunting heretics.

Setting the mood that afternoon for the Spaniard's grim crusade, storm clouds veiled the sun and soon began lashing the sea with sheets of rain. Lookouts, however, made a discovery through the summer downpour: Moored at the mouth of the St. Johns River, four vessels loomed ominously ahead. And their topgallants, flying in the storm gusts, revealed them to be French.

Menéndez grimaced at the news. He had been looking for a French settlement, Fort Caroline, which the Indians told him was nearby. But he had hoped to find it before reinforcements from France arrived. And those ships moored at the river's mouth could only mean that he had not been fast enough.

No matter. Menéndez and trouble were old acquaintances, and he was accustomed to meeting challenges with the cunning and toughness that had endeared him to the

He came, he saw, he conquered: Pedro Menéndez de Avilés founded the first permanent European settlement in North America—St. Augustine, Florida—before the founding of Plymouth and Jamestown.

King of Spain. He readied his squadron for a fight with the French ships, anticipating a victory for the greater glory of God.

Though he could not know it at that tense moment, Menéndez, in the coming days, was going to add a page to the history books. Here, on the coast of Florida, he would take possession of an ordinary bit of ground and christen it St. Augustine. And it—rather than Plymouth, or Jamestown, or any of the other communities that came later and achieved greater renown in the English-speaking world—would become the first European settlement in all of North America to endure continuously into the present.

THE KING'S MAN

Menéndez had come to Florida prepared for a fight. By far the greatest of his assets was the 900-ton *San Pelayo*. Just a few years old and his personal property, this impressive galleass—a vessel boasting extensive sail power as well as oars—provided a gun platform more than capable of wreaking havoc with any challengers.

With the other ships in support, Menéndez intended to loose *San Pelayo*'s wrath on the French. That night, as a favorable wind picked up from the south, he guided his ships to within hailing distance of the enemy and dropped anchor with the intent of engaging them in the morning.

MENENDEZ WAS LANGUISHING IN A SEVILLE PRISON ON CHARGES OF SMUGGLING WHEN HE MANAGED TO FINAGLE THE OPERATION THAT TOOK HIM TO FLORIDA.

It was a noisy night. Now close enough to exchange oaths, the opposing squadrons shouted insults and threats to each other, the vulgarities of myriad Gallic and Iberian dialects reverberating through the darkness. Taunted into action, Menéndez pushed the schedule forward a bit and attempted to attack.

The Spanish ships closed on their quarry, the French cut their anchor cables, cannon fire split the night, and a chase ensued. By morning his enemy had outdistanced him, and Menéndez was forced to try a different tack. Sailing back to the river with the intent of seizing the fort, his original target, he found it defended by carefully deployed troops and three of the smaller French vessels waiting beyond the bar over which the heavy *San Pelayo* could not hope to pass. Menéndez had been checked again.

None of this dissuaded him, for he was here to stay. Born in the northern Spanish maritime culture of Asturias in 1519, Pedro Menéndez de Avilés was a classic *hidalgo*, or nobleman, on the make. He was still a young man when he made his reputation as a master privateer, commanding galleons against corsairs in the Bay of Biscay and the Indies and capturing enough prizes to make a modest fortune.

In time he secured a huge plum escorting his monarch, Philip II, to England for the king's marriage to Mary Tudor, and was made a captain-general of the fleets bringing treasure home from the Indies. Menéndez's success—and overweening ambition— earned him no small number of enemies, especially merchants, who had the power to harm him. In fact, Menéndez was languishing in a Seville prison on charges of smuggling when he managed to finagle the operation that took him to Florida.

Since discovering that French Huguenots had settled in La Florida and raised a stronghold christened Fort Caroline, King Philip II of Spain had determined to kick them out of what he believed was rightfully Spanish territory. Such a settlement posed a threat entirely out of proportion to its modest size and garrison. Corsairs operating out of Fort Caroline were in a perfect position to swoop down on Spain's treasure fleets, whose course on the Gulf Stream took them north along the Florida and Carolina coasts before breaking east for home. Eager to strike a blow against both France and Huguenot Protestantism, His Most Catholic Majesty had sent Menéndez across the ocean to purge Florida of its interlopers.

Though sailing under the flag of his sovereign, Menéndez himself bore most of the risk—he funded the voyage (through creditors, of course) and provided many of its vessels, including his own impressive flagship. His reward for such efforts was laid out clearly in the contract, or *asiento*, which he negotiated and formalized with King Philip. According to the agreement, Menéndez was to become *adelantado* of Florida—a title that made him royal governor of the new territory he was about to subdue, complete with lands and titles that, depending on the success of his leadership and colonizing effort, could make him a very rich man indeed.

To hold up his end of the bargain, Menéndez had to do as much as he could to Christianize the local inhabitants, establish proper municipal institutions along the Spanish model, and keep the territory clear of trespassers from other European powers. It was a mission that appealed to his Catholic piety and thirst for power and riches in equal measure.

AN OMINOUS BEGINNING

On September 8, a boat approached the shore of a sheltered harbor on the Florida coast. Several days earlier, Menéndez had spotted the area and christened it after the saint whose day it was: Saint Augustine. Now, accompanied by a small party of his officers, he was coming to take formal possession of it.

De facto possession had been a reality for several days—the new adelantado of Florida had ordered soldiers ashore to start throwing up defensive works. But today was a day for ceremony and fanfare. Stepping out of the boat into the surf, Menéndez strolled solemnly ashore as cannons thundered and trumpets sounded his arrival. Banners of Spain unfurled into the breeze, and he dramatically kissed the cross. The history of St. Augustine had begun.

Having failed to crush the French outright at Fort Caroline, Menéndez had begun to take a longer view of things. A quick solution to his problems was obviously out of reach, and a base would have to be established for long-term operations—a base that would mark the beginning of his settlement of La Florida.

In time the new governor would see to the creation of municipal institutions. He would dole out lands and titles to his lieutenants and see to the details of "civilization." But that lay in the future. St. Augustine's first purpose would be far simpler and a lot more brutal: to facilitate the extermination of Florida's other European settlers.

Besides a sheltered harbor, the location of St. Augustine—roughly thirty-five miles south of Fort Caroline—had one other asset: a nearby village of Timucuan-speaking Indians who hated the French for their occupation of Timucuan land. These were the locals who had given Menéndez information that led him to the mouth of the St. Johns River, and they would soon prove useful to him yet again.

The French, however, struck first. On September 10, the same ships that Menéndez had earlier chased to no avail arrived off St. Augustine with the rising sun. They couldn't have timed their appearance better if they'd tried. Having just sent *San Pelayo* away toward Hispaniola to pick up supplies and reinforcements, the Spanish were unloading stores off the bar when they were rudely interrupted by the Frenchmen's approach. But rather than launch an amphibious operation as planned, the little French fleet headed south after the *San Pelayo*, intent on catching the great galleass alone at sea. This decision, though quite sound, would prove disastrous for the nascent French community in Florida.

Nature soon intervened dramatically. Within days of the French appearance off St. Augustine, a ferocious storm struck, mercilessly reminding everyone that the elements still reigned in Florida. By the time the winds subsided, Pedro Menéndez de Avilés was making some shrewd calculations.

King Philip II of Spain (1527–98), pictured here, sent Menéndez to Florida to remove French Huguenots out of what he considered Spanish territory.

MARCH TO DESTINY

Within the crude walls of his newly founded settlement, in between bouts of wondering whether his precious flagship had survived the weather and her French pursuers, Menéndez considered the situation as it now stood.

To begin with, the French fleet must have suffered dreadful damage in the storm. For all Menéndez knew, they could be washed up on a Florida beach, sailing on to the Caribbean, racing back north along the coast, lost at sea, or dead. One thing, however, was certain: The French fleet could not have made it back to the area of Fort Caroline since the storm swept it south. Moreover, because so many soldiers appeared to have been on the ships, Fort Caroline's garrison must be seriously depleted.

The adelantado's next move was obvious: He must strike at the French fort itself, and the sooner the better. After consulting with his Timucuan colleagues, who outlined an approach that would allow the Spanish to attack Fort Caroline from its more vulnerable landward side, Menéndez struck north with some five hundred arquebusiers (named for their principle weapon, the arquebus, an early variety of musket) into the wilds of Florida.

Over several days, under a nearly constant, drenching rain, the column—spearheaded by axe-wielding Basques—hacked and marched its way through nearly fifty miles of swollen marshes, grassland, and forest. They spent the night of September 19 beneath the dripping trees, just a short jaunt from their slumbering enemies.

As the sun rose over the St. Johns River on September 20, the arquebusiers trudged quietly through the woods that concealed the southern approach to Fort Caroline. Beneath a steady drizzle, their firearms were useless. The day's work would be done with cold steel. After overcoming a lone sentry, the Spanish, holding two standards aloft, forced the main gate and poured through in a rolling tide of swords and halberds. Shouts of *"Santiago y cierra Espana!"* ("St. James, and close ranks Spain!"), the old Castilian battle cry, roused the slumbering inhabitants to their doom.

Slaughter ensued. Here in the verdant Florida wilderness, seemingly a world away from the religious wars that were igniting Europe, zealots fired up with hatred set about murdering each other. Menéndez, who referred to the Huguenots as members of an "evil Lutheran sect," would later claim that both Protestants and Indians held beliefs that were "probably satanic in origin." Hot with sanctimonious rage, the adelantado's soldiers started stabbing and slashing at every man in nightclothes.

"They made a pretty butchery of it," claimed one French eyewitness who escaped the melee. At least forty others managed to flee, as well, while a slightly larger number

A nineteenth-century hand-colored woodcut depicts Pedro Menéndez de Avilés breaking ground for the Spanish settlement of St. Augustine.

Overleaf: A nineteenth-century engraving of Fort Caroline, the French Huguenot stronghold in Florida.

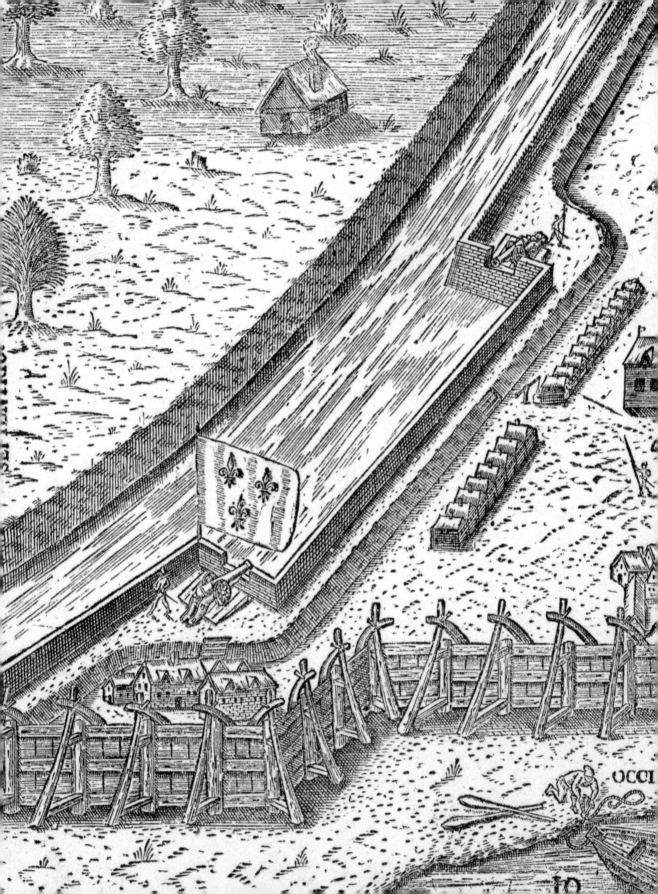

OCCI

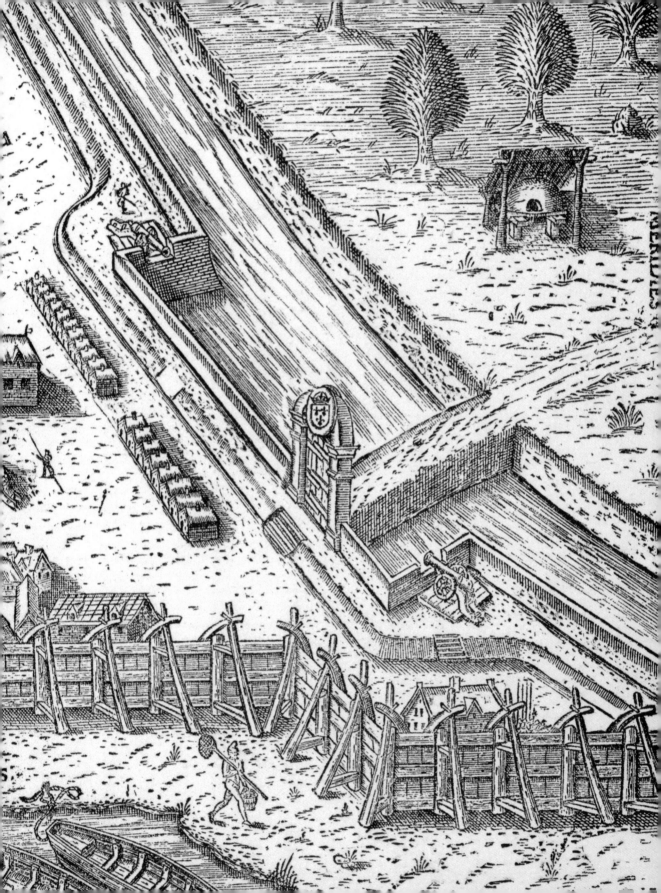

Erected in 1562, Ribault's Column—shown here in a contemporary engraving by Jacques Le Moyne—was intended to commemorate the French presence in Florida. The Huguenots, however, hadn't counted on Spanish determination.

of women and children—protected by the adelantado's injunction against attacking them—were captured when the killing stopped. The final death toll stood at 132. In a single morning of violence, Fort Caroline effectively passed into memory.

A GULF OF ANIMOSITY

Several small French vessels remained moored in the nearby river, as if daring the Spanish to attack. Menéndez came out to parley with them even as Protestants wounded in the fort were being silenced by rummaging Spaniards. On one of the craft, the *Pearl*, the adelantado met with a Huguenot named Jacques Ribault.

There, on the *Pearl*'s confining deck, the two men glared at each other over an endless gulf of animosity. The Frenchman was the son of Jean Ribault, who had commanded the modest fleet of ships sent to reinforce Fort Caroline—the very man whose vessels had challenged St. Augustine before being scattered by the storm, and whose whereabouts were now completely unknown both to his son and to the Spanish.

Making the Most of
What's Available

A succession of nine wooden forts protected the community of St. Augustine through the middle of the seventeenth century, most of which came to a pathetic end. One of them, in 1586, had the good fortune to fall to a raid by Sir Francis Drake rather than to hurricane damage, mutiny, or rot.

Not until 1672 did St. Augustine's landlords get serious and build a fortress of stone. The impressive square stronghold known as the Castillo de San Marcos boasts four bastions and an impressive record: It has never been taken by force.

Designed by the renowned military engineer Ignacio Daza and requiring nearly twenty years to construct, the Castillo was built with an unusual variety of local stone. *Coquina* (pronounced "co-key-na") is Spanish for "little shells," which is precisely what the stone is comprised of: the husks of fossilized shellfish. Quarried on the nearby island of Anastasia, mostly by local Indians, the stone was ferried to the fort and shaped into blocks that were fixed in place by lime. The result was a stronghold with an extraordinary ability. Porous and strangely pliant, the castillo's coquina walls *caught* projectiles rather than *deflected* them, producing a façade that, though pockmarked, seemed invulnerable to the splintering suffered by harder stone. Strange as it may seem, the stronghold defied sieges by English forces in 1702, 1728, and 1740.

✝

To Menéndez, this young man before him, like his father, was a creature beyond the limits of Christian mercy. He was a heretic pirate and trespasser on land owned by the King of Spain and sanctified by soldiers of Christ in the service of Rome. Nevertheless, the adelantado hoped to secure Ribault's vessels without a fight, thereby strengthening his own naval assets in this harsh frontier.

For his part, Jacques Ribault—ignorant of his father's fate and all too aware of what this savage Spaniard was capable of—saw the swift little craft beneath his feet as his only salvation. The Fort Caroline enterprise was dead—time to head back to France, and good riddance. The negotiations broke down, and Menéndez got off the *Pearl* while the getting was good.

Along the river and in the fort itself, Spanish soldiers sprang into action. Guns boomed, and one of the French vessels shivered from a mortal blow, then began to sink.

The others, including Ribault's *Pearl*, cut their cables and went with the current toward the bar. In time they would choose to sail for France, making them some of the select few to escape Menéndez's Florida bloodbath.

As the sun rose that day over a scene of carnage, Menéndez took stock of his conquest and the odd assortment of booty that came with it. There were livestock, wine, grain, silver, and a few pieces of artillery. But the most valuable treasure had made off into the woods. During the attack, a handful of important Frenchmen were able to escape, only to be captured beyond the stockade by hostile Amerindians. Eager to ransom them back in Europe to families who would doubtless pay dearly for their safety, Menéndez negotiated with the Indians for their release. Wealthy hostages would help offset the expedition's expenses.

Over the ensuing days the victorious adelantado saw to the security of the captured fort (which he renamed St. Mateo) and to the equitable distribution of the plunder to his men. Then, eager to return to his base of operations, he marched back to St. Augustine the way he'd come—and toward a fate that would make him a legend to be feared.

BLOOD ON THE SAND

On the steamy dawn of September 29, Menéndez stood on the bank of an inlet about eighteen miles south of St. Augustine. Around him were his chaplain and a company of soldiers, all of whom, like their leader, watched the far shore of the inlet intently.

The previous day, friendly Timucuan Indians had met with the adelantado in St. Augustine, telling him that a group of French castaways had come ashore here. Menéndez raced south, knowing that God had favored his Florida enterprise. The Frenchmen must be members of Ribault's fleet, thrown against the coastline by the ferocity of the storm and now all but defenseless. With Fort Caroline out of the way, Menéndez had only to dispatch the survivors of the storm to purge his new realm of heretics.

The Spaniards hailed their enemies across the water and, in a short time, saw one of them come across to parley. With a prisoner from Fort Caroline acting as interpreter, Menéndez learned that he was speaking with one of Ribault's pilots. He then delivered the news that, he knew, would strike the Huguenot before him like a dagger thrust: Fort Caroline had fallen. The nearest succor for the pilot and his comrades now lay several thousand miles across the ocean in France. Menéndez sent the messenger back to his fellows with a dour message: The new adelantado of Florida was their sworn enemy, bound to hunt them into extermination.

The pilot did as he was instructed and was presently succeeded by another negotiator—a noble who hoped to reach some understanding with the Spaniard. Precisely what

A seventeenth-century engraving depicts the fall of Fort Caroline to the Spanish conquerors.

happened next will never be known. The adelantado either told the Frenchman that he could make no guarantees for their safety, or he promised to spare their lives if they surrendered. Whatever the truth, the Frenchmen agreed to come across the inlet and surrender themselves into Menéndez's custody.

It was the last decision that most of them ever made. The Spanish bound their captives, and then selected seventeen of them—including the pilot—who were deemed useful for their skills or willingness to convert. The rest of them were escorted in small parties of ten or so to a concealed location behind a dune, forced to their knees, and slaughtered.

Nearly a fortnight later, the adelantado's burgeoning intelligence network delivered yet again. Word came to him that another group of stranded Frenchmen had gathered at the very same inlet—and one of them was Jean Ribault himself.

FOR HIS EFFORTS IN THE UNFORGIVING FLORIDA FRONTIER, JEAN RIBAULT WOULD BE REWARDED WITH A PIKE THRUST THROUGH HIS HEART.

Returning in haste to the location that today bears the name "Matanzas" ("slaughters"), Menéndez once again found himself negotiating with Frenchmen who, understandably, were covetous of their lives. From dawn on October 11 until well into the afternoon, the adelantado verbally sparred with his quarry. Only later, as the shadows grew long and the mosquitoes gathered in clouds, was he afforded the opportunity to meet his nemesis.

But even Jean Ribault could not change the implacable conquistador's terms—the Huguenots were to give up unconditionally, without promises as to their fate. Hardened by a crusader's zeal, Menéndez would not truck with adherents of a "wicked sect," and insisted, as he later wrote to his king, that he could only deal with Ribault and his men "as Our Lord should command me." Ribault at last relented.

A number of the French decided against Spanish hospitality and headed south down the beach to an uncertain fate. The others, save for a captive few, were butchered like their fellows two weeks earlier. For his efforts in the unforgiving Florida frontier, Jean Ribault would be rewarded with a pike thrust through his heart.

A TENUOUS BRIDGEHEAD

Between the deaths at Fort Caroline and the liquidations at Matanzas Inlet, Pedro Menéndez de Avilés took somewhere between 280 and 450 lives in the course of his 1565 Florida enterprise.

Bathed in the blood of religious strife and imperial ambitions, the birth of St. Augustine would mark the commencement of two centuries of Spanish rule in Florida—and more than four and a half centuries of white settlement in North America. He could not have known it at the time, but the adelantado's modest little foothold—a roughhewn collection of ditches and embankments in a waterlogged wilderness—would become the first permanent settlement by Europeans on the continent.

The rest of his efforts in La Florida, by contrast, weren't nearly as successful. Menéndez envisioned St. Augustine as merely the first, and not necessarily the most important, of a series of outposts that would turn the great peninsula into more than just the northern guardian of Spain's treasure fleets.

In his lifetime, he hoped to turn the region into an ongoing interest of communities based on agriculture and cattle raising. The forces ranged against such an effort, however, were too strong. Crops failed to grow in the sandy earth, Indians—Guale, Ais, Calusa, and Apalachee, as well as Timucua—often resisted conversion and forced labor, and the vast and prolific wilderness swallowed efforts at colonization and exploration. By 1569, nine of the adelantado's ten settlements had failed.

As for St. Augustine itself, it became the solitary emblem of Spain's dashed Florida dreams. Until 1698, it would be the only substantial, durable European settlement on the peninsula. And it was not the sort of place that attracted waves of visitors. A military post peopled mostly by dissolute soldiers, vagabonds, outcasts, and alligators, St. Augustine acquired an unsavory reputation—appointed leaders often paid substitutes to govern in their stead rather than endure the fetid isolation themselves.

Against this backdrop, one can't help sensing the irony that St. Augustine should be the place where Americans today can visit the first continually inhabited city north of the modern border with Mexico—a community that has flown the flags of Spain, Great Britain, the United States, and the Confederate States of America.

But it is also appropriate. For St. Augustine, christened and created by a man of ruthless purpose, was the North American entrepôt for European avarice and subjugation—a symbol of an age of extremes. And the violence that marked its creation would be repeated again and again in North America in the centuries that followed.

chapter three

Puritan New England's First Major War—and a Harbinger of Things to Come

1637

Ever since designing and building Fort Saybrook at the mouth of the Connecticut River in 1636, Lieutenant Lion Gardener had held on by the skin of his teeth, hoping that Boston would send reinforcements. Now, roughly a year after he first arrived to start construction, he had more reinforcements than he knew what to do with.

There were twenty soldiers under the command of John Underhill, sent weeks ago by the English investors whose claim on Connecticut was the purpose of Fort Saybrook in the first place. But just recently, in mid-May 1637, came a larger force of men from upriver. Led by a veteran of the Dutch Wars named John Mason, these ninety-odd men had been mustered in Hartford, Windsor, and Wethersfield—communities in the Connecticut interior that had just begun to suffer Indian attacks. They were well armed, well provisioned, and eager to meet their enemies.

Another contingent had arrived with Mason, as well: seventy Mohegan warriors. Their sachem was a man called Uncas, who had made a career out of pleasing the English. His people had once been one with the Pequots, with whom the host now massing in the fort hoped to grapple in the near future. But the Pequots, who tended to be suspicious of the English, no longer welcomed Uncas. He and his followers formed their own tribe, called the Mohegans, and maintained their close ties with the English.

The fiery death of détente in New England is shown here in the destruction of the Pequot Indians by Colonial forces.

TEST OF LOYALTY

On this fine spring day, these soldiers and Indians filled Fort Saybrook, an enclosure named for two of the settlement's prominent financial backers (Lord Saye and Sele and Lord Brook) and dominated by a bit of high ground called, appropriately, "Fort Hill" for the two cannons emplaced there. With a campaign into the interior against the Pequots about to get underway, plenty of preparations had to be made. The enclosure was alive with activity.

Lion Gardener, however, had something else on his mind. He had been holding this fort without much help since the previous year, 1636. And it had been a long winter. Since relations with the local Pequots had deteriorated so drastically, Fort Saybrook had been under a state of siege.

Just last month, Gardener had watched a trader named Joseph Tilly tortured to death within sight of the fort. Tilly was flayed, dismembered, and mutilated for three days before succumbing to the attentions of his Pequot captors, who proudly wore his fingers and toes as hatbands. Now Gardener, with the image of Tilly's death fresh in his mind, had a fort full of Mohegans—people who were virtually the same as Pequots as far as he was concerned.

THE MOHEGANS SOON SAW TO THE SUFFERING OF THEIR PRISONER. AFTER TYING HIS LEG TO A POLE, THEY BOUND HIS OTHER LEG WITH A ROPE THEN, AS A GROUP, THEY PROCEEDED TO PULL THE PEQUOT LITERALLY APART.

Would they fight? Or were they loath to take on their erstwhile brethren? And what if they were spies? Gardener, a Scottish engineer whose service against Spaniards in Europe had once earned him a place on the staff of the Prince of Orange, was not one to mince words, especially on a hostile frontier. He didn't care whose feathers he ruffled; he needed to know what this Uncas was about.

"You say you will help Major Mason," said the Scotsman to Uncas, "but I will first see it." Gardener then challenged the sachem to send twenty of his band out after a small group of Pequot who had been spied near the Bass River just the previous night, and to "fetch them now dead or alive." Uncas accepted, and sent twenty of his finest warriors to the task.

A hand-colored woodcut illustrates the murder in 1643 of Narragansett leader Miantonomo by Mohegan sachem Uncas.

His men later returned with several heads and a captive. Gardener was very pleased indeed, and rewarded his newfound friends with a bolt of cloth. He also gave them leave to do whatever they chose with the captive.

The Mohegans soon saw to the suffering of their prisoner. After tying his leg to a pole in the enclosure, they bound his other leg with a rope. Then, as a group, they proceeded to pull the Pequot literally apart. John Underhill, sickened by the spectacle, finally walked over to the victim and shot him through the head.

Such was the state of affairs in southern New England in the spring of 1637. Here, where native and European cultures collided, mixed, traded, and sparred, vitriolic hatred had overtaken reasoned dialogue.

The soldiers at Fort Saybrook had gathered to wage war. Goaded by paranoia, self-righteousness, and greed, the Puritan New Englanders and their native allies had found cause to expand and smite the evildoers who inhabited the wilderness around them. The result would be the first severe conflict between the English and the Indians of the northeast—a conflict whose uncompromising ferocity would lay the groundwork for centuries of animosity between America's warring peoples.

OF DEMONS AND DEMAGOGUERY

Times had changed in the seventeen years since the Pilgrims established Plymouth colony in 1620. With the founding of the Massachusetts Bay colony a decade later, New England had become a hotbed of competing interests. Settlers, merchants, and separatist nobles all jockeyed for control over "unclaimed" territory beyond the two colonies.

The area around the Connecticut River was especially desirable, offering easy access to the interior and its potential for trade and agriculture. Plymouth and Massachusetts colonies, financiers back in England, and the Dutch all made claims along the seacoast, up and down the river, and within the Connecticut interior itself, creating an atmosphere of reckless competition that was bound to lead to trouble.

Of course, plenty of people already lived in Connecticut, and their interests complicated matters further. Chief among the Amerindians who populated the Connecticut River valley were the Pequots, whose relentless efforts to monopolize trade in the valley put them in conflict with other natives, particularly the Narragansetts, as well as European traders. Greed and ambition had essentially turned southern New England into a powder keg. And it remained only for someone to produce a spark.

Trouble came in the early 1630s when the Pequots, jealous of growing Dutch influence, attacked their trading post at the House of Good Hope. Dutch retaliation was as foolish as it was prompt. After kidnapping a Pequot sachem named Tatobam, the Dutch

Beads of Power

Wampum, from the Narragansett word for "white shell beads," held enormous cultural significance long before Europeans showed up on American shores. Beads were the basis of wampum, carefully shaped from marine shells harvested along the Atlantic coast.

White beads, fashioned from the whelk shell, and purple beads, from the quahog shell, were arranged in various patterns and woven into belts.Recording events or solemnizing treaties, these belts, rather than the beads themselves, were wampum. Like portable treasures that communicated messages or events of significance, they were highly valued by the Algonquin peoples that ranged from Maine to Florida—the tribes that dealt in the harvesting and trading of wampum beads. Wampum became a part of other cultures that were linked commercially with the Algonquins, especially the Iroquois, making it a standard of worth respected by numerous peoples across much of North America.

The appearance of Europeans, who quickly understood the enormous influence of wampum, essentially turned the belts into currency. Before long a wampum-based economy evolved in New England—the Dutch even manufactured their own for a time.

✢

demanded an enormous ransom payment for his release. Upon getting it, they sent Tatobam back to his people—after killing him. Outraged at this egregious effrontery, the Pequots set upon a white trader near the mouth of the river, killing him and his crew. The assailants, however, goofed spectacularly. The trader, John Stone, wasn't Dutch. He was English.

Though widely considered a cad and a scoundrel throughout New England, Stone became a rallying cry—evidence of how unscrupulous the English could be when searching for a convenient cause célèbre. Negotiating a treaty with the Pequots in November 1634, Massachusetts Bay demanded that the Indians surrender Stone's assassins and pay a large indemnity of wampum for his murder. For their part, the Pequots insisted that Stone's killers were all either dead or beyond reach. As for the indemnity, it was simply preposterous. No deal.

Overleaf: Block Island's Amerindians give John Endecott and company a warm reception. Hand-colored woodcut of a nineteenth century-illustration.

The issue festered until, in the summer of 1636, another trader named John Oldham turned up dead off the coast of Block Island. Though certainly not the work of the Pequots or their subject tribes, Oldham's murder convinced the seething, paranoid English that some sort of Indian conspiracy was afoot—a notion that segued with a desire to free the Connecticut River valley of Pequots once and for all. Any lingering chance for peace was banished by the Puritan belief that the woodland savages trucked with demons and worshipped the devil. If the good folk of Massachusetts Bay could smite a wicked people and benefit from the confiscation of their land, so much the better.

PERSONAL VENDETTAS VERSUS WAR

The Pequots, nonplussed by the issue over Stone's nationality, were further hampered by an inability to comprehend why a whole people would push the death of an unpopular sea captain to the point of war. Stone's murder, after all, was merely the final in a series of retaliatory slayings—personal vendettas that were ubiquitous in Algonquin culture. What did this have to do with war?

They found out in August 1636, when an expedition of soldiers under John Endecott showed up in Pequot territory on the Connecticut River after making a fruitless sweep of Block Island. The English skirmished with the Indians, burnt their crops, and then departed like furies on the wind.

Whipped up into a rage, the Pequots set about spoiling the region around Saybrook and laid siege to its fort. Upriver, they attacked Wethersfield, killing nine settlers and taking two girls captive. The spark had fallen into the powder keg.

INDIAN ALLIES

On an evening in mid-May 1637, the military leaders inside Fort Saybrook discussed their options for attacking the Pequots. Each of them had firsthand experience of things beyond the imagination of their Indian foes—practices honed in European campaigns in which vast fortified cities were besieged for months or even years at a stretch, costing thousands of lives, bankrupting mighty nations, and deciding the fate of *millions*.

They had seen war on a scale unfathomable to any Algonquin, and had long since inured themselves to extremes of destruction that America's woodland Indians would've considered nightmarish or even mad. They would fight for absolute victory, sustained by confidence in their armor and muskets, and buoyed always by God's grace.

And it was God to whom they now turned for a decision regarding strategy. Should the army sail to Pequot Harbor, as its orders stipulated, and make an amphibious landing close to the Indians' forts? Or should the men sail east, make landfall in the territory of the Narragansetts, enlist as many of their warriors as possible, and then sneak up on the Pequots via an overland route?

John Mason, the army's commander, put the issue to his chaplain (a fellow whose name, interestingly, was "Stone") in the hopes of acquiring divine guidance. The Reverend Stone returned the next morning with an answer: Go to the Narragansetts and attack from the east.

The Lord had spoken. On May 18, the army, roughly ninety strong with some seventy Mohegan allies under Uncas, boarded the vessels that would take them to Narragansett Bay. Two days later they arrived and anchored until the weather allowed them ashore.

The Narragansetts, the mightiest of the peoples of southern New England, had been persuaded to the English point of view in recent months by Roger Williams, a radical theologian who had been ousted by Massachusetts Bay for his insistence on the separation of church and state. Though an outcast, Williams had answered the call by Massachusetts Bay to use his influence with the Indians to keep them neutral—or, better yet, to make them enemies of the Pequot. Because of Williams's brave and extraordinary efforts, Mason and his fellows found a warm reception at Narragansett Bay.

Warm, but skeptical. Miantonomi, chief sachem of the Narragansetts, spoke frankly with his white-skinned guests. The Pequots, he insisted, were "very great captains and men skillful in war," while the English were clearly too few in number. Unable to move their Indian hosts to war, Mason and his men moved on. The following day they encountered the eastern Niantics, once closely aligned with the Pequots, and were given an even cooler reception. Clearly they had entered enemy territory.

MARCH TO PURGATORY

Mason walked along the old Indian trail and reached for his water. He reckoned the hour to be noon, and already the sun was hot and oppressive. Insects careened and buzzed in the humidity, lending an almost claustrophobic atmosphere to the woods around him. It was going to be a long and unpleasant day.

Wiping his brow with a gauntleted hand, he cursed the heat, then checked himself, and quietly thanked God for the good fortune they'd had so far. Early that morning, outside the Niantic village, some five hundred Narragansett Indians had caught up with Mason's column, having decided to join the fight after all. Gathering themselves up in a great circle, they each stepped forward and proclaimed their ferocity and devotion.

Then the army, now almost six hundred strong, struck west for Weinshauks, home of the Pequot sachem, Sassacus.

Mason took two swallows of water and heard someone approach from behind. It was another messenger from the rear of the column with bad news: Men were dropping along the trail from heat exhaustion. The captain could only press on, knowing that food was running out and time was against them. They needed to spot their target by nightfall so as to be able to attack at sunup.

The army marched on until, after another hour or so, they saw a ribbon of burnished silver through the trees. It was the Pawcatuck River. Several Narragansetts went forward to join Mason at the head of the column, guiding him to a ford where the men could cross. And then the Indians changed, becoming somber and even agitated.

THE SMELL OF TERROR

Mason sensed fear, and asked his guides what it was about. One of the Indians looked at him and explained that the ford was a favorite Pequot fishing spot. Back in the column, voices were raised in argument, and the ranks broke up in agitation. News soon made its way up to Mason: The Narragansetts were deserting.

Disgusted, the commander turned to Uncas for explanation, but was told only that the Mohegans would stay. As for the Narragansetts—who knows? Clearly they weren't as good as their word. And clearly the Pequots had instilled in them a visceral terror.

Mason ordered his men to rest and eat a small meal before fording the river. The betrayal of the Narragansetts only galvanized his determination to strike some great blow against the Pequots. Surprise had always been fundamental to the battle plan, as the Pequot numbers were reportedly quite large, and nothing had changed. The English and their Indian allies would have to ambush their foe and make the most of their firepower.

After crossing the river and thanking providence for its cool relief, the army journeyed several miles more before arriving at a flat expanse of newly planted Indian corn. Captain Underhill came up and sat with Mason as they spoke with Uncas and several of the Narragansetts who had chosen to remain. As the guides explained, two fortified settlements loomed ahead on the trail. Weinshauks, Sassacus's capital, lay much deeper in Pequot territory. The column could not possibly reach it before nightfall. The other settlement at Mystic, though somewhat smaller, was closer, requiring a shorter march and lessening the chance of discovery by Pequot scouts.

Mason toyed with the idea of attacking both, but allowed himself to be talked out of it. Dangerously short of food, and exhausted from the day's forced march in the withering heat, the men would need to perform their duty soon or not at all. Mystic it was.

Theologian Roger Williams used his friendly relations with the Narragansett Indians to persuade them not to side with the Pequots.

Presently the column resumed its journey. Mason and Underhill forbade the men from talking and ordered their kit to be stowed and wrapped. Silence would be their truest ally as they penetrated deep into the realm of the Pequots. As the sun dipped beneath the western woods, they came to the edge of a swamp, which the guides insisted was close to Mystic. There, in the hollow between two hills, the exhausted soldiers slept beneath a moonlit sky. The morning would bring blood and fire.

HOLOCAUST

John Mason was angry. The day had begun badly when the whole army overslept, rising just after sunup. So much for advancing on the fort under the cover of darkness. Now, after a two-mile march along a winding path through swamp and forest, he was beginning to wonder whether his guides were deliberately misleading him. The army was supposed to have camped near the Mystic settlement. So where was it?

The Indians came up to the head of the column and pointed to the large hill that loomed ahead, just off the path. "There is Mystic," they said.

The commander sent for Captain Underhill and his men, and the two conferred on tactics. Their conversation was brief and to the point: Knowing that the fort had two entrances, they would attack both ends simultaneously, with Mason commanding one contingent and Underhill the other.

The leaders bowed their heads and led the men in prayer. Then they set off for Fort Mystic in two columns.

Cresting the hill, the men beheld an impressive sight. The Pequot palisade, enclosing some two acres, had been fashioned from twelve-foot tree trunks driven deeply into the ground and solidly supported by an earthen rampart. Strategically placed loopholes ringed the enclosure, from which no arrows flew to menace the advancing English—surprise had been achieved.

The attackers pressed their advantage and rushed the entrances, both of which were blocked with brush and tree branches that had been piled for defense. After firing their muskets over the obstructions and through the palisade, each column forced the entrance before it, crowding into the enclosure with swords drawn. Caught with many of their number still asleep, the Pequots were trapped in a pincer.

WITHIN THE PALISADE, WHOSE TREES NOW POURED SMOKE LIKE ROWS OF CHIMNEYS, THE SCREAMING WAS SHRILL AND UNNERVING. MYSTIC'S RESIDENTS WERE BEING BURNED ALIVE.

Nevertheless, resistance was fierce and immediate. Captain Mason took a stream of arrows to his head, all of which bounced harmlessly off his helmet. Many of the English wore leather buff coats, which were thick enough to stop most arrows. Storming into the rows of wigwams, the soldiers slashed savagely with their swords, dealing ugly wounds to groups of Pequots who looked in vain for some safe place from which to launch a coordinated counterattack.

Then Mason appeared at the entrance to a large wigwam, a firebrand in his hand. Walking along the lanes between the structures, he set fire to one wigwam after another, imploring his lieutenants to do the same. It wasn't long before the enclosure became a conflagration.

Mason and Underhill hastened their men's evacuation from the inferno, ordering them to surround the palisade and shoot any Pequots who managed to flee. Standing

Hundreds of Pequot Indians lost their lives—mostly from immolation—in the colonists' destruction of their village in Mystic, Connecticut, in 1637. Only two colonists died in the attack.

clear of the tremendous heat, the great flames dancing and lunging before them, the soldiers encircled the dying settlement like executioners. Few Indians escaped, and all were shot down like game. Within the palisade, whose trees now poured smoke like rows of chimneys, the screaming was shrill and unnerving. Mystic's residents were being burned alive.

Two of Mason's men lost their lives that day. Another twenty were wounded. Inside and around Mystic, which ceased to exist, somewhere between four hundred and seven hundred Pequot men, women, and children lost their lives, most by way of immolation.

Having scorched whatever comestibles remained in the fort, Mason and his men, lower than ever on provisions, were forced to find the quickest route home to safety, which meant rendezvousing with ships in Pequot Harbor, seven miles to the west. Along the way they torched whatever settlements they came across and skirmished intermittently with the Pequots. The tribe's power, however, had been broken forever, borne away in the smoke of Mystic. As Captain Underhill later wrote, "Sometimes the Scripture declareth women and children must perish with their parents."

SAVAGE PRECEDENT

According to some accounts, the Mohegan and Narragansett warriors present at Fort Mystic's destruction fired their muskets into the air in protest of what their English allies were doing. Horrified by the European manner of war "because it is too furious, and slays too many men," the Indians saw their white-skinned neighbors as if for the first time. The chronicle of interaction between Amerindians and Europeans had turned a corner.

The conflict known to history as the Pequot War petered out after Mystic, leaving an indelible memory in all those who called New England home. Pequots looking for sanctuary from the predatory English were turned away by native peoples who wouldn't soon forget the lesson of Mystic. Indeed, parts of the head of Sassacus ended up being carried to Boston, care of other native peoples looking to appease the English.

In the treaty they forced upon the vanquished Pequot, English authorities sent Pequot captives into slavery both locally and abroad, and even attempted to expunge the name "Pequot" forever from local culture.

Not long before the massacre, well within the memory of the captains who burned women and children at Mystic, the great Wampanoag sachem Massassoit had saved the Pilgrims at Plymouth from certain destruction by offering them food and knowledge to carry them through. The Plymouth authorities had responded by securing ties with Massassoit and his people built on trust. That honeymoon had long since ended,

What could have been: Massasoit is shown smoking with the Pilgrims. He could just as easily have orchestrated their destruction.

replaced in a wide and dangerous wilderness with the baser instincts of people, both red and white, on the make.

Perhaps it was only a matter of time in New England before acquisitive instincts broke the limits of harmony. But the Mystic massacre had laid bare the harshest differences between old world and new in stark terms, setting a new standard for aggression—and ensuring the propagation of hatred and mistrust that would last for centuries to come.

chapter four

The First Female Defendant of the New World Tests the Tolerances of Puritan Righteousness

1637

"Mistress Hutchinson," said Governor John Winthrop in a voice that filled the Cambridge meetinghouse, "you are called here as one of those that have troubled the peace of the commonwealth and the churches here."

The governor sat behind a wooden desk surrounded by the other thirty-nine members of the General Court of Massachusetts, as well as eight Puritan ministers. Like the crowd that sat opposite them in this large, fireless place, the men kept their coats and gloves on against the November cold.

Standing before the court, wrapped in a wool cloak, was a rather ordinary-looking woman of forty-six. Anne Hutchinson was many things, including the mother of twelve children, an active member of the Congregationalist church, and a midwife. But to many she was also a menace, for which alleged crime she was now obliged to answer before the stern-faced men in black who sat before her.

"You are known to be a woman that hath had a great share in the promoting and divulging of those opinions that are the cause of this trouble . . ." As she listened to Winthrop, Anne gave no indication of fear or humility.

Weary with her sixteenth pregnancy, she nevertheless gave the outward appearance of one who hardly felt the heat of animus radiating toward her from the court. She was an intelligent, perhaps brilliant, woman, whose quick mind was matched only by an

Anne Hutchinson, Massachusetts Bay's most famous woman, steps before her accusers and into history in this hand-colored woodcut.

overweening surety in herself—one of the reasons, in fact, for her present predicament in this community that demanded quiet reserve from its female members.

The other issues that got her in trouble were more complicated. Two of the qualities that defined the Massachusetts Bay colony had conspired to whip up a crisis in 1637: First, the community's severe and pedantic religiosity, and second, its acutely felt vulnerability, from both within and without—fighting to maintain its freedom of action from England and its very existence from Indian foes, the colony was paranoid of any divisions that might undermine its need for strength and a united front.

Anne Hutchinson represented the explosive convergence of these circumstances, posing a problem for the colony that it was not properly prepared to face. The result was a clash of wills that brought Massachusetts to its knees, gave birth to a whole new colony to the south, and produced a heroine whom some have since dubbed "America's founding mother."

ONE WHO DARED

Though not present at the proceedings that late autumn day, there was one man whose reputation hovered above the debate like a ghost. John Wheelwright, Anne's brother-in-law, was a minister whose ideas had made him a few too many enemies. Convinced that the colony's other ministers were incapable of interpreting the gospel correctly, he openly railed against them to his own congregation, and espoused a brand of Puritanism that, among other things, seemed to imply a slightly greater equality between the sexes.

For such views he was ultimately banished from Massachusetts, a punishment that now threatened Anne—for she had backed his preaching. Had she been a man, she would have fixed her signature to the petition that was written up in support of Wheelwright before his forced exile.

Open support for Wheelwright was an excuse to come after her. Having already banished the signatories who refused to rescind their opinions, Winthrop's administration now focused on eliminating what they considered the heart of the colony's problem—the woman whose femininity hadn't stopped her from donning the wings of a gadfly.

The governor continued. "You have spoken diverse things, as we have been informed, very prejudicial to the honor of the churches and ministers thereof. And you have maintained a meeting and an assembly in your house that hath been condemned by the general assembly as a thing not tolerable nor comely in the sight of God nor fitting for your sex."

Winthrop had hit upon the genesis of Anne's dangerous conduct—and, in his opinion, of the commonwealth's troubles. Since 1635 she had been holding open meetings in her Boston home to go over the finer points of scripture with whoever chose to attend. And, as it soon happened, many indeed chose to attend.

At first only women showed up, but husbands, intrigued by their wives' accounts, started attending Anne's meetings as well. Their format was simple and straightforward: Anne, sitting in a chair at the head of her "class," would field questions about the most recent church scripture reading, guiding attendees to a fuller, deeper appreciation of the Bible's myriad lessons—at least, as she understood them.

A SPIRITUAL MENTOR

This was bad enough, as far as the leadership of Massachusetts was concerned. But what truly damned Anne in their eyes was her opinion of the ministers in whose hands rested the spiritual health of the colonists. It was widely suspected that Mistress Hutchinson derided their understanding of scripture, just like her brother-in-law had—that she had "traduced" the spiritual leaders of the community.

And when, in December 1636, they had held a meeting with her to discuss spiritual matters, she made her views plain to them. As far as she was concerned, the only minister in Massachusetts besides her brother-in-law Wheelwright who preached the gospel correctly was John Cotton.

Cotton, a longtime friend and associate of Anne's, was present in the Cambridge meetinghouse, and not just as a witness to Anne's trial. One of the most respected Congregational ministers on either side of the Atlantic, he was notoriously aloof and unreadable, as well as brilliant. He would probably have been present at proceedings like these no matter who was on trial. Cotton was something of a spiritual mentor to Anne, whose steadfast piety and intellectual dexterity with the intricacies of scripture had endeared her to him when they were still back in England. Here, in the New England frontier, his connection to her could save her—or seal her doom.

At the moment, however, it seemed not to matter. Governor Winthrop had a dilemma: Anne Hutchinson was as difficult

Anne's brother-in-law, John Wheelright, preceded her into exile.

to convict as she was to tolerate. As a woman, she was not entitled to a public role in Puritan society. How, then, could she have made a deleterious impact on the public?

Accusing her of such a crime was complicated, if not impossible-Winthrop may as well accuse a young child of deliberately undermining the local fur trade. With so much in Puritan culture based on the notion that women were subservient and inferior, the image of a female who could turn so many minds bordered on the ludicrous.

He tried the original tack of the Wheelwright petition. "Do you not assent and hold in practice to those opinions and factions that have been handled in court already, that is to say, do you not justify Mr. Wheelwright's sermon and the petition?" But his opponent was also sharp, and would not so easily be snared. Anne kept insisting that he name a charge, knowing that the governor was powerless to do so. "What have I said or done?" became the buckler with which she parried his jabs.

After all, such a thing as allying oneself with this or that minister was a matter of conscience, and therefore free of the state's punitive consideration. In this way she blunted the court's attacks on her, drawing the debate that frigid afternoon to the thing that seemed most tangible to Winthrop and his fellow court members: Anne's slandering of the colony's ministers.

And in this, the assembled would learn soon enough, lay far more than anyone had bargained for.

STANDOFF

By the end of the first day of Anne Hutchinson's trial, the argument against her had come to rest on a pair of related questions: Had she openly traduced the ministers of her colony? And had she done so based on a belief that Puritan orthodoxy found heretical?

"There were diverse things laid to [Mistress Hutchinson's] charge: her ordinary meetings about religious exercises; her speeches in derogation of the ministers among us; and the weakening of the hands and hearts of the people towards them," announced Governor Winthrop at the commencement of the second day's proceedings.

The governor's antagonism toward the accused was impossible to hide. Winthrop had a lot riding on Anne's destruction. He had been governor before, but in the time since his last term, the Hutchinsonians had become entrenched with the help of his predecessor, Governor Sir Henry Vane, an avowed friend of Hutchinson and Wheelwright. Under Vane's regime, unorthodox beliefs had been allowed to take hold and grow, like weeds in an abandoned garden.

Massachusetts Bay Governor John Winthrop made a point of confiscating the arms and ammunition of Hutchinson's male supporters in the colony.

Harvard College, later Harvard University, was created in 1638 as a religious school to properly instruct young ministers before they could fall under the sway of heretics like Anne Hutchinson.

Forged in Strife

Because Anne Hutchinson and her supporters insisted that only God's grace was required for salvation, their enemies accused them of being Antinomians—people who believed they were under no obligation to obey the laws of religious leaders or mentors.

Whether this was strictly true, most of the establishment of Massachusetts believed it. Consequently, they took steps to prevent later generations from falling under the snare of Antinomianism, or any other disagreeable doctrine, for that matter.

Their plan was simple. In early 1638, a wood-and-mortar building went up in Cambridge, Massachusetts, marking the beginnings of a new college. The idea was to instruct young ministers in the proper interpretation of religious belief before they could fall under the sway of wayward forces (e.g., Hutchinsonianism). In time, the college grounds would expand dramatically thanks to the generosity of an ailing son of a London publican named John Harvard. And so began the story of Harvard University—thanks in part to a brash woman named Anne Hutchinson.

Now back in power, Winthrop meant to purge his precious colony of all opposition. In addition to espousing unorthodox religious beliefs, Anne openly opposed the war on the Pequot Indians that had been raging for months. Such rifts in the community could not go unattended to.

Winthrop's intent was not entirely selfish: With the crown back in England looking for any sign of unrest as an excuse to rescind the colony's charter and exert direct control, the fate of Massachusetts hung in the balance. Winthrop slept easily at night knowing that his war on Mistress Hutchinson was as statesmanlike as it was pious.

And in the cloistered, chilly meetinghouse in Cambridge, that war had taken on a decidedly exegetic flair. Hoping to trap Anne in her own scriptural snare, the court pursued the displeasure that she seemed to have with all the commonwealth's ministers except Cotton. According to the ministers in the court who acted as witnesses, Anne—at the meeting with them eleven months before—had said that she thought only Cotton preached a covenant of grace. The others, so she was believed to have said, preached a covenant of works.

THE CONSEQUENCES OF GRACE

This was a vital point in seventeenth-century Puritanism, as contemporary belief insisted that God selected—before the creation of the universe—those destined to receive His grace and enter heaven. The "saints," as these elect called themselves, could discover in their lifetimes whether they were chosen, a state that Puritans dubbed "assurance." In effect, they came to know inwardly that they had been sealed with God's grace—that they had achieved "justification."

But what about one's conduct during life? If one's classification as a saint was dependent solely on God's unknowable will, what difference did one's conduct really make? This was the line that divided the Hutchinsonians from their critics, for, according to Hutchinson, who believed she was receiving her unique grasp of scripture from the Lord Himself, assuming that "good works" (or "sanctification") were crucial for someone to receive God's grace and get into heaven was heresy. In other words, one's conduct was entirely immaterial to one's chances of being—or becoming—a saint.

As for orthodox Puritans, they believed that grace was paramount, but that good works were still a part of God's plan, if only because the alternative implied that people may do as they damned well please—hardly an enticing prospect for buttoned-down Calvinists. Good works were also evidence of justification. Nevertheless, because grace was still all-important to them, they prided themselves on preaching a covenant of *grace*; anyone accused of preaching a covenant of *works* was committing the heresy of implying that behavior alone could get one into heaven.

Overleaf: Colonists such as these were banished from Massachusetts Bay for heresy.

Against this background, Anne's alleged remarks at the meeting eleven months earlier with the colony's ministers became *the* issue to the governor. According to most of the ministers themselves, she had claimed that only John Cotton preached a covenant of grace-implying, of course, that all the others preached a covenant of works. Further, it was believed that she implied that they were incapable of preaching a covenant of grace because they did not have "the seal of the spirit"—that is, that they weren't even saints.

COTTON MATHER SPEAKS

Anne had insisted all along that her words that night were meant to point out that none of the other ministers preached a covenant of grace *quite as clearly* as Cotton. Nothing was said, according to her, of a covenant of works.

"If they accuse me," Anne now said defiantly to the governor, "I desire it be upon an oath." Winthrop demurred, knowing that the sharp lady was laying a trap. Should the ministers take a solemn oath and then fail to remember precisely what was said eleven months ago, or contradict each other's testimony, they would be damned—and incapable of hurting her.

The tension in the courtroom, already high, increased palpably as arguments for and against the administering of an oath flew back and forth. *The ministers were proven men of God*, said some. *But the gentlewoman's fate is at stake*, insisted others. And so it went. Winthrop, increasingly exasperated and sensing that he still had nothing with which to conclusively convict the elusive woman before him, finally called on John Cotton to offer his testimony of that night. Cotton, temperate and accommodating as always, stood next to his old friend and essentially backed her story.

One of the ministers begged him to recall more: "Do you not remember that she said we were not sealed with the spirit of grace, therefore we could not preach a covenant of grace?"

"I do not remember it."

Winthrop, deflated, knew he was out of options. All he had against her now were her tacit support of the exiled Wheelwright and her improper conduct as a female leader of scripture meetings, neither of which was grounds for more than a formal admonishment.

Standing before him, Anne spoke up. "If you please to give me leave, I shall give you the ground of what I know to be true."

THE TEACHER MAKES HER EXIT

Though initially urged to be silent, as she had not been asked a question, Anne kept speaking as if the whole meetinghouse were now her classroom. "Now, I had none to open the Scripture to me but the Lord . . ."

It was as if the trial had somehow been concluded, and Anne felt the need to explain her thoughts by lecturing to her flock. Lively and intense, the accused proceeded to reveal to her stunned listeners the full breadth of her spirit and closeness to God. Winthrop wanted to silence her again but thought better of it: Perhaps she was about to hand him her own undoing.

With a glint in her eye, and clearly enjoying the rapt attention that showed so clearly on everyone's face, Anne insisted that God, in effect, spoke to her—a shocking thing, to say the least. He had revealed to her through scripture His favor for her. Quoting the biblical passages to which the Lord had led her, she seemed lost in a sort of rapture.

"Therefore, take heed how you proceed against me. For you have no power over my body," she warned the court. "Neither can you do me any harm, for I am in the hands of the eternal Jehovah my Savior."

Anne's rant finished with a prophesy: Should they move against her as they no doubt planned, God would destroy them, their posterity, and all of Massachusetts itself.

Well, then. Winthrop didn't know whether to cover his ears or yelp for joy. The woman hadn't only fashioned her own noose, but she had also obligingly slipped her head through it.

"I LOOK AT HER AS A DANGEROUS INSTRUMENT OF THE DEVIL, RAISED UP BY SATAN AMONGST US TO RAISE UP DIVISIONS AND CONTENTIONS, AND TO TAKE AWAY HEARTS AND AFFECTIONS ONE FROM ANOTHER."

—REVEREND JOHN WILSON, DESCRIBING ANNE HUTCHINSON

No one communicated directly with the deity, not even ministers (and certainly not a woman!). Any claim to do so was blasphemy. Incredulous and alert to a shift in the wind, Governor Winthrop asked her if she, like Daniel, expected to be saved by a miracle. Anne replied that she expected to be spared some calamity by providence, which then sparked a debate over whether "providence" was the same as a "miracle," which Cotton, for one, denied. But such pedantic chatter was academic at that point.

As far as the Winthrop faction was concerned, Anne's revelations were delusional, and clearly the cause of all the discord that her teachings had sown. She was a heretic, plain and simple—a neatly packaged excuse to move on to sentencing.

The Merciless Heretic

During the autumn 1637 crisis over Anne Hutchinson's beliefs, Governor John Winthrop's government made a point of confiscating the arms and ammunition of all those males in the colony who were known to foster sympathies for Mistress Hutchinson. Most of them were subsequently banished.

This, beyond the courtroom attacks on Hutchinson herself, was instrumental in securing the power of Winthrop and his allies. What transpired in the final months of 1637, in other words, was essentially a coup—a multitiered effort on the part of the recently elected governor to rub out the last vestiges of the old order that had existed under former Governor Sir Henry Vane.

One of the most well-known Hutchinsonians to lose his stature in the community was none other than John Underhill, who had lately done so much in the war against the Pequot Indians. Though most Hutchinson supporters shared Anne's displeasure with aggression against the Indians, Underhill harbored no such misgivings, and he led his men at the Mystic, Connecticut, massacre despite his other beliefs.

In 1643, after years of fruitless wandering in the colonies, he accepted an offer to lead soldiers in New Netherland, the Dutch colony centered on modern-day New York City and Albany. He soon proved his worth to his new employers, becoming one of Dutch Governor William Kieft's most valuable dogs of war.

In February 1644, Underhill complemented his awful work at Mystic with a repeat performance in southern Connecticut near Greenwich. In the midst of a brutal winter, Underhill—given command over all the Dutch forces—launched an attack on a palisade-village of Weequaesgeek Indians at Pound Ridge, near the border with Connecticut. As at Mystic, Underhill ordered his men to surround and torch the settlement, creating an extermination.

The Hutchinsonian was vivid in his depiction of the scene: "What was most wonderful is, that among this vast collection of Men, Women, and Children not one was heard to cry or scream."

Interestingly enough, Underhill made a return to Massachusetts in 1640, pleading that his sentence of excommunication be lifted. Church officials agreed after hearing his public confession—a performance he subsequently repeated for the General Court, which released him from most of his penalties.

✢

Anne Hutchinson's fiery life was brought to a violent end when she and her youngest children were massacred in a raid by Siwanoy Indians in 1642.

After more debate, which included an attempt by several Hutchinsonians to decry the injustice of the proceedings, the General Court voted. "Mistress Hutchinson," boomed Winthrop, "the sentence of the court you hear is that you are banished from our jurisdiction as being a woman not fit for our society, and are to be imprisoned till the court shall send you away."

CAST OUT

In fact, the colony of Massachusetts Bay wasn't done yet with its most famous outcast. The trial in Cambridge that November was a civil trial, conducted by the state.

Anne had yet to endure a religious trial. Held in March 1638 in Boston, its outcome was virtually assured; after all, she was already a convicted heretic who had been banished by the colony. The courtroom drama, also lasting two days, galvanized the community's move to rid itself of her. Cotton, faced with the possibility of being associated with Anne, made an effort to distance himself from her in the proceedings, removing her only remaining hope of succor.

As if all this weren't taxing enough, Anne's pregnancy was progressing poorly, hitting her with bouts of exhaustion that boded ill for the delivery. Toward the end of the trial the Reverend John Wilson spoke for many when he declared, "I look at her as a dangerous instrument of the Devil, raised up by Satan amongst us to raise up divisions and contentions, and to take away hearts and affections one from another." Anne Hutchinson was excommunicated.

Her last words as she exited the church were, "Better to be cast out of the Church than to deny Christ."

A NEW COLONY

Following Anne's sentence of banishment in November 1637, she was placed under house arrest until her church trial the following March. But she was not the only one whose future was altered irrevocably. In addition to her husband, Will, and their children, many of Anne's most prominent supporters, male and female, were disenfranchised or worse, creating a whole faction of outsiders looking for a new home.

They were not idle. Representing a variety of professions and beliefs, they had one central thing in common: They had been exiled from a society that brooked no alternative views to its rigid brand of religious orthodoxy. Grasping the greater significance of their plight, they decided to do more than merely flee Massachusetts Bay to the four winds—they decided to found a new colony. And this one would be a mirror image of the intolerant community they were leaving behind.

As Anne languished in her captivity that long, terribly cold winter, her husband and the others laid the foundations for the new home that would afford them freedom of conscience. In the spring, having settled on Aquidneck Island (then known to Europeans as Rhode Island), they composed and signed the Portsmouth Compact, bringing into being the colony that Anne Hutchinson's plight had wrought.

Roger Williams, an earlier outcast who settled Providence Plantations, lived just to the north, and he was instrumental in the colony's creation. According to the laws written down for the colony shortly after its settlement, "No person within the said colony, at any time hereafter, shall be in any [way] molested, punished, disquieted or called into question on matter of religion—so long as he keeps the peace."

A TRAGIC ENDING

Anne's struggle, whatever its motivation, had changed the complexion of New England forever. But her own life was struck with tragedy. In May 1638, she went into her sixteenth labor, hoping to add a thirteenth child to her magnificent brood. A troubled pregnancy from the start, marred by pain, weariness, and nausea, the outcome was in doubt. Six weeks shy of the expected delivery date, the forty-six-year-old gave birth to a frightening anomaly that bore no resemblance whatsoever to an infant. Though she bled profusely, Anne survived the ordeal.

Her enemies, however, pointed to the strange occurrence as proof of the woman's sinful nature. Was such a ghastly event not evidence of God's displeasure?

In fact, Anne herself would be undone by far more earthly matters. In 1642 her husband, Will, died. With Rhode Island's future in doubt among the eternally squabbling, land-hungry New England colonies, Anne took her youngest children and moved west to Dutch New Amsterdam, which would one day become New York City. There, in Pelham Bay, she made a home for her family. And there, the following year, she was massacred along with most of her youngest children in a raid by Siwanoy Indians. Only one child, nine-year-old Susan, survived the slaughter. Adopted by the Indians, she would eventually return to New England to form a family of her own.

Survived by six older children (including the fortunate Susan), the "American Jezebel," as she came to be known by her detractors, made a mark upon the raw land she adopted as her own.

Anne Hutchinson's religious inflexibility was probably as great as that of the men who accused her of heresy. Nevertheless, her willingness to take them on—her courage in transgressing the boundaries of her gender and in testing the limits of religious tolerance—set her apart as truly extraordinary. Perhaps it's too much to call her the originator of American religious freedom. But her struggle certainly played a role in laying its foundation.

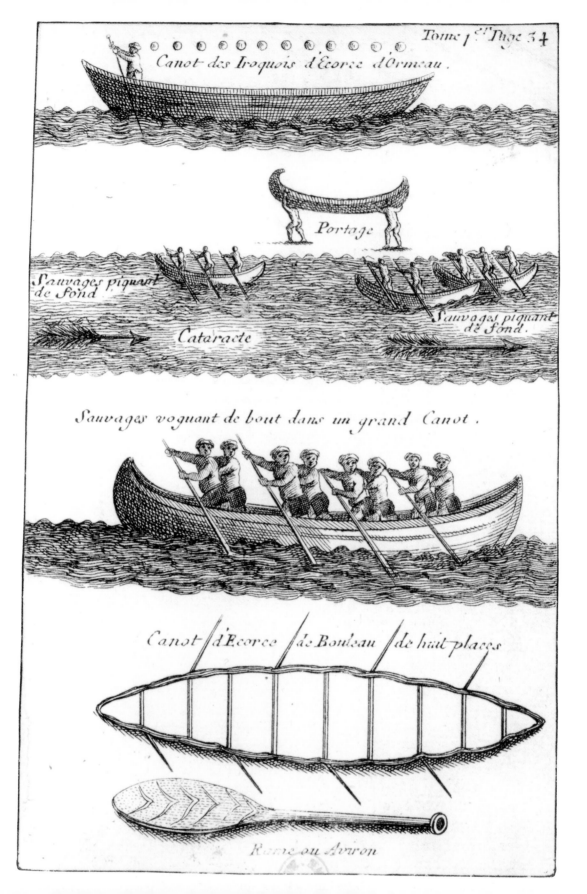

Canot des Iroquois d'Ecorce d'Ormeau.

Portage

Sauvages piquant de Fond

Cataracte

Sauvages piquant de Fond.

Sauvages voguant de bout dans un grand Canot.

Canot d'Ecorce de Bouleau de huit places

Rame ou Aviron

chapter five

The Five Nations Invade the West and Solidify an Iroquoian Empire

1654

The Seneca town of Sonontoen, in today's western New York State, swirled with activity. The day was bright and animated—children roughhoused between the longhouses, cook fires filled the air with enticing aromas, and young and old gathered to appreciate the spectacle that made this a day to celebrate: At the center of town, a large group of men were being tortured to death.

Throughout the long day, their captors clubbed, sliced, stabbed, yanked, and dismembered them in a carnival atmosphere, drawing cheers and chants from the ebullient crowd. These were choice enemies, whose torment was intended to compensate for an unacceptable crime—and to fortify the heart and spirit of the Seneca people.

Hanging over the community was the specter of war, whose promises of future suffering whispered into every Seneca ear as their victims this day twisted and winced under the knife. But Iroquois honor had been trampled upon. And today's festivities, whatever the consequences, were a necessity.

It was spring 1654, and the Five Nations of the Iroquois had long since grown accustomed to war. Organized into a confederacy, the Seneca, Cayuga, Onondaga, Oneida, and Mohawk comprised a league unlike anything in North America.

Five years before they had smashed the Huron, old enemies, and alarmed the French in their St. Lawrence fastnesses. From the Finger Lakes to the Richelieu River,

Canoes like these helped the Iroquois advance their nation—and on at least one occasion, shield their warriors from an onslaught by another tribe.

from Lake Ontario to the Virginia frontier, Iroquois influence spread like a rising tide. But their domain would not be safe as long as enemies—or potential enemies—lurked in the west.

Since the Europeans had arrived, the Iroquois had grown rich in trade goods like broadcloth, liquor, guns, and glass beads. But the white man always wanted only one thing in exchange: furs. And it wasn't long before nearly all of Iroquoia was trapped out.

Now, to maintain their control over trade with the Dutch along the Hudson, they needed to secure newer sources of beaver. And that meant expansion—a convenient complement to the traditional excuses for war, such as the taking of captives and avenging of old wrongs. The Eries, fellow speakers of the Iroquoian language, would fall like the Neutrals before them, opening the way to further conquests toward the Great Lakes. And the Iroquois now had their *casus belli*.

A Seneca man had been murdered in a feud with an Erie even as thirty Erie ambassadors were in Sonontoen to secure peace between the two peoples. Outraged, the Seneca decided to turn their Erie guests into victims. Five escaped, leaving the remaining twenty-five to be tortured in retaliation for the dead Seneca—as in so many things, the Iroquois favored extreme acts to set an example of ferocity for all to dread.

Now the war kettle was over the fire. Every one of the twenty-five Eries would end up consumed, either by flame or by the Seneca themselves. The Seneca knew that the cycle of retaliation would continue to escalate—but they had no idea just how far.

In the coming summer, they would find themselves launching an invasion the likes of which hadn't been seen since the desolation of Huronia. Having acquired a position of supremacy and a taste for wielding it, the Five Nations would set in motion a tide of violence that would ripple clear into the American plains, forever altering the balance of power in North America.

THE PRICE OF MOURNING

His name was Annenraes, and he was a great captain of the Iroquois, respected throughout the Five Nations. But he was no longer among his own people.

In the wake of the massacre of their delegation, the Erie went on the warpath, burning an Iroquois village and wiping out a raiding party. Among the few to be captured was Annenraes, who was taken back to the Erie as a great prize. His burning would do much to even the score with the Seneca.

But he was an extraordinary leader, gifted and eloquent. The Erie village soon understood that they had caught a man of tremendous worth. In very little time

Europeans and Native Americans trade in beaver pelts in this eighteenth-century image.

Annenraes won his enemies over, and they came to enjoy his company around the fires. He became as much an honored guest as a prisoner of war. And the idea of burning him to death was soon forgotten; he would be returned to his people as a gesture of peace that would bring honor to the Erie.

Now, as he feasted with his captors, he swelled with pride—how extraordinary must he be that he could invoke such mercy! This was a great story in the making, one that his children and his children's children would tell for generations to come.

Leaders of the village presented him with gifts of tools, wampum, and clothing. They were happy to have settled on a solution that all would welcome: Annenraes was to be given symbolically to the sister of one of the slain Erie ambassadors, replacing her lost brother with a captive of immense importance. Then he would be released. Custom will have been observed, and the Iroquois captain would live to help heal the wound between the Eries and the Senecas. Though the woman had been absent from the village, they were sure she would accept their proposal when she returned. All was warm and cordial, and the feasting continued.

As the hour grew late, several of the village elders left the banquet, having heard that the grieving woman had returned to the village and was waiting in her lodge. They found her there, wretched and sullen, and told her of their decision. But the woman protested emotionally, insisting that she could never stop her grieving until her brother's savage murder was avenged.

LIKE THE MEN FOR WHOSE MEMORY HE WAS SACRIFICED, ANNENRAES ULTIMATELY WENT TO THE FLAMES. AND WITH HIM WENT THE LAST BEST HOPE FOR THE ERIE PEOPLE.

The men urged her to reconsider: This would sink them further into a long fight with the Iroquois, who were mighty and terrible in war. But she only sobbed, demanding satisfaction. How could they keep one such as Annenraes in their midst and let him go after what the Seneca had done? How could they call themselves men? No, they must give the man to her. The great Iroquois's life was forfeit. It was her right.

Back at the feast, Annenraes looked with concern as the elders returned and stood by his side. Silent and grim, they insisted the captive come with them, and escorted him out into the cool night. Before long they were all standing in the woman's home, and Annenraes was quietly and quickly stripped of all the handsome gifts he'd so recently been given.

Awareness came flooding over him like an ice-cold waterfall, and his heart sank. Knowing he had but hours to live, all of which would be filled with the cruel caresses of his enemies, he prophesied the end of the Erie for what they were about to do. Nothing could save them now, he cried.

Like the men for whose memory he was sacrificed, Annenraes ultimately went to the flames. And with him went the last best hope for the Erie people.

BLOOD TIDE

News of the execution of Annenraes swept across Iroquoia, and what had been an Erie struggle with the Seneca became a struggle with four of the Five Nations; only the Mohawk, easternmost of the League peoples, would remain neutral. The Seneca, largest and westernmost of the Confederacy peoples, found a sympathetic audience at the Onondaga council fires for an assault on the Erie. This would not be a raid. All four of the nations provided warriors, creating a veritable army. And an army was needed: The Erie could field between three thousand and four thousand warriors, an awesome host.

From Oneida Lake to the Genesee River, scarlet poles appeared in almost every village—stark signifiers of war's arrival. Braves chanted, feasted, and pledged their ardor in the coming struggle. Though their numbers could never match those of the Erie, the Iroquois had acquired countless muskets over the years in their trade with the Dutch at Fort Orange, and they had become adept at using them.

Just as important, the Hudson River trade had also brought them iron tools and weapons. Unlike so many of their neighbors to the west, the Iroquois fought with steel hatchets—as handy at destroying palisades and longhouses as they were at hewing limbs and cleaving skulls. They also knew that a frightful reputation went before them in battle, a spiritual advantage that more than compensated for their smaller numbers.

The country to the west—a rich land whose large cougar population led the French to refer to the Erie as the "Cat Nation"—fell into chaos at the arrival of the invaders. Twelve hundred Iroquois braves had answered the call; hundreds more would follow throughout the summer.

Incredibly, they caught their enemy unawares, moving in smaller war bands through the wilderness like the many streams that eventually make a river. Striking with terrifying speed out of the east, garishly painted warriors loped from one village to the next, burning everything in their path, gathering a ghastly harvest of scalps. Surprise and ferocity were the Iroquois' primary weapons, playing on the fears of Erie villagers who fled before the onslaught. Throughout the territory from the Niagara River all along the southern coast of Lake Erie, the old footpaths funneled refugees farther west and south.

The Erie sachems knew that a reckoning was in order, and they worked to gather their warriors to make a stand. After five days of flight, the Erie leadership gathered their desperate people and quickly enforced order. Then, after choosing an ideal piece of ground, they began to build in earnest.

FATE OF THE CAT NATION

The army made a ferocious spectacle as it emerged from the woods. Tattooed and painted in vibrant hues, shouting and whooping like woodland beasts, the Iroquois advanced slowly on the Erie fortification before them, determined to force some weakness to present itself.

Since pouncing upon the Eries like a summer cyclone, they had driven out all before them, leaving a landscape of smoking desolation. Crops had been destroyed, villages gutted, and captives taken and tied for the return journey. Through a week of war they had encountered only scattered resistance, obliterating every war band sent against them. Clearly, it seemed, the Erie were preparing for a showdown. And this was it.

The people of the Cat Nation had not been idle. Like all Indians of the northeast, the Erie were adept at throwing up elaborate wood and earth defenses in very little time, whether for permanent settlement or as impromptu entrenchments. Over the previous day, with the enemy hot on their heels, they had constructed a palisade large enough to enclose the core of what remained of their people: between two thousand and three thousand warriors, along with countless women and children. This was truly a fortress of defiance, massive in scale and stoutly built of tree trunks, the gaps between which offered innumerable loopholes for the loosing of arrows and gunshot.

League confidence had been high since taking up the hatchet, but this was no ordinary obstacle. Already outnumbered, they now faced a superior foe behind daunting works. The bulwark before them negated every advantage they had enjoyed till now. Logic dictated that they treat with these people to find some accommodation.

Two war sachems led the Iroquois host, and they now stepped out before their braves. Their dress already set them apart. Before embarking upon this war, the elders of Onondaga—the most influential of the Five Nations—had entertained French Jesuits from New France. Intent on converting the Iroquois to the Catholic faith, the Black Robes had bestowed gifts on their hosts, including French clothing and uniforms. The two captains who now faced the might of the Erie people presented themselves in an outlandish fusion of European and native garb, a display intended to unnerve the Erie by its shear strangeness.

In fact, one of them was a successful convert of the priests. He now spoke up to implore the Erie to reason, claiming that the "master of life" now fights for the Iroquois. The defenders were unimpressed, admitting ignorance of this so-called "master" and proclaiming in their confidence that they acknowledged the power of none but their own weapons.

Unlike many of their neighbors to the west, the Iroquois fought with steel hatchets—as handy at destroying palisades as cleaving skulls.

Overleaf: An attack on a heavily protected Iroquois fortress is depicted in this early seventeenth-century engraving.

With this, the sachems grew incensed and returned to their men. Within moments, the great throng of Iroquois charged the palisade from all sides, howling with fury and brandishing their weapons in a terrifying display. Almost at once came a hail of missiles from behind the wooden walls, dropping many of the attackers. The waves of Iroquois kept coming until, nearly at the wall, they loosed a storm of musketry, focusing on the loopholes but unable to harm their tormenters. Others hacked at the wooden barrier while still others attempted to scale the walls using their fellows as steps. But the Erie settlement stood firm and unbroken.

SLAUGHTERHOUSE

Fire from within the defensive barrier remained furious, decimating all who made a charge for the wall's base in the hopes of establishing some lodgment. Still the Iroquois came on, pouring their fire and rage into the defenses.

By this time they had begun to bring out their secret weapon: counter-palisades. Built like scaled-down, portable versions of the palisade they were now attacking, each could be carried by several braves like an extraordinarily large shield, providing cover and, when placed side by side, offering an ad-hoc defensive barrier from which close-range fire could play on the enemy.

The Iroquois produced more and more of these from the rear, creating islands of protection that slowly began to surround the great Erie fortress. But despite their improved situation, they still failed to make a breach. The day wore on, hot and stifling, the wounded staggering and crawling from the great clearing that surrounded the Erie.

A stalemate settled over the plain. Iroquois warriors, sweating and impatient with the day's progress, began shouting to each other for ideas from behind their great wooden shields. Before long one started circulating that held the hope of success. Out from the woods whence they had all come marched warriors bearing, of all things, canoes.

More and more made their way to the front lines as the Erie, clearly running short of arrows and gunpowder, maintained a desultory fire. The boats, which had borne the Iroquois along the streams and lakes to hasten their advance, would now be used for a very different purpose. When enough had been brought forward, a great war whoop went up from the Iroquois ranks, and a line of braves hastened forward while holding the canoes before them like shields (much lighter than the counter-palisades).

At the base of the palisade, a series of furious battles commenced as the Erie poured violence at oblique range on the Iroquois struggling to maintain their positions at the wall. But the defenders were flagging; presently, the assailants were able to get their canoes upright, leaning them against the palisade like scaling ladders.

The rest of the Iroquois streamed forward, screaming their wrath. Frail and a little wobbly, the upright canoes nevertheless delivered their burdens up and over, allowing the Iroquois to pour over the walls like a flash flood.

Within the palisade, the scene erupted in gore. Having refused to surrender peaceably, the Erie had damned themselves utterly, and the Iroquois now enforced a ruthless judgment. The palisade had been built too well: With so few entrances, each narrow enough to easily defend, the fort now trapped its builders as surely as it had defied its attackers throughout the hot summer day. Iroquois warriors, presented with a profusion of prospective victims, fell upon the screaming populace with exhausting brutality. Few of the unfortunate Erie were able to escape, turning the enclosure into a slaughter pen.

Before the day was finished, the remaining Erie made a futile counterattack and were nearly destroyed. For all intents and purposes, their people had been broken.

SWEPT ASIDE

The fight that fateful day against the Erie fort cost the Iroquois dearly, and they spent weeks in the vanquished country before returning to their homes. Victory, however, was theirs. Though the war would continue for another year, the Cat Nation had ceased to be a formidable people. In the end, they migrated west, putting as much distance between themselves and the Iroquois as possible.

Their destruction opened the way west, like a great barrier swung wide. As it had in the north, east, and south, Iroquois hegemony would spread west, bringing more peoples, trade routes, and trapping grounds under their control. In the following two years they launched offensives into present-day Michigan, across Lake Michigan into what is today Wisconsin, and north, beyond Lake Huron and down the St. Lawrence.

With varying degrees of success, they would fight peoples of the Great Lakes region like the Mascouten, Poulak, and Ottawa, as well as northern foes like the Necouba and Abenaki. The causes of these wars varied, but all of them put the long arm of Iroquois might in bold relief. By the 1660s they were raiding the Sioux on the northern plains, the Shawnees to the southwest, and the Susquehannock on the banks of the Chesapeake.

Though the Iroquois suffered defeats during these years, their victories were more numerous and decisive, placing them in a uniquely strong position. Seeking refuge within the Iroquois circle, client peoples welcomed "governors" from Onondaga, extending the frontiers of a bona fide empire. And all of this was achieved by a league of nations whose population was relatively tiny: Rarely did the total number of Iroquois warriors exceed two thousand. Little wonder that some called them the "Romans of the New World."

The Longhouse

Although Europeans referred to the peoples of the League as "Iroquois," the Indians knew themselves as Haudenosaunee, meaning "People of the Longhouse." This distinctive and remarkable structure, so closely linked with the Iroquois in the popular imagination, was once ubiquitous throughout the northeast.

Ranging anywhere from thirty to almost four hundred feet in length, the Iroquois longhouse was a communal building whose sections housed individual families belonging to the same clan. The larger the clan, the longer the building, though longhouses invariably measured around twenty feet wide and twenty feet high.

They were built of tree trunks cut from second-growth forests, whose smaller trees allowed a greater variety of tensile strength. While stout, inflexible posts formed the walls and ends, greener trees were used to form the bowed rafters, which had to be bent to form the distinctive domed roof.

Over this skeletal structure was fastened a "skin" of bark, preferably from the elm tree, which was harvested from older forests to ensure large sheets. These sheets of bark, once flattened and dried, could make a surprisingly durable barrier against the elements. With the help of tools that were made of stone or animal

Built of wood, the Iroquois longhouse ranged from thirty to almost four hundred feet in length and housed individual families belonging to the same clan.

bone, the sheets were tied to the frame with strips of younger bark that had been soaked in water for flexibility. Once dried, they shrank, securing the fastening.

The longhouse's interior was as warm and welcoming as it was utilitarian and practical. Each family, depending on its size, was allotted roughly twenty feet of the structure's length, with each section placed end to end. A common corridor ran from one end of the longhouse to the other, with each family's section partially walled off from its neighbors. There were only two entrances, one at either end, either of which could have a roof or other enclosure that could double as a shed. Hanging from the high ceiling were har-

vested corn, tobacco, or sacks of beans, while more foodstuffs were stored in communal areas at either end.

Each family had its own fire pit, whose smoke was released through an opening in the bark roof that could be closed during periods of inclement weather. The organization afforded closeness and a degree of privacy with in families while simultaneously emphasizing the importance of, and connection to, clan.

Tree of Peace

It is worth noting that much of the success of Iroquoian diplomacy rested on a martial reputation that, some historians believe, was uniquely brutal and relentless relative to the League's myriad neighbors. Whether that's true, the Iroquois themselves certainly believed their past to be a violent and destructive one—that they possessed an alarming penchant for warfare that formed the unlikely genesis of the Confederacy itself.

At some date that will forever remain nebulous (perhaps the mid-sixteenth century), the five nations decided that embracing each other, rather than constantly fighting each other, made a great deal of sense. According to tradition, the great founder behind this development, Deganawida, made a circuit of the various Iroquois people, and was eventually joined by an outcast named Hiawatha.

As they traveled from one village to the next, the two proposed a "Great Peace" that would end the constant wars of mourning and allow the Iroquois to create something greater than themselves. The five nations ultimately agreed, converging on the territory whose sachem, Tadodaho, was the only one to resist the idea: the territory of the Onondaga. Ironically, the Onondaga would become the heart of the League after Tadodaho was told that he could preside over the League as its chairman. They became the keepers of the council fires and the Tree of Peace, a white pine planted by Deganawida that represented the coming together of the various nations.

✣

By the last quarter of the seventeenth century, anyone wanting to do business in the northeast on a large scale had to treat with the Iroquois. Their position was unique: Though bordering on the European powers in New England, on the Hudson, and along the St. Lawrence, their vast realm had protected them from the fate that had befallen other Indian nations whose smaller territory was easily manipulated or even annexed by land-hungry white speculators.

They maintained a constant, carefully controlled trade with the European powers while acting as middlemen to Indians farther west who did not have direct contact with European colonies. And their ability to mobilize large numbers of warriors,

The outcast Hiawatha grapples with an opponent in this nineteenth-century hand-colored woodcut.

both from the League itself and from client nations, ensured their security for decades to come.

In the end, the Europeans, whom the Iroquois had expertly played off each other for years, pulled the League apart as their military and economic power grew. The Mohawks in the east became relentlessly Anglophile, while those in the west, particularly the Senecas, were drawn into the French camp. Such a situation compromised the centuries-old solidarity centered at Onondaga, spelling the doom of Iroquois supremacy.

chapter six

The English Steal a Colony and Gain a Metropolis

1664

New Amsterdam bustled with panic in the hot August air. From the gabled homes off Heere Wegh (later known as "Broadway") to the boisterous, pungent taprooms along Pearle Street, people worried and speculated in a dozen languages. English gunboats had appeared in the harbor amid rumors of an invasion. What would happen next? Bombardment? All-out war?

One man stood out from the others for his grim determination. As he limped purposefully through the streets, Pieter Stuyvesant—the same peg-legged director-general of New Netherland who had wiped New Sweden from the map less than a decade before—seethed with rage.

He had heard rumors that the English were planning a preemptive strike against New Netherland, a fact he hastily passed on to his employers, the Dutch West India Company. The company responded with reassuring calm that there was a squadron of English ships headed his way, but that he need not worry about it. According to England, the squadron's mission was to exert greater control over its colonies in New England. No act of aggression should be expected. Besides, no state of war as such existed between the two great powers.

Clearly, the information from Westminster had been a ruse to lull the Dutch into a state of unwary calm. And what galled Stuyvesant was that it had worked. Satisfied with the security of New Amsterdam, he had traveled north to Fort Orange, the other principal hub of New Netherland, to deal with the local Mohawk Indians, only to learn that

English vessels had parked themselves menacingly at the mouth of Manhattan's harbor in his absence. Racing back south on the Hudson River current, he found a town in chaos.

This was a moment—a morass of danger, paranoia, and international brinkmanship—for which Pieter Stuyvesant, soldier-administrator extraordinaire, thought himself ideally suited. On that note he was dead wrong. In the gambit that was about to decide New Amsterdam's fate, Stuyvesant alone posed the greatest danger to the community's safety. Nevertheless, the jewel that survived his ham-fisted reign and red-faced defiance—the colony that would pass to his nation's enemies—owed much to Stuyvesant for the resilience that made it, ultimately, one of the world's greatest cities.

ROYAL LAND-GRAB

Stuyvesant, characteristically, met the threat out in the harbor head on. In the claustrophobic confines of New Amsterdam's fort, he dictated a brief letter to the warships floating off his island like great wooden predators waiting for signs of weakness. What was their intention?

The answer came the following morning, and it was as blunt as blunt could be. Stuyvesant was to surrender the island of Manhattan and all its inhabitants to the English. Ever the pedant, Stuyvesant returned the letter because it was unsigned. Another letter followed soon enough, dutifully signed by one Richard Nicolls, commander of His Majesty's forces in the harbor. And it merely emphasized its predecessor's brusque terms.

Nicolls was a forty-year-old man-at-arms who had long since hitched his wagon to the house of Stuart, the family that now sat on the throne of England. He had stayed with the Stuarts and fought with them in exile during the years when Oliver Cromwell ruled England, and he had returned to Britain when Charles Stuart assumed the throne as Charles II. Nicolls, however, was principally the creature of the sovereign's brother James. And it was James, Duke of York, on whose behalf this overt act of real estate thievery was being committed.

Playing the dedicated warrior to his brother's dissolute patron of the arts, the Duke warmed to games of conquest. Appointed Lord High Admiral by Charles and spurred by voices in parliament who were "mad for a Dutch war," James presided over a great scheme whose goal was nothing less than the total reorganization of the Atlantic world.

English forces would kick the Dutch out of their slave posts in West Africa, exert more uniform, direct control over the colonies in New England, and, most important,

The British had to get through Pieter Stuyvesant, director-general of New Netherland, to get at New Amsterdam, and very nearly did.

seize the capital of the Dutch empire in the New World itself: New Amsterdam, key to the Hudson and to all North America. By royal caveat, James was to inherit all the land to be pilfered from the Dutch—a vast empire that stretched from Maine to Delaware.

Little regard was given to the consequences of this preemptive strike, but the Stuarts had an idea of what lay in store for them. And it would shape the course of world history.

AN OLD VETERAN'S OBSTINACY

The foil for England's plan played his part to the hilt. Upon receiving Nicolls's demand, the director-general of New Netherland prepared himself for the ultimate sacrifice. Since the 1630s Pieter Stuyvesant, now in his fifties, had been a devoted employee of the West India Company.

After starting as a clerk, he had worked his way up through the company's ranks through hard work and conspicuous discipline, and was made governor of Curaçao in 1643. There he had led a daring, if unsuccessful, attack on Portuguese St. Martin, during which his leg was carried off by a cannonball. From the Caribbean to the Chesapeake, he had fought for the United Provinces (later known as The Netherlands), and not for nothing. Now, in the face of overwhelming force, he would stand defiant.

There would be no capitulation.

After all, he was director-general, and directors-general didn't make history by surrendering. Stumping along the bastions of his tumbledown fort, he looked out upon the mongrel population he was sworn to protect. They hailed from all over Europe, and some from beyond that. There were Jews, Lutherans, Catholics, Calvinists, and atheists. Settlers from the United Provinces lived alongside Germans, English, Scots, free and enslaved Africans, Swedes, and French.

This, he muttered to himself as he paced, is what comes from free trade. It had been the West India Company's idea, not his. He would've preferred a structured society of Dutch settlers and Company employees, all marching to the same drum and—more important—worshiping at the same Dutch Reformed church.

When he had first arrived seventeen years ago in 1647, New Amsterdam had been a filthy cockpit of disorder. The new director-general set about turning it into a proper outpost of civilization. He enforced the removal of trash from the streets, outlined new building codes to alleviate the town's vulnerability to fire, gave Manhattan its first hospital, and organized a nascent police force. He fostered local industry, turned the town into the continent's entrepôt for the slave trade, and presided over a healthy rise in population—by 1664, around 1,500 people called New Amsterdam home, three times as

English plans to take over the New World called for James, Duke of York, and future king, to inherit all the land pilfered from the Dutch—a vast empire that stretched from Maine to Delaware.

The Stadhuis, or city hall, in New Amsterdam is shown here in a seventeenth-century watercolor.

many as when Stuyvesant first assumed office. And most of them looked upon their director-general (or governor) more as a tyrant than a leader.

Why? Because he had brought structure, security, and definition. When they need-ed cleanliness and efficiency, he had given it to them—and all he had ever wanted in return was obedience. Prosperity had made the people—these myriad people from far-flung, heretic lands—brash and ungrateful. And so they whined and chafed like chil-dren, demanding freedoms they didn't deserve. And he, as father figure of an outpost on the edge of chaos, was forced to bear down and do his best, follow his righteous instincts—even if those instincts worried the Company itself as well as the citizens of New Amsterdam.

He knew better than his charges, and they would have to suffer for it. They had wanted religious tolerance, local government, and popular representation, and he had

Richard Nicolls, henchman of James, Duke of York, became the first governor of New York. Here, he presides over the establishment of a local racecourse.

The Dutch Come Back for Round Two

On May 28, 1672, Richard Nicolls stood on the deck of a Royal Navy ship off the Suffolk coast as it raced into battle against the Dutch. Standing next to him was James, Duke of York—who had the ugly misfortune of watching his famed henchman get savaged by a cannonball in the heat of action. It proved to be the end of Nicolls.

Called the Battle of Southwold Bay, the fight in which the Dutch revenged themselves on Nicolls for his 1664 triumph across the Atlantic was part of the Third Anglo-Dutch War. And while Nicolls lay mauled and bleeding to death, the scheme to reverse his conquest of New Amsterdam was already in the planning stage.

In the spring of 1673, a dashing Dutch mariner named Cornelis Evertsen led a squadron of ships to the Western Hemisphere to hit the British empire where it hurt. After stealing sugar and slaves in the Caribbean, Evertsen blew into the Chesapeake like a bad dream and captured the English tobacco fleet in its entirety. By July he was eyeing New York itself.

Evertsen had not arrived to parley, and he wasted little time loosing his fury on the English occupiers of Manhattan. He bombarded the fort, sent marines ashore, and captured the colony very neatly. New York was renamed New Orange, and the new landlords toiled to bring back Dutch administration. All for naught.

Two years later, the exhausted States General of the United Provinces settled a peace treaty with England that gave New York back to the English.

come down hard on non-Calvinist faiths—particularly Quakers—and dismissed the town's council. He had demanded strict observance of the Sabbath and absolute obedience to his governance. All of this, he believed, was his responsibility.

Now the reborn society that he'd worked so assiduously to build was about to be taken from him by brigands from a renegade power. Who were they kidding? Did anyone seriously think that Pieter Stuyvesant was going to lie down over something like this? No. It was time for a little fire and brimstone.

A TOWN BESIEGED

A stalemate of several days ensued, and August faded into September. Ensconced within his quarters in Fort Amsterdam, Pieter Stuyvesant read—for the hundredth time—a letter addressed to him from Nicolls that was already a couple of days old.

The second appeal from Nicolls, it offered generous terms for the town's capitulation, including a stipulation that guaranteed "every man in his Estate, life, and liberty"—all the citizens of New Amsterdam had to do, in other words, was accept the transfer of sovereignty to England, and nothing would change. They could maintain their property, way of life, chosen faiths, and uniquely tolerant culture. All that would change would be the flag flying over the fort.

Stuyvesant had kept the letter a secret. Knowing his people's penchant for cowardice and liberty, he chose not to offer them an opportunity to save their necks and cost him his moment of glory.

He had calculated the odds. Stuyvesant had at his disposal some 150 soldiers, a paltry store of powder and shot, and a fort that was clearly showing its age. Nicolls, on the other hand, had many times that number of men and a lot of good artillery with copious stores of fresh powder. And that wasn't the only problem.

Patriots from New England had gathered on Long Island in support of Nicolls's ships. Arrayed along the shore of Brooklyn in plain sight of the fort, these aggressive English partisans presented themselves in martial array, the tips of their pikes glinting threateningly in the late summer sun. Stuyvesant could not gauge their numbers precisely, but they clearly offered a baneful supplement to Nicolls and his force.

But if the director-general was worried about them, what he saw next gave him very serious concern indeed. Summoned by a guard to the parapets, he spied a boat rowing toward the dock, its crew clearly waving a white flag. The director-general limped out to receive the party, which he presently learned was led by John Winthrop, governor of Connecticut. Winthrop carried a letter reiterating Nicolls's previous offer, which remained just as generous as before. And this document—handed to Stuyvesant in front of numerous witnesses—could not be kept secret.

Winthrop, who had known the Dutch director-general for years, begged him to carefully consider the lenient English terms and avoid any needless bloodshed. New Amsterdam's capture was a fait accompli, insisted the Connecticut Yankee, and defiance would only lead to the slaughter of innocents. Their meeting did not go unnoticed by a town on the verge of calamity. Letter in hand, the director-general stumped his way up Pearle Street, over the brackish brown water of the Heere Grecht canal, all the while feeling the eyes of his fellow citizens upon him. He was headed for City Hall (the "Stadhuis"), where, he knew, his greatest trial awaited.

THE TRAGEDIAN IN HIS SIGNATURE ROLE

Inside New Amsterdam's Stadhuis, a crowd of apprehensive city officials clamored for answers. Before them stood a sweating Stuyvesant, the exhaustion of the last week showing clearly in the way he leaned heavily on his good leg. But if his face was slick with perspiration from the heavy air, it also showed a degree of calm assurance that stood utterly at odds with the frantic throng that now confronted him. The promise of destruction had given him a sort of peace that his frightened fellows could neither sense nor understand.

Voices from the crowd spoke of rumors—that the English were offering generous terms, that they were willing to let the colony go on as it had. What did Manhattan stand to gain by fighting? Death? Mutilation? The horrors of plundering invaders?

As nerves stretched to the breaking point, the assembled men began demanding that Stuyvesant show them the letter that he'd been given by Winthrop. They suspected what it was: proof that this whole nasty international incident need not end in the death of women and children. And they knew what their director-general wanted to do. He had told them: Fight to the last. To him, that was the only option with honor.

So Stuyvesant produced the letter. And then, before the assembled leaders of New Amsterdam, he tore it up.

Shouts of outrage shook the rafters. For seventeen years, the city's eclectic mass of brewers, traders, prostitutes, farmers, and seamen had tolerated the tyrannical excesses of Pieter Stuyvesant. All their requests for greater participation in government had fallen on deaf ears. Now they'd been trapped in a mad death-drama of his making. And that, not surprisingly, was too much.

Overleaf: Enduring the unendurable: Pieter Stuyvesant surrenders New Amsterdam to the English.

The End of New Sweden

One of Pieter Stuyvesant's proudest achievements was the destruction of New Sweden. Centered on the Delaware River and comprising parts of the present-day states of New Jersey, Pennsylvania, and Delaware, the colonial enterprise of New Sweden was begun in 1638 by a nation that was experiencing its golden age.

Under the leadership of King Gustav Adolph, who died in 1632 while campaigning in Germany during the Thirty Years War, Sweden had become a Protestant powerhouse, leveraging its unique military prowess into a position of supremacy amid the powers that bordered the Baltic Sea. Riding this wave, Sweden established colonies on the American coast, joining the rarified group of European empire-builders.

Alas, it was a short-lived enterprise. In 1654 the Swedish expanded along the Delaware by taking over Fort Casimir, a Dutch establishment. Though the conquest was bloodless, the Dutch took notice up in Manhattan. Pieter Stuyvesant reacted the following year by sailing up the Delaware with an impressive armada of ships and more than three hundred armed men. Within weeks, he received the surrender of Sweden's strongholds in the region. New Sweden became a memory.

Incredibly, Stuyvesant's antagonists insisted that he give them the pieces of the letter. He superciliously complied, and the burgomasters set about fitting them together into a readable whole. New Amsterdam's predicament had achieved the absurd.

The director-general's day would not get any calmer. Nicolls, having grown impatient with the progress of affairs, made the bold decision to move his ships up from the narrows and close enough to Manhattan to shell it. News of this development galvanized Stuyvesant.

Walking as fast as his groaning wooden stump would allow, the director-general raced into the fort, up the stairs, and out onto the top of the bastions. There he saw the malevolent spectacle of the English ships, close enough now to take his other leg off with a lucky shot. It was the moment that his career had been leading up to. Here, with the earthen solidity of the fort beneath his feet, he felt his heart race with the prospect of a fight, however hopeless. Not far from him, soldiers awaited the order to fire their guns. The director-general of New Amsterdam considered precipitating the destruction of his city.

The townspeople, however, had not given up on their ban of suicide. At this very pregnant juncture in Manhattan's history, two of the colony's leading clerics decided to shape the course of events.

Dominie Megapolensis and his son, also a churchman, ascended to the battlements and spoke with Stuyvesant. No one will ever know what words passed among the three men, but the effect was clear. The director-general, convinced of the profound futility of his situation, was talked out of his dream of Armageddon and escorted by the dominie out of the fort. Reality was gradually returning to the colony's highest office.

CHANGING OF THE GUARD

Monday, September 8, was a turning point in Pieter Stuyvesant's life—and in the history of North America. At eight o'clock in the morning, he stood inside the fort that he had grown to know so well. And though soldiers of the Dutch West India Company surrounded him, he felt like the loneliest man in New Amsterdam.

Both his besiegers and his fellow besieged had been working toward the same thing: his surrender. Spurred by his unforgiving vision of duty and praying for some succor from Europe, the implacable Dutchman had brought his community to the brink. And then, in a stunning blow, the burgomasters had presented the director-general with a petition of ninety-three names demanding that he accept Nicolls's surrender terms. Prominent among them was Stuyvesant's seventeen-year-old son, Balthasar.

And so, two days before, he had been obliged to arrange, at his own farm outside of town, a meeting between the two opposing camps to arrange the surrender of New Amsterdam. The humiliating end had come at last.

As the sun climbed and the shadows shortened inside the walls of Fort Amsterdam, Stuyvesant, impressive in his glinting cuirass, brooded over his fate. He had signed the surrender document that very morning, his hand probably shaking in the effort. He would have preferred death to this.

Above him flew the flags of the United Provinces and the Dutch West India Company, the standards for which he had struggled so hard and so long. Now they would be carried out of this place and across the sea. With an effort, he gave his last command as director-general of New Netherland and ordered the little column of soldiers forward. Drummers beating, it wound its way through the open gate and toward the waterfront. There, before a thousand onlookers, the party slowly boarded a ship, the *Gideon*, and bore away the fate of the Dutch empire in North America.

The Fortunes of World War

Nicolls had won a major victory indeed: bloodless and decisive. New Amsterdam became New York, and Fort Orange, up the Hudson, was renamed Albany. The Duke of York's big gamble had paid off.

But it was about to reap the whirlwind. James and his sovereign brother, as well as all the bloody-minded gentlemen who surrounded them, had allowed themselves to be duped into thinking that the United Provinces were on the way out. Perhaps—but not nearly as quickly as Westminster had hoped. In fact, the Dutch still had plenty to teach their rivals across the channel.

The conflict that quickly ensued, known to history as the Second Dutch War of 1665–1667, didn't make very good newspaper copy in England. Despite several significant English victories at sea, the Dutch recaptured their bases in Africa, scored their own

impressive record of maritime triumphs, and, most sensationally, dealt their foes the single worst naval disaster in British history.

In June 1667, a Dutch fleet under the great Michiel de Ruyter sailed up the Medway in England, pounced on the fleet anchored at Chatham, sank much of it, and towed the massive HMS *Royal Charles* back home as a trophy. (The great warship's coat of arms remains a Dutch museum piece to this day.)

But there were a couple of other Dutch victories, as well—and they would have a profound effect on the destiny of New York. In the great global commercial wars in which England and the United Provinces clashed, New Amsterdam, though significant as a naval base and a strategic entrepôt to greater markets, earned *nothing* compared with other places around the

The conflict between the English and Dutch didn't stop with the surrender of New Amsterdam. In June 1667,
a Dutch fleet under Michiel Adriaanszoon de Ruyter delivered England its single worst naval disaster.

world over which empires were willing to spill their blood and treasure.

In 1667, the Dutch captured two of these significant places: Suriname, along the South American coast, and Paulu Run, a flyspeck of an island in Indonesia. The former produced sugar, while the latter was the world's primary source of nutmeg—two commodities whose outrageous profit margins in the markets of Europe made Suriname and Paulu Run some of the most valuable real estate on the globe. Little wonder, then, that the Dutch, flush with victory, were happy to trade New Amsterdam at the peace conference of Breda for these two remote locales and their enormous financial potential.

The Dutch could not have foreseen what Manhattan would one day become, of course. But it is interesting to consider that the island's colony—turned by liberal, Dutch free trade into a colorful, uniquely cosmopolitan society; given structure and organization by a strutting autocrat who nearly blew it to pieces; and incorporated into a British empire that would allow its population to truly explode—should find its destiny in exchange for exotic locations that are now all but forgotten.

As for Pieter Stuyvesant, he couldn't stay away from Manhattan forever. He eventually returned, thrived as a farmer and converted "New Yorker," and died peacefully in 1672.

chapter seven

One Indian Sachem Ignites a Conflict That Changes New England Forever

1675

On June 8, 1675, Plymouth colony sealed its own fate. Before an assembled crowd, three local Indians were led to a gallows and hanged in succession. Though the first two executions came off without incident, the third produced a surprise. The condemned in question, the youngest of the three, was spared when the rope unexpectedly broke, sending him tumbling to the ground before gasping onlookers.

As the young man was helped to his feet, English officials pressed him one last time to change his testimony in light of his miraculous reprieve. So he did: The two men swinging above him, his father and his father's friend, had indeed murdered the Christian Indian named Sassamon. As for himself, the overwhelmed young Indian insisted that he'd only been a spectator to the act. In accordance with English law, which looked mercifully on victims of botched executions, his life was spared.

To the Puritan witnesses that day, the confession seemed like divine confirmation that justice had been served. The murderers named Tobias and Mattachunnamo had been properly punished—and then outed, no less, by Tobias's own son. Would that everything in seventeenth-century New England were that simple.

In fact, *nothing* in seventeenth-century New England was that simple, as events would soon prove. The jury had earlier convicted Tobias and his fellows of murder based on the testimony of a single eyewitness (needless to say, the account of Tobias's son, though a corroborating testimony, was given *after* sentence had been passed). According to law, however, two eyewitnesses were required.

But as everybody in Plymouth knew, tensions between the English and their Indian neighbors had been at a fever pitch for months. And at the trial of Sassamon's alleged killers, one witness was enough in a rush to justice. The blithering admission from Tobias's son, his neck still red from the rope, served as a convenient confirmation. Sassamon, after all, had been an informer for the English, risking his life among his fellow Wampanoags to bring word of their actions back to the governor of Plymouth colony. His death, coming on the heels of his reports of Wampanoag war preparations, could not have been an accident.

It probably wasn't. But the June 8 executions were received with outrage throughout most of the local Indian communities.

RACE WAR

One man in particular looked upon the event with grave concern: Metacom, head sachem of the Wampanoags. Known to many as King Philip (it was common for sachems to adopt an English name), he was the leader whose stockpiling of arms was reported by Sassamon to the governor.

For years his people had sworn loyalty to the English, only to see the old Wampanoag lands shrink before the growing power and population of Plymouth and its fellow colonies. War had begun to seem preferable to further humiliation. And the executions of June 8—more proof of Plymouth's perfidy and ruthlessness—offered him and his people the perfect excuse. Indeed, Tobias had been one of Philip's closest advisors. War dances began in earnest.

Metacom, head sachem of the Wampanoag Indians, was known as King Philip. It was common for sachems to adopt English names.

Philip would have preferred to dictate the course of events himself; now events controlled him. Before long all of New England, from the remote coasts of Maine to the sprawling swamps of Rhode Island, would be swept up in violence. Within a year, the countryside would be dotted with charred, empty settlements, offering grim testament to the severity of race war.

"King Philip's War," as it came to be called almost immediately, stopped English expansion in its tracks, broke the remaining power of local Amerindians, and established a pattern of paranoia and mistrust between English-speaking America and native peoples that would thrive for centuries.

ESCAPE FROM MOUNT HOPE

We will never know whether Philip ordered the death of Sassamon. What is known is that the great sachem, whose own Wampanoag people were known as the Pokanoket, had been anticipating a war with the English for months, perhaps years.

Things had taken quite a turn since Philip's father, the revered Massassoit, had helped the Pilgrims avoid starvation during their first winter in the North American wilderness. Now those days of trust seemed like ancient history; in the span of a single generation, animosities between the Wampanoags and their English neighbors had festered to the point of violence.

On a balmy night toward the end of July, just weeks after war had broken out in earnest between his people and the settlers of Plymouth, Philip stood on the banks of the Taunton River, in present-day Rhode Island, watching the waters roil south in the moonlight. He had performed a marvelous coup by bringing his people here.

When hostilities broke out, the Pokanokets had a tough decision to make. Their home, the Mount Hope peninsula in today's Rhode Island, hung like a misshapen wine sack beneath Swansea, where English forces had gathered to sweep south. Should Philip and his people have stayed there, they'd have been hunted down on the peninsula and trapped like deer for the slaughter. Philip, desperate to take his fight north to other Indian peoples who might become allies, had fooled his enemies by making a daring dash across Mount Hope Bay to the mainland. From there he'd led his people north through swamps deemed impassable by the English.

His journey had only just begun, however. Should his people make it across the racing waters of the Taunton, they would need to traverse the ten miles or so to Providence, then turn north to central Massachusetts, where potential allies waited in the territory of the Nipmucks. Every stretch of the long trek was fraught with danger—

A Wampanoag warrior is dressed in full regalia in this nineteenth-century illustration.

and with every mile, Philip lost warriors to desertion. Not every Wampanoag warrior relished war with the dreadful English.

Before the yawning expanse of the Taunton River, Philip made his decision. Time, after all, was of the essence. And this, the river's narrowest point for miles in either direction, was good enough for fording—it was perhaps an eighth of a mile to the far bank. Here they would cross.

IN THE SPAN OF A SINGLE GENERATION, ANIMOSITIES BETWEEN THE WAMPANOAGS AND THEIR ENGLISH NEIGHBORS HAD FESTERED TO THE POINT OF VIOLENCE.

Men, women, and children all lent a hand in building makeshift rafts for the crossing. The crude wooden platforms were made strong enough just for the brief passage, carrying Philip's warriors and their families to safety in the night. By dawn, the last rafts were sent floating down the current, their final passengers having scurried into the forest. The Taunton, Philip's greatest obstacle to freedom and a war of mobility, had been crossed.

The Indians sped west toward Providence, keeping to a breathless pace along ancient paths. Though Philip had left the very old and very young behind before crossing the Taunton, his force was still burdened by families that made passage through the countryside slower than it would have been with just warriors. Nevertheless, the threat of pursuit drove them on.

Soon they were across the Seekonk River and heading north. As the sun sank beneath the horizon on July 31, Philip and his people, content that they had outdistanced any pursuers, made two camps for the night—one under Philip, and the other, some three-quarters of a mile distant, with Weetamoo, Philip's sister-in-law and fellow sachem.

DISASTER AT NIPSACHUCK

Dawn brought the chatter of muskets. Rousing his swiftest warriors, Philip sprinted toward the ominous racket—Weetamoo's camp must be under attack.

By the time he arrived on the scene, the noise of fighting had grown to a frightful level. Philip crested a hill and beheld what he had hoped desperately to avoid. On the undulating plain before him, a large group of Englishmen, recognizable at a distance from their broad hats and woolens, were, when they weren't pausing to fire their long guns, scattering a hapless throng of Weetamoo's people, cutting them down with swords.

Just as alarming as the raging English were the Mohegans that ran alongside them, swinging maple-wood war clubs to deadly effect, their faces painted like demons. Old

Those Who Disappeared into Slavery

For Amerindians and English alike, warfare in seventeenth-century North America was characterized by shocking excess. If the Puritans were horrified by the native penchant for mutilation and scalping, the Indians found the European willingness to wage total war with enormous casualties almost insane.

Both peoples came from a tradition of accepted torture, though very different in practice, which we today would find profoundly disturbing. But one of the most tragic consequences of King Philip's War was the fate that befell so many of the Indians captured by English forces: slavery in a distant and alien land.

In August 1675 a group of Indians, several hundred strong, surrendered to Plymouth authorities with the promise of amnesty. Governor Josiah Winslow, however, refused to accept the agreement, and arranged to sell the prisoners into captivity. They ended up in the slave markets of Cádiz, Spain. Such was the fate of countless Native Americans who found themselves in the custody of the English during the war.

Hundreds disappeared on trading vessels, most of them bound for the Caribbean, where they would live out their lives in forced labor. To the English authorities, the solution killed two birds with one stone: Enemy natives were exiled out of the region, and their sale to independent slavers raised revenue to offset the cost of the war.

✢

allies of the English, the Mohegans made peerless scouts—it was undoubtedly they who had first discovered the Wampanoag camp in the early morning hours.

Philip's warriors had caught up with him on the crest. He heard their war whoops, sensed the fury pouring from them like sweat. The English and Mohegans must pay dearly for this. Several of his men instinctively aimed their muskets and fired off a desultory volley, stopping many of the raiders in their tracks and drawing their attention. Philip gave the signal for his fighters to scatter. The English, more than one hundred of them, did likewise in response, their Mohegan colleagues out on the flanks leaping through the brush to find positions of advantage.

Expert shots, Philip's men kept up an impressive hail of fire. Most of them had firelocks—newer muskets that relied on the spark of a flint to discharge the shot, rather

The English and Wampanoags clash at Hadley, Massachusetts, in 1675, during King Philip's War.

than a chord of smoldering slow match. But if plenty of the English still depended on their old matchlocks, there were more of them. And the swarms of lead snapping through the tall grass soon started taking a toll.

The Pokanoket sachem had to do something. As the morning grew longer and hotter, English numbers and firepower pushed his warriors to the very edge. He had already been short of powder and shot; now he was getting short of his most important asset of all: fighting men. By nine o'clock, more than twenty of his precious warriors lay dead or dying on the field. His struggle was in jeopardy of being destroyed before it even had a chance to truly get off the ground.

Rising in a flash, he shouted to his men to fall back, exhorting them toward the Nipsachuck Swamp. The Indians ran for their lives, some of them hobbling frantically with wounds. The swamp—traditional sanctuary against the Europeans, who often operated at a disadvantage in the trackless, choking gloom—was Philip's last hope. His exhausted men huddled there, nursing their wounds and counting the dead: twenty-three had been lost, including some of the bravest. They had virtually no food, and the morning's fight had seriously depleted their paltry store of powder. Surely the English would come on and finish them here.

But the English never came. Perhaps the swamp dissuaded them after all; perhaps they had no idea that Philip stood with only forty remaining warriors at his side. Never one to question a gift so dearly purchased, the sachem led his men away to the north, snaking into freedom along the Blackstone River. The struggle would live on.

THE DOGS OF WAR

Snow blanketed the ground, reminding the sachem how long it had been since he'd escaped certain destruction at Nipsachuck. Since that tragic day six months ago, Philip had run like a fugitive through the breadth of New England, sowing conflict wherever he went, his entourage of warriors shrinking with every week.

But now Philip's prospects were considerably brighter: Here, at Schaghticoke, north of Albany, New York, he hoped to spend the winter husbanding his resources amongst the Mahicans, his hosts. Already, more than two thousand warriors had rallied to his cause. He had once only dreamt of such numbers.

Indeed, much had happened that once seemed the stuff of dreams—or nightmares. Philip's spark had set much of New England on fire. Back on the Mount Hope peninsula, he had once hoped to bring as many other native peoples as possible to his cause. Chief among them was the Nipmucks, into whose territory the renegade sachem had fled after the fight at Nipsachuck. Traditional allies, the Nipmucks threw their lot in with Philip. Other peoples, however, had no desire to risk their fates in a war with Plymouth, whose leaders had quickly secured the military help of Massachusetts Bay colony and Connecticut, as well.

But the English, ironically, proved an unlikely ally in Philip's cause. War with the Wampanoags had awakened in them a latent fear of Indians that now raged out of control and that drew no distinctions. Old friends fell like tenpins before a clumsy, reckless war policy. The once-neutral Norwottucks, ambushed by a large force of Massachusetts men, joined the fight, as did the Pocumtucks.

Soon the whole Connecticut River valley was a battlefield. English militia forcibly disarmed Agawam Indians near Springfield, Massachusetts, driving them angrily into the arms of their aggressive Nipmuck neighbors. And so it went; where Philip's crusade failed to strike a chord, heavy-handed English tactics more than compensated.

Greatest of those who now opposed the English were the once-neutral Narragansett people, ruthlessly attacked in December in what came to be called the Great Swamp Fight. Theirs was the largest contingent that now wintered with Philip at Schaghticoke.

As the sachem walked among the wigwams of his huge army in the early morning cold, he beheld many other faces, as well. There were Abenaki and Sokoki, having traveled south from Maine, as well as Canadian Indians from even farther afield, with French gunpowder in their pouches and straw twigs through their noses. There were Mahicans, of course, masters of this great gathering place, and a group of loyal Wampanoags who had followed Philip from the beginning.

With all of these people, he would return to New England in the spring and finish what he'd started. Victory would only make his host grow larger.

Columns of smoke climbed skyward from cooking fires beyond number, their swirling gray clouds twisting and merging in the sharp February chill. Peace and plenty reigned here in the valley of the Hoosic River.

And then, with heart-stopping suddenness, the forest behind him erupted with the screams of a thousand throats. From out beyond the vast cluster of wigwams, in seemingly every direction, the trees disgorged a mad rush of Indian warriors, their battle cries now merging with the rattle of musketry in a dreadful cacophony. Philip shook off his fright, instantly gauged the scale of his predicament, and prepared to run for his life. His army, and his cause, had been ambushed.

These were no ordinary assailants who had surrounded his encampment and who now butchered and rampaged before his eyes. Daubed from head to toe in a phantasm of colors, with painted faces at once beautiful and demonic, these were Mohawks—ancient foes of the Wampanoag and their Algonquian brothers, and the most feared fighters in the northeast. Seemingly all of them carried firelocks, loading and handling them with frightening agility, then dashing along the rows of crumbling wigwams

Colonists attack the Narragansett-fortified village in 1675. Between 5,000 and 10,000 colonists and Native Americans lost their lives during King Philip's War.

through curtains of their own musket smoke to bash and scalp and plunder. The carnage was consuming.

Accompanied by his wife and young son, as well as a few of his most trusted henchmen, the sachem of the Pokanokets ran and ran, dodging the trees with nervy desperation. That he had escaped at all seemed incredible, a thought that only made his legs pump faster.

Philip knew that all was lost now. What he didn't know—couldn't know—was that the success of his cause had bred its very destruction. The leaders of New England may have developed a broad suspicion of natives, but the Hoosic River wasn't New England. And to Sir Edmund Andros, governor of New York, not all Indians were alike. Having wisely and assiduously cultivated a close relationship with the mighty Iroquois Confederacy, he relied on their help to purge the region around Albany of what he rightly considered a serious threat from a rogue sachem who had sunk Plymouth, Massachusetts, Connecticut, and Rhode Island into chaos. Calling on the Mohawk, easternmost of the

Iroquois and often considered the most warlike, he armed them from his own arsenals with all the guns and powder they needed. The Mohawks themselves did the rest.

The forest echoed with screams of the murdered, and Philip's little party kept on running. They had spied the butchery of fleeing friends through the snow-clad trees, only to turn and fly in horror. On and on they moved, and in time the noise of fighting grew steadily more distant. Exhausted and disconsolate, they headed away from the sun, due east. Back to New England—and an uncertain fate.

RECKONING

King Philip had become a spectator in the war that bore his name. Making their way east from the catastrophe on the Hoosic, Philip and his people lived like refugees in the midst of a brutal, New England–wide conflict. In the north, the great Abenaki threatened to push Maine's English trading posts into the frigid Atlantic.

The smoke of torched villages choked the Connecticut River valley, while the settlements of central and east Massachusetts—those that hadn't already been burned to the ground—barricaded themselves against the constant threat of Indian attack. As the months passed, Philip longed to return to the homeland from which he had launched the original enterprise—back to the Mount Hope peninsula. And it was there, after countless hardships, that he found himself in August of 1676.

His entourage had shrunk to a mere handful; even his wife and son had been captured by the English. The road back to Mount Hope had been an awful one. Over the past weeks, scarcity of food had compelled Philip to adopt a grim severity: He had ordered many of the youngest put to death, both to conserve food and to avoid betrayal by their constant, hungry crying. This was total war in all its brutality—a war Philip had clearly lost. On the night of August 11, he allowed himself a fitful sleep in what seemed a secure place.

It wasn't. Early the next morning, Philip bolted upright into consciousness with the bark of guns. As he had done so many times before, the sachem gathered his musket and kit and ran.

He didn't get far. The man who had arranged the ambush in which Philip now found himself was one Benjamin Church, about whom much would be written in the centuries to follow. Church had become a devotee of guerilla warfare, proving to the leaders of New England that he could do more with the help of dedicated, loyal groups of friendly Indians than he could with a force made up of only English and a few native allies. With the help of an angry turncoat, Church and his lithe force had caught Philip unaware, surrounding him with a cordon of stealthy sentries. And Philip ran right into one of them.

His name was Alderman, one of the Pocasset Indians who had sworn themselves to the English cause with the help of Church's unorthodox diplomacy. Beside him was a young Englishman, who pulled his trigger when Philip came into view that fateful day in the swamp. When his gun misfired, Alderman discharged his own musket, dropping the running sachem into the mud. King Philip was dead.

That he had been felled by a fellow Wampanoag was telling indeed. The war had forced a reorganization of society, challenging racial boundaries that once had reigned supreme. Men like Church insisted on employing large groups of loyal Indians with a few English followers, a strategy that his superiors were slow to accept in their dogged orthodoxy and racism. Nevertheless, the society that sponsored Church—one in which losses, however terrible, could gradually be compensated for by a mother country across the ocean—could learn and grow from the horror of King Philip's War in ways that Philip and his supporters could not.

If New England had been transformed, however, it had also been deeply scarred. Estimates of the war's cost in lives and property vary widely, though it is quite possible that more than 2,000 English men, women, and children had lost their lives out of a population of slightly more than 50,000. Amerindians fared much worse, losing somewhere between 3,000 and 6,000 lives out of a population of perhaps 20,000. Such staggering losses make King Philip's War the costliest conflict, in terms of death rates, in American history.

Thirteen English settlements throughout New England had been burned to the ground, abandoned, or both—some 1,200 buildings had been leveled. Not until the eve of the American Revolution would the region regain the level of prosperity it had enjoyed before that fateful June of 1675.

As for Philip, his corpse was drawn and quartered and his head stuck on Plymouth's palisade, where it would remain for twenty years. Alderman, the great sachem's assassin, was granted Philip's hand as a gift; the proud Indian kept the ghastly relic in a jar of alcohol as a valuable keepsake.

Taking the violence of the Pequot War to a new level of destructiveness, King Philip's War sent New England's native peoples into a downward demographic spiral from which they would never return, and decided the future of the region's English, as well.

Weakened and bankrupt, Plymouth and her fellow colonies had no choice but to rely on the efforts of the home country to pull them back from the brink of total collapse. As a result, New England's distinctive, autonomous culture was drawn more closely than ever into the burgeoning British empire—a bond that would take another war, exactly one hundred years later, to break once and for all.

Metacom met his end in August 1676 at the end of a musket fired by a Pocasset Indian sworn to the English cause.

Overleaf: Weakened and bankrupt from the war, Plymouth, shown here in a seventeenth-century map, had to rely on England to bring it back from total collapse.

chapter eight

A New England Carpenter
Changes the Calculus of War
with the Indians

1675

A rattlesnake started buzzing just ahead, and the men came quickly to a halt. There may have been hostile Indians in these woods, but dealing with rattlers was another thing entirely. Time to back it on up and turn around.

Thirty-six-year-old Benjamin Church heard the grumbling of his men and reversed the little column's course, leading it back to the main trail. They had been following what looked like the tracks of Indians now for quite a while, only to stumble upon an angry reptile. Perhaps this hunt for natives was a lost cause.

Once back on the trail, Church reminded his twenty-man force that they were on a mission of reconnaissance. If it came to a fight, so be it, but he had come over to Pocasset territory to try to talk sense into his neighbors, not to shoot them to pieces. Given the present state of affairs, however, the pragmatic Church knew how much of a long shot that truly was.

It was July 1675—just a month after Wampanoag Indians and English settlers had started killing each other around Swansea, Massachusetts, beginning what would become known as King Philip's War. When the English forces had moved south onto the Mount Hope peninsula in Rhode Island in search of Philip and found nothing, Church and another colonial leader, Captain Matthew Fuller, crossed east over Mount Hope Bay to the territory of the Pocasset Indians on the mainland. While the rest of the army built

Plymouth Governor Josiah Winslow's order to burn the Narragansett Indian fort marked the greatest battle of King Philip's War. Hundreds of Narragansetts burned to death.

a fort on Mount Hope, Church and Fuller embraced a more assertive strategy, hoping to scare up a reaction where Indians were known to be.

Once ashore, the group split up: Fuller went north, toward the Pocassets, led by Philip's sister-in-law, Weetamoo, while Church headed south, toward the home he had built in the realm of the Wampanoag Indians known as the Sakonnets. Their sachem, a woman named Awashonks, was believed to have already thrown her lot in with Philip and Weetamoo. But Church, having long since developed a friendship with her, was sure he could talk her out of it if he had the chance.

Church and his men hadn't been on the trail long before they came upon an old field of peas belonging to a farmer named John Almy. Somebody spotted a couple of Indians walking through the field; Church shouted and motioned to them that he wished only to talk, but the two figures started running.

The English chased them through the peas only to watch the two Indians jump a fence and disappear into the trees of a wooded slope. Hot on their heels, Church had hardly gotten beyond the fence when the forest gloom exploded with musket fire, sending great gouts of smoke rolling over him and his men. They'd been ambushed, and very neatly.

So much for talk.

As stunned by the fact that nobody had been hit as he was by the mortal danger he'd led his men into, Church heard his men firing blindly into the smoke and darkness and ordered them to stop. The party retreated, and Church had some of his men deploy along the fence while he and the rest retreated far enough into the field to reload their pieces and prepare for the attack that now seemed inevitable.

Soon the smoke was clearing on the wooded rise, and Church could see a veritable swarm of Wampanoags moving through the trees to cut him and his column off from the river—their only possible avenue of escape.

Their best hope now lay in the meager protection of an old stone wall down by the shore, to which Church and his men now fled while flying musket balls hissed all around them. Once over the crude barrier, they made themselves as difficult to hit as possible while getting the attention of the boats in the river, there to cover operations in the bay. The Wampanoags advanced steadily on their desperate foes, spreading out along a perimeter of rocks and thickets and taking up positions in an old ruined house.

The two sides exchanged fire for hours in the summer heat, and Church's men began to run dangerously low on ammunition. One attempt was made to rescue the besieged column, but the sloop's master could not get close enough to the shore and was then driven off by fire from the Indians. Succor did not come until evening, when another pilot boldly brought his ship up, let down a buoy, and sent it floating to Church with a canoe attached to it. Ten trips in the little craft were required to bring the twen-

A nineteenth-century illustration depicts the Pease Field fight in July 1675.

ty men to safety, by which time the sloop's sails were full of bullet holes. Church was the last to depart.

Miraculously, none of Church's men died during that day's long agony, which went down in history as the "Pease Field Fight." Benjamin Church, a carpenter who had established a homestead for himself here, at the far southern tip of Plymouth colony, now found himself at war with his Sakonnet neighbors. But they would not remain enemies forever. Church, making the Sakonnets an integral part of his new approach to fighting other Indians, would become a New England hero and, arguably, the original American frontier legend.

That, however, was still a year away...

INTO THE GREAT SWAMP

Five months later, in the predawn darkness of December 19, 1675, a Sunday, Benjamin Church stomped his feet to keep warm and tried to recall the last time he had ever been so cold. All around him stood men from every colony, a great throng of armed Englishmen milling about in the snowdrifts, their breath billowing in the gelid air. Many complained of frostbite. By day's end, many more would be fighting to stay alive.

Led by Governor Josiah Winslow of Plymouth, this army—one thousand strong, with contingents of Mohegans and Pequots—had spent the night beneath the falling snow. Now, just before first light, they prepared to leave this trampled field dotted with smoldering campfires to go where no army of white men had ever gone before: into the Great Swamp of the Narragansett.

Church, who had signed on as the governor's advisor, had his doubts about the operation, and not just because many of the men were too cold to pull a trigger. By now virtually every tribe in New England had taken up arms against the English, with several notable exceptions: the Mohegans and Pequots, who were old friends and allies of the English, and the tribe whose enormous population and elusive intentions had made them the subject of intense speculation around every campfire in New England—the Narragansetts.

Although bound by treaty to Plymouth, the Narragansetts—who held unchallenged sway over the southernmost stretch of New England west of Philip's home at Mount Hope—had been harboring refugees from hostile tribes almost since the war began. Infuriated by this, Plymouth officials had demanded that the Narragansett hand over any Wampanoags they may have taken in. The reply from Canonchet, sachem of the Narragansett, was famously flip: "No, not a Wampanoag nor the paring of a Wampanoag nail."

That was too much for the English, who set about organizing the greatest military operation in their New World history up to that time. Having taken up the sword with such ardor, most New Englanders now found it difficult indeed to slash selectively. The mighty Narragansetts would have to be taken down sometime; why not now?

FIRE AND ICE

Church wasn't so sure, especially since the English were hardly in need of more enemies. And as the long column marched

Benjamin Church penetrated the wild areas of New England in pursuing Native American enemies. His strategy, based on speed, stealth, and intelligence gathering, produced few battles and many captives.

all morning through the frozen wastes, the men raw from the bitterest winter in memory, the operation began to look almost suicidal.

The intense chill, in fact, did offer an important benefit: the swamps were as solid as shale, making movement enormously easier. And the winter landscape, devoid of leaves and blanketed in snow, was ideal for finding and fighting elusive Indian foes. Nevertheless, the men had barely more than a day's food left, a dangerous limitation indeed for a large force in frozen enemy territory.

Guided deep into the heart of the vast bog land by a turncoat Narragansett named Peter, the army was on the point of exhaustion when, around one o'clock in the afternoon, Peter announced that they had arrived: not far ahead was the elusive capital of the Narragansett, for so long the subject of gossip and conjecture. Shots were already being exchanged between the column's vanguard and Narragansett pickets. Anticipation rippled through the ranks, dispersing fatigue and drawing the men forward in a disorganized mob. And what they beheld upon coming out of the trees gave every one of them pause.

CHURCH OBSERVED A PALISADE WALL STANDING BEHIND A BARRIER OF INTIMIDATING THICKETS, SEVERAL YARDS DEEP. BLOCKHOUSES AND FLANKING POSITIONS BUILT OF TANGLED TREE BRANCHES SUPPORTED THE WHOLE STRUCTURE.

Spread before the English was a massive system of elaborate wood and earth fortifications, solid and majestic in the frosted mire from which the whole bulwark rose, it seemed, almost organically. Though the English wouldn't know it until later that blood-soaked day, the fortress enclosed some five acres of high ground, 300 to 500 wigwams, and an estimated 3,000 Narragansett men, women, and children.

Nowhere did the fortress appear vulnerable, until someone noticed a narrow yet conspicuous stretch of defensive wall that stood only four feet high. Guarded by a block-house within the wall's circumference that promised a hot reception for anyone foolish enough to rush it, the position seems to have been a deliberate invitation to assaulting foes. If so, the English took the bait—with a vengeance.

Two companies of Massachusetts men rushed the four-foot wall, only to be savaged by an eruption of Indian musketry. They went to the ground in a writhing carpet of dead, wounded, and terrified. Both of their captains had been quickly slain.

More men from Massachusetts Bay flew into the maelstrom, including a company led by Samuel Moseley, younger than Benjamin Church. Outspoken, controversial, and merciless, Moseley was already a legend. The previous summer, the sea captain had made his entrance in King Philip's War at the head of a rough band of Dutch privateers; after capturing them off the New England coast, he had offered them clemency in exchange for their services fighting Indians. It wasn't long before he impressed all of New England with his daring exploits and wild-eyed disdain for Indian lives. Now, rushing over the wall and into the fort, he and his men wavered before a deadly hail of bullets.

THE SETTLEMENT BLAZED, BUILDING INTO AN INFERNO THAT AWED THE ENGLISH AS THE CRIES OF HUNDREDS OF IMMOLATING MEN, WOMEN, AND CHILDREN CARRIED OVER THE SWAMP.

They were soon reinforced by more of their fellows from Massachusetts, whose assault managed to capture one of the fortified positions guarding the short wall. Then the men from Connecticut came rushing in, forcing the Indians further back. Fighting in the fort was now general and ferocious, the Narragansett warriors desperate to defend the settlement and its innocents.

Given command over a group of soldiers by Governor Winslow, Church made his way into the fort, only to watch a friend of his, Captain Joseph Gardner of Salem, die in his arms with a bullet through his head. Convinced, despite his friend's fate, that the fort was more or less secured, he led his men back out into the swamp to confront a group of Narragansetts intent on flanking the assaulting English. Surprising them with a well-timed volley, he and his men drove the Indians back into the fort, where a struggle ensued over control of one of the blockhouses. There, in the melee around the crude wooden structure, a ball struck his leg and threw him down. Church's thigh gaped with an ugly wound.

Struggling with the help of his men to get out of the fort, Church saw sheets of flame spreading through the settlement and despaired. English soldiers, firebrands in hand, were walking from one wigwam to the next, committing the Narragansett town to scorching oblivion. Church hobbled over to Governor Winslow as fast as his bleeding leg would let him. Why burn the fort? he asked fervently. With so many wounded, and the nearest friendly settlement some sixteen miles distant in the unbearable cold, better to take advantage of the Indian's food and shelter than destroy it.

But Winslow, convinced by more impetuous voices bent on scorching heathen ground, would not be swayed. The settlement blazed, building into an inferno that awed the English as the cries of hundreds of immolating men, women, and children carried over the swamp. Like the horror at Mystic forty years earlier, it was a gruesome, unforgettable spectacle.

An undetermined amount of men, women, and children were slaughtered in the Great Swamp Fight in 1675.

And it was followed by a long, nightmarish night. Burdened by a score of dead men and ten times that many wounded, the English column limped and staggered in the crippling cold through sixteen miles of trackless snow and forest toward Wickford, the closest friendly settlement. More men died in the night and in the days that followed, bringing the greatest battle of King Philip's War to a grisly denouement.

The bloodiest single day of the war, the Great Swamp Fight, slaughtered an undetermined number of men, women, and children; turned New England's largest Indian nation into an inveterate foe of the English; and failed—despite all its violence—to kill the majority of Narragansett warriors. Church survived, but he was a changed man. Whether it was the wound, or the battle's sickening excess, or the fact that he needed to do things his own way, he was convinced that a new approach was needed to bring this awful war to an end.

BURYING THE HATCHET

On an early June day in 1676, Church, standing at an outcropping of flat stone not far from his home, squinted at the glittering Sakonnet River in the distance. Along its shore, not quite a year ago, he had battled for his life in the Pease Field Fight and escaped by "the glory of God and His protecting providence" to fight another day. Now, on the plain of tall grass surrounding this jagged altar of stone, those same Indians surrounded him, guns and war clubs in hand.

He had returned to the land of the Sakonnet on his own authority to strike a deal that would make him a controversial figure back in Plymouth and Boston. Before him stood Awashonks, who had agreed to meet her old acquaintance at this spot, knowing that he was a man of honor. Church, rum in hand, suggested they start with a drink, and they each swallowed their share. Then they got down to business.

The Englishman was looking for allies, but talk of the past nearly got him killed. When he admitted to being present at the Pease Field, several warriors bristled menacingly, having lost brothers at that legendary skirmish—warriors whose lives may well have been cut short by Church's marksmanship. But the carpenter pressed on, saying that Plymouth, with his help, would pardon the Sakonnets and embrace them as friends, just as Plymouth had already embraced the Pequots—another people who had once been bitter enemies but who now fought alongside the English. All they had to do was fight for him. Awashonks, backed by her leading warrior, Nompash, was won over to her charismatic neighbor.

The following month, having acquired official recognition of his special arrangement with the Sakonnets from Governor Winslow, Church and his party of English henchmen rode back to his new allies and caught up with them along the western shore of Buzzard's Bay, just west of Cape Cod. After a feast by the water, the Englishmen were treated to a night of war dances. The Sakonnets were ready to follow their new leader wherever he would take them.

STALKING PREDATORS

And he took them into harm's way. Eschewing the conventional tactics of the Puritan colonies that relied on securing an area with fortifications and settlements, Church penetrated the wild areas of New England and went after the enemy. A purely offensive strategy based on stealth, speed, and intelligence gathering, Church's approach produced very few battles and a great many captives.

Enemies were surrounded long before they knew they were being stalked, then rushed from all sides and compelled to surrender at gunpoint. The captain's force consisted overwhelmingly of Sakonnet warriors, augmented by a cadre of English stalwarts

Lock, Stock, and Barrel

Early firearms were temperamental, inaccurate, and cumbersome. The weapon that became the standard shoulder arm from the late fifteenth century in Europe was the matchlock, so called on account of the cord of slow match required to fire it—a long coil of smoldering wick that accompanied musketeers whenever they were close to battle. Once in a fight, a musketeer would load his weapon and pour a little powder into the priming pan. Then he would blow on the tip of his smoldering slow match to make it glow, secure it in the jaws of a brace called a "serpentine," and pull the trigger, causing the serpentine to depress into the pan and ignite the powder, which fired the musket.

Needless to say, it was a long procedure fraught with danger on account of the fact that one had to run around before and during battle with a length of smoking twine—in an environment replete with gunpowder.

By the early seventeenth century, however, a new firing mechanism was overtaking Europe. Called a "snauphance," or "firelock" (and, ultimately, "flintlock"), it did away with the combustible slow match, replacing it with a "cock" that gripped a shaped piece of flint. Pulling the trigger sent the flint slamming against a "steel," or "frizzen," which showered the pan with sparks and ignited the charged weapon.

The firelock allowed a combatant to load and prime his musket hours before encountering an enemy. Once in battle, all he had to do was cock the piece and pull the trigger. Although it was more expensive, the firelock took hold in the New World relatively more quickly than it did in the Old, on account of the weapon's simplicity and utility in ambushes. By the time of King Philip's War, most warriors—English and Amerindian alike—were carrying firelocks.

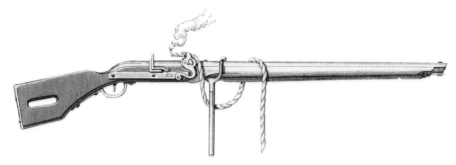

The matchlock with slow match, shown here, was so called because of the slow match required to fire it.

and, most important, Indian captives who were offered their lives in exchange for joining Church's ranks.

There were others who took to the woods and fought like the Indians, including Samuel Moseley, who continued to be a rival of Church's. But nobody—not even the colorful Moseley—captured the public's imagination quite like Church, who seemed to be everywhere at once, and whose list of successes continued to grow. By the time he had tracked King Philip and produced his corpse for the bloodthirsty crowds of Plymouth, he was already something of a legend.

But in a war that had long since raged beyond Philip's ability to control events, his death could not bring an end to hostilities. Other, more dangerous foes remained at large.

THE OLD WARRIOR IN DEFEAT

On a cool September night, a month after the death of Philip, Church found himself hugging the ground and peeking over the ledge of a steep rock face near Rehoboth. He and a dozen of his men had been led there by an old Indian who claimed to know the location of the great Annawon, fiercest of the late King Philip's warriors.

And there Annawon was, below them, his weathered face a mask of flickering orange in the firelight. With him were a group of loyal followers; women busied themselves pounding the corn for supper while Annawon's young son sat a short distance from his father.

Church had two good reasons to be there. First, both he and Governor Winslow knew that there could be no peace while fighters such as Annawon remained at large. And second, Annawon was precisely the sort of man Church could use up north, in Maine, where he had been asked to fight the Abenaki. A gnarled old warrior who had fought with Philip's father, Massassoit, Annawon was something of a legend, and for good reason. He was brave, deadly, and loyal.

Looking down into the encampment, Church started calculating. He needed to take Annawon alive. Beside Church were the old guide who had brought him there and a girl who had been found with him, both of whom had been in Annawon's camp and were known to the old warrior. As he looked at them, a plan began to form in his mind.

Moments later, the old man and the girl began to climb down the rock face in the darkness. Behind them went Church, a hatchet in his belt, followed by his Sakonnet warriors. As the group slowly and carefully made their descent, grasping at crevices and old roots, Church and his men hoped to conceal themselves as much as possible behind and above the two Indians, should Annawon or any of his people look their way.

Images of King Philip, shown in this hand-colored engraving, proliferated, but no one knows for sure what he looked like.

When they were near enough to the ground to make a last jump, Church looked toward Annawon's son. Near him, leaning against a bench, were the Indian's muskets.

Church leapt toward the boy and brandished his axe, instantly drawing the startled attention of Annawon. Seeing that he could take no action without endangering his son, the old warrior sank in defeat, resigned to the success of Church's gambit. The Sakonnets gathered up the muskets and secured the campsite.

A GNARLED OLD WARRIOR WHO HAD FOUGHT WITH PHILIP'S FATHER, MASSASSOIT, ANNAWON WAS SOMETHING OF A LEGEND, AND FOR GOOD REASON. HE WAS BRAVE, DEADLY, AND LOYAL.

Within hours Church's men had captured neighboring camps full of Annawon's followers, announcing to them that their leader had surrendered and wished them to do the same. Back at Annawon's site, Church invited his famous prisoner to sit with him at the fire and share a meal. The Englishman promised to do what he could to secure clemency for Annawon and his people, but admitted that the fate of Annawon himself was out of his hands—Plymouth and Boston had had more than their fair share of executions in recent months. Nevertheless, the great warrior, noble in defeat, offered Church rich belts of wampum and other items that had belonged to Philip, including a powder horn and blanket.

The men talked late into the night, knowing that they were bearing witness to the end of an era.

THE CHANGING FACE OF WAR

Much to Benjamin Church's regret, Annawon's head ended up on the palisade of Plymouth fort, right next to Philip's. The carpenter would fight the dreaded Abenaki in Maine without the help of King Philip's mightiest warrior.

And he didn't really need him, if Church's reputation was even close to the truth. Church didn't die until 1717, having built a name for himself as English America's first Indian-fighting celebrity. His son Thomas would galvanize that reputation by culling Church's notes and producing *Entertaining Passages Relating to Philip's War*, a book that went on to great renown.

There is little doubt that the book somewhat inflated Church's deeds and significance. But there is also little doubt that he was widely respected in his own time for helping to reinvent how war was fought against hostile Indians on the frontier.

Conventional European leaders had hitherto attacked only when they themselves were attacked, preferring to use "friend" Indians as auxiliaries in a white man's fight that was based on fortified strongholds. They preferred the tactical defensive. Church, on the other hand, took the fight to the enemy, coming upon them in the night when they least expected it—a tactic he learned from the Sakonnet warriors he so eagerly befriended and, perhaps more important, trusted.

In time the frontier would be rolled back and conquered by Europeans. And—contrary to popular opinion—it would be artillery, professional soldiers, carefully designed fortifications, and spit-and-polish officers with years of experience that would accomplish it. The irregular fighter, however, would always be there with them, as a scout, pioneer, and so much more. In the vastness of North America, one could not have one without the other.

Others of his kind would later find greater renown. But long before there was Robert Rogers or Daniel Boone, there was Benjamin Church.

chapter nine

Race War and Naked Ambition Ignite the Virginia Frontier

1676

The Indians had retreated deep into the stygian murk of the Dragon Swamp. They were Pamunkeys, a nation friendly to the English of Virginia, who were longtime trading partners and even protectors. But recent events had taken a turn for the worse—and it was Englishmen from whom they now fled.

The man who stalked them was Nathaniel Bacon, a relative newcomer to Virginia. Tall and brooding, he had an air of haughty assertiveness that had made him a controversial figure in the two brief years since his arrival with a wife, a small fortune in sterling, and a dubious reputation. Though exiled from England by his own father-in-law for being something of a swindler, Bacon had become a member of the planter establishment and a natural leader to his fellow frontiersmen.

A small army of those uncompromising men now followed Bacon through the humid viridescence of the marsh, and they had come as slayers. The Pamunkeys may have been considered friendly by the political elite of Virginia, whose pockets were filled by the Indians' fur trade. But to those who lived in the Pamunkeys' midst, far from the bustling ports along the Chesapeake, they were heathen savages—and all heathen savages were enemies to be exterminated. To frontiersmen like Bacon and his fellows, there were no friendly Indians.

The oligarch and the rabble-rouser: Sir William Berkeley and Nathaniel Bacon face off in Jamestown in this nineteenth-century illustration

The English now eyed their enemies, glad in their hunger and exhaustion for the end of the hunt. But the Pamunkey seemed unconcerned, even resigned. Their queen, committed to the old pro-English policy, had commanded her people not to harm the white men even if they advanced upon them. And that's just what happened next.

Attacking from all sides, Bacon's men waded into the Indians with axe and musket, sending up a wave of violence through the wilderness. The Pamunkey, however, merely fled. The English slew many and captured more for the slave trade, falling on their flee-ing opponents like wolves on sheep. The action continued for as long as Bacon's men could find fugitives to bag or cut down.

This was why Nathaniel Bacon had risen to prominence—this is what he had come to do. Virginia, worked into a frenzy by rumors of King Philip's War up in New England, had become a land imprisoned by hatred of Indians.

But the colony's governor, William Berkeley, stood for a status quo that men like Bacon could not accept: an entrenched system of oligarchy that favored commercialism, distanced Virginia from English home rule, and rewarded some Indian nations at the expense of others. Citing frontier security as his casus belli, Bacon was going after *all* Indians and, in the process, taking on the whole structure of political power in Virginia. What followed has been called, justifiably, a revolution.

A CASCADE OF CRISES

For months, there had been trouble with the Susquehannock Indians all along the Virginia frontier. These outbursts of violence and mounting retaliations by both sides had turned a countryside already paranoid with tales of New England's strife into a land of unbridled panic.

The Pamunkey, however, weren't aligned with the Susquehannock—nor were the Occaneechee, the other Amerindian nation that Bacon and his men had attacked. Wild-eyed with racism, the frontiersmen had committed themselves to a campaign of exter-mination, even against those peoples long considered allies. Governor Berkeley had proposed building forts along the frontier—an idea that seemed outdated and far too expensive.

Besides, it was widely believed that the governor and his fellow old guard oligarchs were protecting some Indian tribes because of lucrative trading deals. Why should the upper class royalists get fat while the planters on the frontier boarded up their houses against raids in the night? Such notions, fanned by record-low tobacco prices and years of economic stagnation, were enough to make many listen to Nathaniel Bacon when he spoke up.

The marriage of Pocahontas to John Rolfe in 1612, is depicted in this 1867 lithograph.

Planting the Seeds of Servitude

In 1612 John Rolfe, the Jamestown gentleman who would become famous for marrying Pocahontas, raised the first commercially viable crop of tobacco in England's struggling Virginia colony. Interestingly, just seven years later, it was Rolfe who also produced our primary account of the first appearance in English America of African slaves—"20 and odd Negroes" brought by a Dutch trading vessel to Jamestown.

Columbus and his men were the first Europeans to encounter tobacco when the local Arawaks of San Salvador offered it to them as a gift. Though the curious "dried leaves" were discarded as useless, it wasn't long at all before some of Columbus's men took up the habit and brought it back to Europe.

By the early seventeenth century, tobacco use had exploded, inspiring King James I of England to pen his famous "Counterblaste to Tobacco," denouncing the habit as "lothsome to the eye, hatefull to the Nose, harmefull to the braine, [and] dangerous to the Lungs."

Immigration to the New World, however, had not kept pace, creating a labor shortage for tobacco growers—and another opportunity for those in the slave trade, which had long been operating in older colonial empires. Labor intensive, from planting and weeding through harvest and drying, the delicate tobacco plant played a fundamental role in feeding Virginia's hunger for captives brought from Africa.

And what he had to say was straightforward enough: Move on the Indians, take over their lands, and ensure the security of Virginia. For doing so on his own volition, the governor branded him a rebel—to which Bacon's neighbors responded by electing him a burgess from Henrico County. Though the two men had initially gotten along when Bacon first arrived in Virginia, mutual distrust had now made them enemies—and divided their colony. What had begun as a difference of opinion between two headstrong men was now a dangerous standoff over the fate of English Virginia.

WHAT HAD BEGUN AS A DIFFERENCE OF OPINION BETWEEN TWO HEADSTRONG MEN WAS NOW A DANGEROUS STAND-OFF OVER THE FATE OF ENGLISH VIRGINIA.

When Henrico County's new burgess showed up for the Assembly in Jamestown, he was arrested, brought before Berkeley, and given a pardon in exchange for a full confession of his misdeeds. Bacon was hardly chastened, however; in fact, he now demanded an officer's commission to legally carry out the Indian war that Berkeley so intensely wanted to avoid. He would get it—by force. Returning to Jamestown with a well-armed contingent of rabid supporters, Bacon compelled the authorities of the capital to make him commander in chief of the army.

The die had been cast. Before long, two armed factions faced each other for control of the colony: Berkeley's group of diehards, exiled to the Eastern Shore, across the bay; and Bacon's swollen army of malcontents, now in control of most of Virginia (including Jamestown itself) and committed not only to displacing the Indians but also to abolishing the old order that had attempted to live in peace with them.

CIVIL WAR IN VIRGINIA

Emerging from the Dragon Swamp at the end of summer 1676 with his Pamunkey captives, Bacon was confronted with bad news: Berkeley had begun his counteroffensive from his base on the Eastern Shore. And he was going right for the jugular: Jamestown.

Bacon had bound his men to him with an oath to fight a war with the governor's forces should it prove necessary. It now proved necessary. Bacon had already filled the countryside with handpicked administrators, undertaken a widespread and largely successful propaganda campaign, and turned many neutral-minded landowners to his cause. Now he would find himself fighting the Berkeleyans to the knife.

To build himself a counterinsurgency force, Governor Berkeley had promised a free hand with rebel property to all who rallied to his standard. His cause was more pop-

A tobacconist trade sign from London's Fleet Street is shown here in this eighteenth-century watercolor.

ular in the ports along the bay and on the Eastern Shore, where gentlemen merchants and ship captains looked to the sea for their livelihood and revered the stability of royal authority. Several hundred strong, Berkeley's mercenaries stormed ashore and compelled Jamestown's rebels to fly by night, surrendering the town without a shot. The governor himself joined them on September 8.

Though Berkeley's men were keen to grab up all the plunder they'd been promised, the governor managed to get enough of them to dig a defensive trench along the isthmus that connected Jamestown to the mainland, and back it up with a palisade. And it was that defensive work that confronted Bacon and his men when they showed up less than a week later.

As Virginia's most famous rebel greeted the morning of September 14, he did so from a crude trench. He'd had the men scoop it out during the night to provide some protection in the siege to come and to block any escape for the Berkeleyans onto the mainland. The isthmus had now become a no-man's-land between two parallel and antagonistic defensive works.

Next to him, stooping in their makeshift swale, the men stared at the enemy palisade in the distance and fought off exhaustion from the night's labor. They were an

eclectic bunch: independent farmers grown weary of taxation, frontier planters and fellow Indian-haters, indentured servants looking to better their prospects, and Africans released from bondage to fight Virginia's old order.

THOUGH IT BEGAN AS A CONFLICT OVER COLONIAL SECURITY, BACON'S REBELLION HAD BECOME MUCH MORE—A RALLYING POINT FOR A COLONY OF IMPOVERISHED AND DISILLUSIONED ENGLISHMEN.

Though it began as a conflict over colonial security, Bacon's rebellion had become much more—a rallying point for a colony of impoverished and disillusioned Englishmen, many of whom were willing to heap blame on a governor and oligarchy that clearly weren't suffering as much as they.

The economic factors behind Virginia's recent troubles were remote and vague, but a wealthy governor who continued to do business with Indians, who suggested defensive measures against the Susquehannocks that were as silly as they were expensive, and who quickly punished all who dared to challenge his authority, made for an easy target indeed.

And so a general struggle against "tyranny" was on—and Bacon was all too happy to fill his ranks with slaves looking for a way out of their hopeless predicament. Indeed, African Americans would remain the staunchest supporters of the rebellion, even after its leader's death.

Bacon, intent on maintaining some sort of initiative, sent a group of his men forward against the palisade. In an act more of mockery than military sense, they thrust their muskets through the gaps in the wooden wall and fired on Berkeley's garrison. Reinforcements continued to come in from the countryside, and Bacon set them to work buttressing their meager defenses with wood fascines and taller earthen ramparts.

Suddenly, a battery of cannon away in the palisade came alive with thunder and smoke. In a flash, a shot came hissing overhead. Another report, and the rebel earthen ramparts quaked with the impact of an incoming ball. Bacon and his men hugged the ground, but the trench wasn't deep enough yet to cradle them all properly. Then someone shouted and pointed toward the river, where enemy sloops were approaching. The vessels opened fire, and lead shot began cutting down the unfortunate amidst explosive plumes of sand and earth. Bacon, seeing the panic in his men, ordered a general withdrawal to the mainland.

The point of no return: In this atmospheric image, published in Harper's Magazine *in 1901, a stern-faced Nathaniel Bacon leaves Jamestown burning in his wake.*

He had come too far to give up this easily, however, and that night he ordered his men back into their positions on the isthmus. It may have seemed like folly, given Berkeley's superiority of artillery. But Bacon quickly bolstered his defensive position with deeper trenches and ramparts. And at sunup, the Berkeleyans made their greatest mistake.

As the rebels waited nervously in their churned and pounded works, signs of activity began to animate the palisade. Something was afoot, and the Baconians began to mumble speculatively to each other. Then it came: The gate swung wide, drums sounded the advance, and a throng of Englishmen came marching toward Bacon's trench.

The rebel leader had hoped for this. With its command of the waters and superiority in cannon, Berkeley's Jamestown would likely endure a very long siege—unless the governor did something rash. And this was it. Bacon's men leveled arms and loosed a storm of fire into the oncoming fighters, blunting their momentum with a wall of fire. When the smoke cleared, wounded men writhed on the field amid their kit and banners in a grisly tableau of defeat. Berkeley had gambled and lost.

THE GLOVES COME OFF

Drenching rain had by now become a constant over Jamestown and its besiegers, complementing the tension and intermittent violence with discomfort and sickness. In this increasingly morose atmosphere, Nathaniel Bacon pressed every advantage he had against his foes within the town.

As the Berkeleyans recovered from their abortive assault on the isthmus, those who looked out at the rebel lines were greeted with a sight that would've shocked even hardened veterans of seventeenth-century warfare. Standing on the ramparts in front of the trench was a line of loyalist women captives, their skirts soaked and sodden in the downpour. Kidnapped during upcountry raids by Bacon's foragers, they now presented a human shield behind which rebel soldiers toiled to construct a battery.

Bacon looked up at the women's backs and clenched his jaw. Over the summer, he had done much more than fight Indians. He had presided over the creation of a revolutionary "association" that branded all those who opposed it—namely, the Berkeleyans—traitors, their property subject to seizure for the cause. There was no turning back—and ploys like this, in which even the womenfolk of the other side were liable to practical use, must now be considered justifiable.

The following day, Bacon showed off more of his captives. These were Pamunkeys from his campaign in the Dragon Swamp, and he paraded them out before the ramparts like goods for sale. His intent was to send a message to the defenders in Jamestown:

Governor William Berkeley confronts angry colonists in this nineteenth-century illustration.

Here, in the flesh, was proof of his Indian-fighting skill. While Berkeley was hell-bent on crushing English "rebels," he, Bacon, had been out doing what he'd always said was his chief goal: taking on savages. Was Berkeley's cause really worth fighting for? Who wanted to die for an Indian-lover?

To many of Jamestown's defenders, the answer to that question was "not me." Grumbling had already begun in the town when, on September 18, Bacon unleashed what he hoped would be his trump card: The battery was completed.

STORM AND FIRE

The rain continued, and Bacon decided to warm his camp with the fire of cannons. The time had come to cut loose on the capital of Virginia.

As his men sighted their guns and prepared the powder and shot, the rebel leader considered his situation. The strength of his position had kept Berkeley's ships and artillery at bay, and the failed sortie must surely have wounded Jamestown's spirits. But Bacon still had no real navy to speak of, and word had reached him of raids being conducted along the rivers and estuaries by sea captains loyal to Berkeley. The quicker Jamestown fell, the better.

The guns barked away, hurling balls into the town. In time their scorching muzzles hissed in the rain, and the smoke settled over Bacon's camp like a great shawl. For the better part of two days, the rebel battery lobbed shot into Jamestown, oblivious of the effect it was having. And then, very early on the morning of September 20, scouts brought word of a change in fortunes.

Berkeley and his army had abandoned Jamestown. The sun had yet to rise when Bacon, alerted to the news, roused his men and led them out of the network of stinking furrows that had been their home for almost a week. Entering the town, the rebels were quick to see that much had been carried away with the enemy's retreat. Other facts, however, weighed more heavily on Bacon's mind. To begin with, how could he hope to hold this town, attached to the mainland by a narrow strip of land, without sea power to match his opponent's? He couldn't. Berkeley and his men had sailed downstream in vessels that were anchored within easy striking distance; a counterattack could come at any moment.

And so Bacon settled on the only course open to him. That night, his men set the capital to the torch, turning it into a flaming spectacle in the darkness to terrify friend and foe alike.

It was the last significant act that Bacon would ever undertake.

Sir William Berkeley surrenders to the Commissioners of the Commonwealth.

REVENGE—BUT FOR WHOM?

Bacon's men then dispersed into the countryside, occupying the estates of their enemies in preparation for winter quarters. But the rebel leader himself had reached the end of his tether. Living and campaigning through weeks of rain had made him a target for foes much deadlier, if smaller, than William Berkeley.

Infested with lice and crippled by the "bloody flux," or dysentery, Bacon succumbed on October 26. His death came at the end of acute and humiliating misery: "Swarms of Vermyn that bred in his body he could not destroy but by throwing his shirts into the Fire as often as he shifted himself." Thus the fate of rebels.

His cause outlived him through the winter. What Bacon had set in motion had swelled into a great, unwieldy surge away from the past—there were even those in the rebellion who spoke openly and enthusiastically of independence from England, perhaps with the help of the Dutch. Whatever the true direction and purpose of the revolution (and historians argue to this day about it), the countryside was full of Baconian partisans who now had too much to lose, especially former slaves and those of the servant class. They would fight to keep what they had won by force.

Berkeley came after them with a flaming vengeance. Assiduously deploying his growing navy, he undertook a series of systematic amphibious campaigns, crushed the rebel strongholds, took their leaders into custody, and hanged them for "taking arms against the King." The gallows had never been busier in Virginia.

Though swelled with personal revenge, Berkeley undertook his multipronged offensive with the assumption that he was the living embodiment of crown authority in Virginia. But the crown itself had other ideas.

The soldiers and royal commissioners who showed up in January, sent from England to sort out the mess that had become Virginia, ended up heaping almost as much blame on Berkeley as they did on the rebels for letting things get out of control. The result fell right in line with the effort by King Charles and his brother James to bring the American colonies under firmer, more direct royal control, just as they would do in New England.

Whereas Bacon and his followers wanted to fight the hold that Berkeley and his fellow grandees had on the life and security of the colony, Berkeley wanted to protect that old order for what it had offered Virginia for more than two generations: relative freedom and autonomy for the colony. Both sides, Baconian and loyalist, lost to a resurgent imperial agenda.

Though the real significance of Bacon's Rebellion remains a matter of contention to this day, the events of 1676 clearly showed two things: first, that notions of colonial independence, however inchoate, had taken root in the soil of Virginia as surely as tobacco had; and second, that the combination of Amerindians, frontier settlers, and English authority—all living in each other's midst and a long way from London—was an unstable one.

One hundred years after England's gambit to tie her Chesapeake treasure more closely to herself, the stresses within that awkward establishment would lead to another, more complete revolution.

chapter ten

Bostonians Forcefully Reject the Royal Prerogative in New England

1689

By the second half of the seventeenth century, the English colonies that hugged the long coast of North America presented a picture more of diversity than of unity.

Settled individually by ambitious, independent-minded entrepreneurs, the various colonies competed with each other in almost all spheres nearly as much as they competed with the French or the Dutch. Their charters varied widely: Some were royal ventures; others were established by private backers.

And their interests seemed constantly at odds. Plymouth resented the greater population and commercial power of Massachusetts Bay. The Anglican settlers of distant Maine disliked the Puritans of Massachusetts almost as much as they felt neglected by their government in Boston. New York, having staked its future on a close alliance with the Iroquois Confederacy, scoffed at the blatant anti-native stance of its New England neighbors. The loyalist grandees of Virginia were uneasy with the Catholic leadership of Maryland. And the colonies of Connecticut bickered with New York over their shared border. In fact, the only thing that most of them could agree on was that Rhode Island was a pariah.

Defensive considerations, however, were always an issue in the unforgiving frontier. Ever wary of Indian attack, as well as threats from the Dutch and the French, four colonies founded the New England Confederation in 1643: Massachusetts, Plymouth, Hartford, and New Haven.

The organization, such as it was, facilitated mutual defense by creating a board with two delegates from each colony. Each of the colonies retained its independence of action, however, and none of them was above simply ignoring Confederation decisions—particularly Massachusetts Bay, whose population was greater than that of the other three combined. The Confederation was hardly an expression of solidarity.

If the New Englanders themselves balked at the idea of union, however, it became quite popular across the ocean. It was there, thousands of miles from the reality of North American fractiousness, that royal officials would help the house of Stuart do from above what its New World subjects could not do—would not do—voluntarily.

In the end, however, the efforts of empire to rule the "Dominion of New England" merely united New Englanders in their hatred of unification—and solidified the passion for political and religious autonomy that would, ironically, lead their descendants to create a new and independent federation some ninety years later.

A MAN OF SOME IMPORTANCE

December 20, 1686, was a Monday, and though Boston shivered in the winter weather, the harbor was alive with pageantry. Moored impressively at the quay, the fifty-gun *Kingfisher* solemnly disgorged her most esteemed passenger—a stately looking gentleman whose scarlet coat and lace identified him as one graced with royal favor. Behind him came his retinue of officers, equally impressive in their uniforms, all proceeding onto *terra firma* while guns from the harbor forts gave them a noisy salutation.

The party was grandly received by eight companies of Massachusetts militia in full regalia, as well as a Congregational minister, Increase Mather, whose blessing invoked divine approval of the event. Boston's official elite came forth to welcome their new chief executive, and they escorted him into town, making a colorful procession for all to see (and *some*, at least, to cheer).

Then came the ceremony that marked a new era in Massachusetts and New England: Standing before the assembled, his hat remaining superciliously on his head, Sir Edmund Andros presided over the swearing in of the council whose primary function was to facilitate the dissemination of order and justice that flowed, as from a fountainhead, from his very person. The royal governor had arrived.

There were many in Massachusetts who did not welcome the very important-looking fellow in scarlet who seemed so naturally disposed to the air and trappings of authority. Not that his arrival was a complete surprise, of course. The previous summer

Soon after his arrival in New England, Sir Edmund Andros, an Anglican, boldly sought the use of a Puritan meetinghouse for a church service. His request was turned down.

Edward Randolph, a Stuart retainer with a long history of animosity toward the Massachusetts Puritans, had arrived in Boston with royal instructions outlining the dissolution of the colony's charter.

Empowered by King James II to replace it with a royal administration, he promptly appointed a council and gave it a president, Joseph Dudley. A Harvard-educated Anglican convert who was sympathetic to the crown's agenda, Dudley was intended merely as a stopgap before Edmund Andros could arrive. Until then, Dudley was given the onerous task of telling the General Court, venerable legislature of Massachusetts, that it had officially ceased to exist. The good subjects of New England were now to be ruled rather than governed.

The General Court—gifted, like all oligarchies, in the art of self-preservation—had dismissed Dudley's mandate as naively autocratic. But it was they who were being naive; if they thought Dudley was being autocratic, the regime of Sir Edmund was about to give them an education they'd not soon forget.

The new governor got an early start at alienating his people. Not long after the conclusion of the day's ceremonies on December 20, Andros approached the Puritan leaders of Boston with a fascinating request: Could he and his fellow Anglicans borrow one of the local Puritan meetinghouses for a church service that afternoon?

Andros's request, breathtaking in its temerity, weighed heavily on the troubled brows of the local Puritans until it was politely turned down (by Increase Mather, no less—the governor accepted the refusal). Puritan congregations, after all, prided themselves on the gulf they put between their own beliefs and those of the Church of England; allowing an Anglican service to be performed in one of their own meetinghouses bordered on willful heresy. It was hardly a hopeful beginning to the reign of Sir Edmund Andros.

POWER AND PRIVILEGE

The discomfort surrounding Andros's arrival in Boston was emblematic of broader issues that were slowly tearing New England—and the whole British empire—apart. As deeply held religious beliefs segued with volcanic political divisions, the situation on both sides of the Atlantic during the reign of James II quickly became very complex.

Sir Edmund Andros stood at the confluence of all these forces, representing an unlikely combination of loyalties: a dedicated servant of the house of Stuart whose sense of duty compelled him to stand fast at the side of James II—a *Catholic* monarch whose designs on bringing all England back into the Papal fold were as offensive to Andros's Anglicanism as they were to Increase Mather's Puritanism.

Increase Mather (1639–1723), on hand to welcome Royal Governor Edmund Andros, later appeared in England before William and Mary to fight for his removal.

Job vander
Spijll, 1688.

A troubled brow: A Catholic by conversion, James II had no shortage of critics.

For their part, the Puritan elite of New England rejected Sir Edmund on three counts: first, because he was an Anglican; second, because he showed his moral relativism by maintaining his Stuart ties in the face of the king's Catholicism; and third (and most important), because he had arrived to abolish all the privileges that local control and distance from London had given them.

But did the self-reliant folks of Massachusetts really have much to fear from their new royal governor? In a word, yes. Andros had come to administer an entirely new and unprecedented polity: the Dominion of New England. And in every detail of his orders from the king, Andros represented the curbing of American liberties.

The impetus for such a drastic development came from the king's displeasure with his subjects in America. Chief among his many complaints was their flaunting of the Navigation Acts, a suite of maritime laws intended to thwart the growing Dutch dominance in the Atlantic carrying trade. According to the Acts, all trade to and from America was to be conducted via English holds—and almost all American products had to go through English ports before being sold to foreign buyers. American colonists, notoriously opportunistic, largely despised the laws as an attack on their commercial livelihoods, and ignored them.

Determined to bring America in line and to streamline its defenses under a single royal authority, James II sent Andros to preside over a newly created province: the Dominion of New England, originally comprising the colonies of Massachusetts Bay, Plymouth, New Hampshire, and Maine. The charters of these colonies were annulled, their assemblies dissolved. But that was merely the beginning.

The governor-general was given complete control over the appointment of his own advisors and agents. He was empowered to create and pass laws on his own, and was given the strength to enforce them—as captain-general of the Dominion, he had supreme authority over all the armed forces. As for sheriffs and judges, they were to be selected by him.

Taxation was also his personal purview: He could decide the level of taxation and dispose of the revenue as he saw fit. In fact, he was answerable only to the crown through whose munificence he had risen to such dizzying heights. Nothing like it had ever been seen in New England.

Andros, a longtime henchman of the Stuarts, had been governor of New York—the personal property of James when he was still the Duke of York. Now that the Duke of York was sitting on the throne as James II, he hoped to advance the royal agenda even further in New England than he had on the Hudson. And Sir Edmund was just the man for the job.

It wasn't long before Andros tackled his other agenda: expanding the Dominion to neighboring colonies. Within a year of landing in Boston Harbor he had absorbed Rhode Island and Connecticut. By the summer of 1688, New York and the Jerseys (East and West) had been annexed as well. It was a veritable gubernatorial empire.

WALKING ON THIN ICE

St. George's Day—April 23, 1687—was also the second anniversary of the king's coronation. To celebrate, Governor Andros sanctioned a day of explosive festivities. There were fireworks and martial displays of gunnery, and bonfires appeared throughout the city of Boston.

Such saturnalia was normal in Europe—the festivities throughout England and Scotland that day were indulgent indeed. But Boston wasn't England or Scotland. In fact, the Puritans who had originally settled the colony were very proud of that fact. They didn't even allow celebrations of the sort that now literally exploded around them; such things were anathema to God's pious flock. But the austere paradise they'd created for themselves had been corrupted by years of Anglican and royalist immigration. And now the heretic newcomers even had a governor they could call their own.

Displays of worldly excess were bad enough. But Andros crossed the line in many other ways as well. A perfect example could be seen every December 25, when he walked through the town on his way to Christmas Mass accompanied by a small armed guard. It was bad enough that he publicly celebrated Christmas, a holiday that didn't exist for Puritans, who conducted business every December 25 as if it were any other cold, wintry day, but the fact that Andros did so with an armed soldier at his side was downright sickening.

AS THE GOVERNOR LABORED TO ADVANCE THE ROYAL AGENDA, HE SOWED THE SEEDS OF HIS OWN DOOM.

Powerless to stop the disintegration of their decades-old theocracy, the Puritan elite of Boston came to view the Dominion of New England as a punishment from God for their sins.

Anyone searching for evidence of the deity's judgment needed to look no further than the city's soldiery. Regular troops were literally unknown in New England until Christmas Eve 1686, when sixty red-coated professionals stepped onto the Boston quay like instruments of providential retribution.

For the average town in Europe or Britain, the presence of a garrison could mean a good boost in the tavern trade. But to the sanctimonious population of Boston, Fort Hill's warriors were a nuisance and a moral liability. They drank, cursed, smoked, toiled on Sundays, and spurned prayer meetings. Boston wasn't New York, where a broad spectrum of peoples mingled, married, and did business in an atmosphere of tolerance and turpitude. Here in the Bay, one's behavior was everyone's business. And the soldiers who now strolled the streets with impunity seemed like a curse from the Almighty.

Surrounded by such obvious manifestations of his sovereignty, Governor Andros settled into a familiar pattern of swaggering inflexibility. He overruled real estate transactions that had preceded his appointment, betrayed non-Anglican supporters to whom he had once made promises, dismissed the advice of local magistrates, and stood loyally behind his most hated lieutenants—not least Edward Randolph, who was appointed to the governor-general's council and whose rigid adherence to royal policies, particularly during his stint as customs agent, earned him many staunch enemies.

Perhaps most vexing of all, the courts under Andros were all but dismissive of the rights of colonists. This stemmed from a belief by all metropolitan authorities that the rights of Englishmen to such things as habeas corpus and representatives in govern-

Sir Edmund Andros, shown here, settled into a pattern of swaggering inflexibility as governor of New York.

ment did not extend to those living overseas; colonies, to be precise, existed for the benefit of the mother country, and did not enjoy the full measure of English protection from tyranny. Andros and his commissioners were clear on this point, and they never considered an alternative view.

Any chance of discovering the dim view in which his people held him disappeared with Andros's habit of listening only to close friends and trusted associates. And as the governor labored to advance the royal agenda, he sowed the seeds of his own doom.

THE CHICKENS COME HOME TO ROOST

Early on the morning of April 18, 1689, Sir Edmund Andros stood on the bastions of Fort Mary, on Fort Hill, and heard a disconcerting noise: the angry shouts of a mob. And by the sound of it, the crowd must have nearly filled the streets of Boston.

Sheriff James Sherlock assured the governor-general that there was nothing to worry about, but Andros worried anyway. After seeing to the fort's security and making sure that all the soldiers were alert and on the lookout for any danger, he tried to get some word from the town and prepared for the worst. Joining him within the security of the fort were other prominent members of his council, including Edward Randolph, whose face had taken on a decidedly worried aspect since hearing the roar of the throng.

Andros and his commissioners were down in the governor's quarters when the shouting grew close, convincing them that the town's people must be at the gates. The governor listened breathlessly for what seemed an eternity, hoping desperately to hear a volley of musketry from his soldiers. But it never came—and all he and his fellows could hear was the din of an enraged rabble, now louder than ever.

Furious, Andros went out and fulminated at his redcoats for their timid uselessness. He and his government were now hostages to an insurrection.

This was Sir Edmund's worst nightmare, made all the more painful by the fact that he had seen it coming. For days, rumors had been flying through the Dominion that James II had been deposed. Determined to rid themselves of the Stuarts once and for all, an uppity parliament had turned to Mary, James's daughter and a staunch Protestant. Her husband, William of Orange, Stadtholder of the Netherlands and a champion of Protestantism, raised an army and accepted parliament's "invitation" to invade the country and oust the last Catholic monarch of England. William and Mary, so the rumors went, were now joint monarchs of the empire.

Andros looked out at the seething rebels before his fort—*my God, there are thousands of them*—and knew the rumors must be true. The Puritan elite of the Dominion had been plotting against his government since the beginning, and had obviously seen James's overthrow as an opportune time to strike. But the crowd—nearly all commoners—was huge. Could the Congregational ministers have set something this large in motion? Was their hold over the ordinary folk that strong?

Seeing militiamen in the ranks below, the governor flushed with anger and considered the fort's artillery. One salvo from the guns with small shot would rip the churning crowd to ribbons. That would teach these perfidious devils. Should he do it?

News arrived that the *Rose*, a Royal Navy ship moored at the docks, had been besieged as surely as Fort Mary, her captain having been arrested when he went ashore

Mary, daughter of James II, reigned as Queen Mary II alongside her husband, William of Orange, the Dutch Stadtholder who became King of England.

to parley with his assailants. The ship's remaining officers, however, continued to defend her valiantly, threatening to open up on the town with her gunnery.

Andros looked out in the direction of the *Rose* and spotted a boat rowing toward the fort. The governor went down to hail it, and discovered that it had been sent by the *Rose* to spirit Andros to safety. But before he could attempt an escape, the rebels seized the little craft and its crew, discovering an array of weapons and grenades within. The governor was well and truly trapped.

By early afternoon, Andros gave in to necessity and went out to speak with the leaders of the crowd. Suppressing his volcanic disdain for the men who now confronted him, Andros was read a letter that outlined the situation as interpreted by the leaders of the revolt.

ONE OF THE REBELS BOLDLY WALKED OVER TO EDWARD RANDOLPH, RAISED A PISTOL, AND JABBED IT INTO HIS STERNUM. IF HE DIDN'T VOLUNTEER TO ORDER THE SOLDIERS OF FORT MARY TO STAND DOWN, HE WOULD HAVE HIS CHEST BLOWN APART.

Written by the Puritan leaders of the town and their allies (mostly merchants, who, though not Puritans themselves, had suffered commercially since Andros's accession), the letter claimed that municipal leaders had taken control of the ravening rustics to ensure the governor's safety. Unless he surrendered himself to the committee forthwith, they could no longer guarantee his welfare. Andros's response was legally correct, if nothing else: No one had the right to convene a committee of any sort except him, so he was duty-bound to ignore their demands.

Andros nevertheless greed to be escorted to the Town House, where all this could be officially handled. After returning to the fort long enough to burn his papers, the governor-general and his entourage of jittery advisors were taken under armed guard to the town's most important municipal building, there to stand before the people who accused them. As they marched through the clamoring throng, those armed militia who had once answered to the governor officially continued to view him with quiet reverence, refusing to let their innate respect for authority be swept away with the tide of emotions.

Once in the confines of the Town House, Governor Andros was reminded that he "might thank himself for the present Disaster that had befallen him." Now a prisoner, the old Stuart stalwart accepted his fate with the dignity and composure expected of one so experienced in matters of state and war.

The rebel leaders, however, had a final matter of business to attend to: the surrender of Fort Mary. Andros, his agile mind sensing a beautiful irony, pleaded that, as a

The Charter of Connecticut was hidden in this old white oak, protected from Edmund Andros' attempts to confiscate it.

Tree of Knowledge

Sir Edmund Andros's arrival in New England marked the commencement of a new era. To ensure the success of that new beginning, he made a point of visiting the constituent colonies of the Dominion to personally confiscate their charters. Connecticut, however, posed a problem.

According to legend, the leaders of Connecticut were so protective of their rights as an independent colony that they went to extraordinary lengths to thwart the governor-general's attempt to destroy the physical embodiment of those rights. On the evening of October 26, 1687, Andros and company showed up in Hartford and met with local leaders at Butler's Tavern. As the argument heated up over the charter, the candles went out (or were overturned—you decide) and the document disappeared in the ensuing darkness. A Captain Joseph Wadsworth, so the story goes, then ran with the charter to the Wyllys estate and hid it in the hollow of a very old white oak tree. Andros never did get his grasping hands on it.

The august oak remained standing, a proud testament to Connecticut defiance, until the summer of 1856, when it was finally felled by a summer storm.

prisoner, he had no authority whatsoever to command troops to do anything, much less give up a fortified possession of the crown.

IN THE COMING WEEKS, SIR EDMUND WAS IMPRISONED IN THE FORT HE ONCE CONSIDERED HOME. ACCORDING TO SOME ACCOUNTS, HE ATTEMPTED AN ESCAPE BY DRESSING IN WOMEN'S CLOTHING.

An awkward tension settled over the room. Then one of the rebels boldly walked over to Edward Randolph, raised a pistol, and jabbed it into his sternum. If he didn't volunteer right now to order the soldiers of Fort Mary to stand down, he would have his chest blown apart.

With very little further ado, Randolph accompanied the insurgents to the fort and secured the garrison's surrender. It wasn't long before mob leaders convinced the *Rose* to give up, as well as the garrison in Castle Island out at the harbor's mouth. The collapse of royal authority in Boston was complete.

ACCOMMODATION

In the coming weeks, Sir Edmund was imprisoned in the fort he once considered home. According to some accounts, he attempted an escape by dressing in women's clothing. He continued to wear his gentleman's boots under the dress, however, which gave him away. As for his erstwhile master back in Europe, James went into exile and, after attempting and failing to beat his successor on the battlefield, went into forced retirement.

Interestingly, Andros's fate wasn't nearly as grim—despite the fact that his detractors had been at work in England even as he was facing rebellion in New England. Increase Mather, who had been on hand to bless the governor's arrival, was present in London to give a (very skewed) account of Andros's regime to William and Mary during their rise to power. Parson Mather's agenda was crystalline: to have Andros removed and to reinstate the charters and representative assemblies that the Dominion had obliterated. Although he was willing to work with the colonies on that front, King William was adamant that Governor Andros be returned to London without harm, ostensibly to stand trial.

Andros did return to England, but he never stood trial. In fact, he ended up serving the new regime as Governor of Virginia from 1692 to 1698. Clearly a survivor, that one.

In the crumbling Dominion of New England, rebellion continued to spread—New York was next, and even Maryland succumbed. For the people of Connecticut,

Massachusetts, Plymouth, and Rhode Island, original charters were reinstated and elected assemblies brought out of retirement. For the new heads of state back in England, this was a problem, if only because it meant a return to the old ways of contraband markets, squabbling petty-states, and helter-skelter defensive plans. But William and Mary were hard-pressed to condemn the overthrow of the Dominion; after all, they themselves were usurpers of a legitimate monarch.

If Sir Edmund Andros came out of all this looking bad, the opposition that overthrew him can hardly be seen as heroes. What seems to have taken place in New England between 1686 and 1689 is a clash of irrational extremes: arbitrary royal prerogative versus entrenched theocratic provincialism. Andros's mission in America was to enforce the mercantilist vision of empire that English monarchs had hitherto only dreamt of—to turn America into a means of enriching the metropolitan home, and little more.

On the other hand, the "liberties" that Increase Mather and his Puritan fellows were fighting for amounted to the right to persecute distasteful religions—to protect the hallowed enclave of parochial extremism that the founders had created an ocean away from Europe. They had had their own way, on their own terms, for too long to give it up for the sake of order.

What emerged from the fracas was a polyglot America with all its factionalism and commercialist ardor. It was the first dedicated, concerted attempt to rope Americans closely into the empire. And it failed. Interestingly, the next attempt would fail as well, bringing into being a wholly new country whose underpinnings lay, perhaps, in the angry discord of 1689.

chapter eleven

A Colonial Minister's Ordeal Highlights the Clash of America's Cultures

1704

The din of hatchets on the front door woke John Williams from a deep winter sleep. As his wife stirred beside him, the minister of Deerfield, Massachusetts, got out of bed and darted into the front room, the frigid February chill nipping at his bare shanks. The harsh noise had instantly banished the sleep from his head, and he soon stood wide-eyed and alert before a door that shuddered from the blows of shouting assailants. His home was under attack.

It must have been shortly before sunrise. In the darkness, the bright flicker of torches played on the window glass, and Indians could be heard whooping out in the yard. Williams barked an order to the two dozing soldiers on the second floor, who quickly scrambled for their arms, cursing the cold under their breath.

The minister then ran back into his bedchamber with Isaiah 38:10-11 on his lips—
I shall go to the gates of the grave: I am deprived of the residue of my years ... —and reached over the bed-tester for the pistol he kept there.

By the time he was pulling the striker back to full cock, a terrible cacophony in the neighboring room announced the entrance of a band of Indians, who quickly broke into the bedchamber in a flood of martial fury. A group of them stood about staring at Williams, who promptly jabbed the pistol into the chest of the nearest and unhesitatingly squeezed the trigger. Nothing happened.

The house of John Williams, minister of Deerfield, Massachusetts, was invaded and ransacked by Amerindians aligned with French forces in Canada during Queen Anne's War.

As he would later write in his account of the attack, the misfire undoubtedly saved his life—the victim's fellows would certainly have split his head open for killing one of their own. Instead they bound him and his wife, and set about tearing through the house in search of booty and more captives.

One of the two soldiers upstairs had leapt from a window and sprinted off in search of help. The other had been captured. From outside came the screams of women and infants and the intermittent crackle of gunfire. The smoky stink of burning houses filled the minister's nose, and he wondered whether this was truly, at long last, the end of Deerfield—the end of everything.

Williams and his family were about to undergo the greatest trial of their lives. The attack on Deerfield, part of Queen Anne's War (the second of the "French and Indian Wars," and the North American component of the War of the Spanish Succession), was a milestone in the ongoing conflicts between the English and their French opponents in New England, not least because of the number of captives taken in the raid.

Most prominent of the more than one hundred English captured that fateful morning was John Williams. In the weeks that followed, he and his unfortunate kin underwent an odyssey of immense adversity that encapsulated the bizarre, complex reality defining the frontier between hostile empires in the New World—a reality that spanned the conflicting interests of numerous divergent cultures through a seemingly unending cycle of war, peace, accommodation, and bondage.

Williams's story—shocking, pathetic, heroic—is emblematic of America at the *fin de siècle*.

ON THE WARPATH

Deerfield was vulnerable in times of war. Perched at the confluence of the Connecticut and Deerfield rivers, it was a target along excellent avenues of approach for war bands from Canada. And its remoteness on the northern frontier of Massachusetts made reinforcement difficult at best.

When news of war with the French arrived, Parson Williams appealed to the colony's leaders for an overhaul of the community's stockade. Measures were taken—in addition to reinforcing the palisade, Massachusetts sent twenty soldiers to garrison the town.

In fact, these actions may have done more harm than good. Secure in the presence of soldiers, the folk of Deerfield settled into a dangerous calm with the onset of winter. As snow drifted three feet and higher, nobody could imagine the French or their native allies braving such conditions to come nearly three hundred miles from Montreal to harass a little hamlet on the outskirts of New England.

Deerfield, Massachusetts, burns after being raided by Amerindians in 1704.

The French had other ideas. In 1701 they had arranged the "Great Peace," in which Indian nations tied to New France affirmed their loyalty and willingness to wage war against the English. The governor had also arranged an uneasy peace with the Iroquois League, which traditionally guarded the broad left flank of English New York and New England. The warpath south was secured.

In the fall of 1703, Pennacook Indians, eager to avenge attacks by the English on their villages in Maine and New Hampshire, approached the governor of New France with a proposal for striking at Deerfield. He responded by tapping a thirty-five-year-old lieutenant named Jean-Baptiste Hertel de Rouville to organize and lead the operation. Born in the town of Trois-Rivières along the St. Lawrence River, de Rouville hailed from a prominent noble Canadian family. Along with his brothers, he held a commission in the *troupes de la marine*, the regular soldiers of New France, and had acquired years of experience living and fighting with Indian allies. Fort Chambly, literally surrounded by the Hertel estate, served as the mustering point for this, his first independent command.

NOBODY COULD IMAGINE THE FRENCH OR THEIR NATIVE ALLIES BRAVING SUCH CONDITIONS TO COME NEARLY THREE HUNDRED MILES FROM MONTREAL TO HARASS A LITTLE HAMLET ON THE OUTSKIRTS OF NEW ENGLAND.

It was to be the largest operation yet mounted by the French and their allies against an English settlement. In addition to several of his own brothers and fifty other French Canadians, de Rouville's force—250 strong—included Pennacooks, Hurons, Mohawks from the Montreal region, and Abenakis. While the Pennacooks and Abenakis were going south for revenge and mourning, their fellow natives were after plunder and captives. It was an army of unprecedented diversity, attesting to the French gift for working with Indians to compensate for their much smaller numbers in North America relative to the English.

After an arduous trek through the frozen wilderness, de Rouville's cold, weary men spent a shivering night sleeping without fires on a plain just across the Deerfield River from their target. Two hours before dawn the next morning, they donned their snowshoes, crossed the river, and skulked toward a slumbering Deerfield.

After de Rouville's scouts brought word that the town's watch had either disappeared or fallen asleep, he gathered his *troupes* and militiamen together, along with those Indians who'd been converted to the Roman faith, and prayed. Then they were off.

Protecting only the heart of the settlement, Deerfield's stockade enclosed some twenty structures, including the house of Parson Williams. In wartime those living beyond the protection of the wooden fortification abandoned their homes and slept in structures erected for that purpose within the inner defenses.

Snow had been blown into great drifts that went right up the side of the palisade, offering the raiders a way in. After making their way up and over, several of them opened the north gate, and de Rouville's men poured through. Deerfield's doom had arrived.

A NEW REALITY

Murder and chaos reigned in the Williams household. As the minister and his wife were ordered to dress, the Indians rounded up the rest of the family. Six-year-old John and his infant sister, Jerusha, were slain with one hatchet blow each to the head. They were not deemed fit for the long journey to Canada. Then the raiders dispatched Parthena, one of the family's two slaves.

By now the sun had been up for over an hour, and the Indians bound the surviving Williamses—there were eight of them, including five children; the minister and his wife, Eunice; and Frank, the family's surviving slave and widower of Parthena—and stepped out into the violent morning. Funnels of black smoke churned skyward from flaming houses, and the rumble of musketry was steady now. Clearly someone was giving the raiders a fight.

As they made their way toward the gate, shoved and taunted by their captors, the Williams family saw more raiders making their way out, many of them wounded, some of them herding large groups of Deerfielders. The minister saw a man off in the distance with a white coat and tricorne hat, the glint of sunlight below his throat betraying the metal gorget of an officer. *That must be the leader*, he thought, struck by the ease with which French gentlemen made common cause with heathen savages. But Lieutenant de Rouville gave him no notice.

Williams and his family were taken across the river and onto the plain where all the other captives were being taken in preparation of the long journey north. They were deprived of their shoes and given moccasins, a necessity if speed was of the essence.

Back across the river, shouts and gunfire announced the arrival of a relief force from nearby Hatfield. Rushing out of the stockade in pursuit of the retiring French and Indians, the furious English, awkward in the drifts without snowshoes, fired wildly at their enemies. Eventually they massed for a proper counterattack, but were driven back by a stubborn and well-organized rearguard of French and Indians. The battle was over.

The captives' misery, however, had barely begun. Williams's earlier observation about stiff English resistance during the raid now seemed correct: Many of the raiders were badly wounded, and the party's simmering anger at that fact was now taken out on the captives. Not long after commencing the journey north, the Indians killed another infant.

Williams, his family divided up among different "masters," delivered himself into God's hands and looked upon this horrific event as punishment for the community's sins. That night the army, now burdened with more than a hundred captives, bedded down early in makeshift shelters. Bound and incapable of leaving his crude wigwam, he heard a commotion in the camp and feared for his family's safety. Later he learned that several of the Indians had gotten drunk on captured liquor and killed Frank, his slave. Freedom was dearly purchased indeed amid the heathen.

INTO THE WILD

The morning brought interesting news: One of the captives had escaped, a twenty-three-year-old man named Joseph Alexander. Williams now got to meet with the officer he'd spied during the previous day's fighting. De Rouville approached the minister and insisted that he tell his fellow English that any further attempts at escape would force the commander's hand—all the remaining captives would be burned to death.

The force was soon up and traveling again, maintaining a daunting pace through a wilderness of crusted, melting snow and frigid watercourses. The minister was shared by two Abenaki captors, one of whom forbade him from talking with anyone. The other, however, was more lenient, and soon afforded Williams a brief opportunity to fall back and speak with his wife, who had become the possession of another Indian.

Eunice had been recovering from the birth of their latest child, now dead, when the raiders fell upon Deerfield. Now, as her feet froze and bled from the impossible pace, her flagging constitution battered by exhaustion, she dared to mention to her husband that she might not be able to make it. It was only the second day of the journey to Quebec, and so much more hardship lay ahead. Her chances were clearly remote.

"She never spake any discontented word as to what had befallen us," Williams later wrote, "but with suitable expressions justified God in what had happened."

The minister was soon forced to resume his place in the column. Before long they were crossing a stream as swift as it was cold, its swirling waters several feet deep. On the far bank they ascended a rise and Williams, exhausted, was allowed a brief respite.

As the rest of the column filed past, he asked after the fate of his wife, who, he knew, must have found the water quite challenging. He was told that, after falling to her knees in the stream, she had gotten back to her feet, stumbled onto the far bank, and collapsed. It was at that point that her captor fell upon Eunice and brained her with a hatchet.

A nineteenth-century illustration of white fear: Fundamental to Amerindian nations, captive-taking spirited numerous young Europeans into an alien culture that many of them came to embrace.

Williams was undone with grief, but he knew he had to carry on. His five children, spread along the column among varying captors, now depended on him as never before. He was determined to look after them, as he'd promised his wife before taking his leave of her for the last time. Later that day, a prominent Indian captain spoke to the minister's master about killing and scalping him. Williams, as he did in all endeavors, appealed to his Lord.

ON MARCH 4, THE PACE WAS TOO FAST FOR FOUR OF THE WOMEN CAPTIVES, WHO WERE PROMPTLY SLAUGHTERED AFTER FAILING TO KEEP UP. TWO MORE STRAGGLERS WERE KILLED ON THE SIXTH.

"I lifted up my heart to God, to implore his grace and mercy in such time of need; and afterwards I told my master, if he intended to kill me, I desired he would let me know of it; assuring him that my death, after a promise of quarter, would bring the guilt of blood upon him." His master decided not to kill him.

Nevertheless, death marched right along with the captives and their tormentors, creating a moving tableau of brutality. Though Williams and his congregation were occasionally allowed to gather for prayer meetings, the tenuousness of life challenged the very limits of their faith. On March 4, the pace was too fast for four of the women captives, who were promptly slaughtered after failing to keep up. Two more stragglers were killed on the sixth.

The following morning, as John Williams sat in his wigwam preparing for the day's labors, a young woman named Mary Brooks came to him, a look of consternation on her face.

"By my falls on the ice yesterday, I injured myself," she explained to her minister, "causing a miscarriage this night, so that I am not able to travel far." With certainty, she proclaimed that her master would kill her within hours. This they both knew. She asked only that Williams pray for her, "that God would take me to himself." Later that day the Indians killed her.

Over the following two days, the column broke up into smaller groups that headed off toward different Indian villages. Williams was parted from his children and, with his masters, traveled in the direction of Lake Champlain. He had no way of knowing whether he would ever see his family again.

A VALUABLE CAPTIVE

On a spring day in 1704, in the Indian village of Odanak on the St. Lawrence River, John Williams sat in his wigwam and ruminated over scripture. Suddenly his master appeared at the entrance and ordered the minister to attend Mass with him. Williams refused.

The Abenaki twisted his mouth into a scowl, strode into the wigwam, forcefully lifted his captive by the shoulders, and dragged him outside. Williams, it seemed, was going to Mass whether he liked it or not.

And he definitely did not. As far as he was concerned, dealing with insistent Catholics was the most challenging hardship he had encountered, even in the wake of the long, torturous trek that had brought him there. After watching his surviving children disappear from view, Williams had been brought up the length of frozen Lake Champlain.

Clearly valuable to his captors, who hoped to sell or ransom him, the minister gradually received better and better treatment. The Abenakis gave him the choicest pieces of meat from their game, and they fashioned a pair of snowshoes for him to move more easily over the late winter snow.

But his masters never failed to remind him how close to death he was, or how fully his fate relied on their goodwill. Many an evening one of them would say goodnight to Williams by pointing a pistol at him and threatening to fire it—the very pistol that had nearly ended the minister's life that awful morning weeks ago.

A CLASH OF FAITHS

In time, they arrived at Fort Chambly, where Williams encountered French officers and civilians who were often as decent to him as they were critical of his Protestant faith. On several occasions, he had dined with kindly French who understood the plight he was in. But the French also knew how important their native alliances were, and the notion of depriving Indians of their captives was unthinkable.

Soon it was further down the St. Lawrence to Odanak, where a large Catholic mission presided over a vast, diverse group of Indians, many of whom were refugees from English encroachments onto their lands. It was here that the minister's captors lived—his journey had at last come to an end.

But Odanak, known as St. Francis to the Jesuits who ministered there, presented threats to Williams's well-being that were far more frightening to him than waist-deep snow or the promise of slow death in an icy wasteland—a fact that now worried him acutely as his Abenaki master dragged him like a deer carcass to church.

Williams at last relented. Until now he had been able to avoid attending any "popish" rituals, but his master obviously wasn't taking no for an answer. He followed the Indian reluctantly into the chapel and promptly found a spot near the door from which to observe the offensive proceedings.

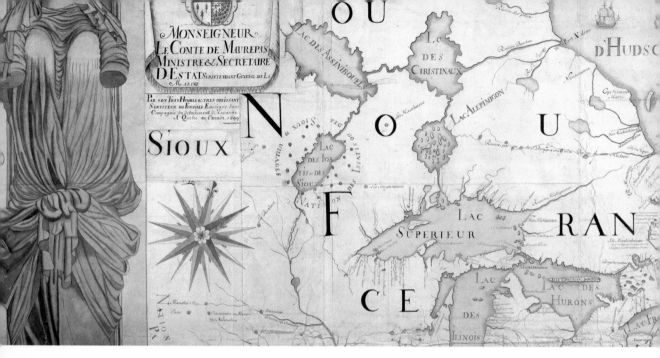

A 1699 engraving shows much of New France.

Indian Allies, Not Subjects

As the rivalry between European empires in the New World heated up during the late seventeenth and eighteenth centuries, an unsettling fact became clear to the leaders of New France: The population of their colony was utterly dwarfed by that of the English possessions along the Atlantic seaboard.

Additionally, the nature of New France itself—a province of fur traders whose business brought them in close and constant contact with the Indians of the interior—created a dependence on indigenous cultures, rather than a conflict with them over land. Taken together, these circumstances compelled the French government to embrace alliances with Indian nations to compensate for the exploding English population.

New England unwittingly greased the wheels of this process with its community-based, agricultural economy, which required the constant displacement of Indians on an expanding frontier to thrive.

Tied as they were to their Indian allies, the French found themselves forced to accept—or even adopt—native idiosyncrasies that would otherwise have offended their Old World sensibilities. Chief among these was the practice of taking captives, a fundamental element of Indian societies. Though many French and Canadians were loath to see white Christians disappear into a "savage" culture—to "go native"—they were also nearly powerless to stop it. As Governor Vaudreuil was fond of pointing out to English emissaries who came north to ransom captured family members, the Indians were allies, not subjects.

Nevertheless, the situation was hardly that simple. In fact, Vaudreuil and others in New France were playing a clever game of deception for the sake of their vulnerable colony. The taking of captives from New England served several purposes, the most obvious of which was its capacity to unnerve English on the frontier and to keep them constantly in fear. It was, in essence, a form of terrorism.

Just as important, however, was the transfer of labor from the population-rich English possessions into New France. English captives were often bought from Indian villages, which were happy for the compensation, and then adopted into French Canadian society to appease the evangelical impulse through their conversion to Catholicism. They could then be employed on farms (which were always looking for labor in New France), as urban workers, or household servants, or put to work using skills they had learned in New England and that were in high demand in New France, such as constructing mills.

Although most captives returned to New England in peacetime (at least, those that could be ransomed from cooperative French and Indian communities), many chose to stay. Of the eighty-six to eighty-nine Deerfield captives who survived the journey into Canada, between sixteen and twenty remained as Catholic converts in French communities, primarily Montreal. Perhaps seven remained with their Indian captors.

✣

What he saw amazed and revolted him. At the head of the crowded room stood a Jesuit, whose Latin mutterings were clearly unintelligible to the native congregants. Several translators tried to keep up with the Jesuit, creating an atmosphere of babbling confusion. Presently, Williams departed with a mocking smile on his lips—a mask of disdain that did nothing to further win over his hosts.

Williams, however, was steadfast. As a minister in the English Protestant tradition, the Catholic penchant for saints, Latin, and the cult of the Virgin was a veritable highway to hell. That the Jesuits and their converts were nearly as steadfast in their attempts to convert him didn't help his situation, which grew for him into a long vigil over the fate of his soul. Canada was like a vast, alien land, full of foreign speakers and guileful, popish minions intent on enslaving him to the Whore of Babylon—what Puritans called the Vatican.

Not long after his first Mass, Williams received a couple of visitors to his wigwam, almost certainly at the request of his master. One of them, named Ruth, was an Englishwoman taken captive during King Philip's War and a resident of Canada ever since. The other was another English captive who spoke only in an Indian dialect that Williams could not understand.

CANADA WAS LIKE A VAST, ALIEN LAND, FULL OF FOREIGN SPEAKERS AND GUILEFUL, POPISH MINIONS INTENT ON ENSLAVING HIM TO THE WHORE OF BABYLON—WHAT PURITANS CALLED THE VATICAN.

As the two women spoke intently with his master, the minister watched and wondered what they could be talking about. At last, their conversation came to an end, and the warrior turned to his captive, commanding him to cross himself. Williams refused—crossing oneself, like all other forms of symbol making, was considered idolatrous by him and his fellow worshippers. The master insisted again and again, but Williams only parried each attempt with a zealous refusal.

"Mr. Williams," said Ruth in very good English, "you know the Scripture, and therefore act against your own light; for you know the Scripture saith, 'servants, obey your masters. He is your master, and you his servant.'"

Williams glowered at the woman and called her ignorant. He insisted that he was not to disobey God merely to obey his master, pointing out her argument as so much savage sophistry. Ruth translated his words to his master, who then grabbed Williams's hand and tried to force him to make the sign of the cross. Again, Williams stood his ground, and wrested his hand free. The Abenaki, fury growing on his face, yanked the cross from around his own neck and told the minister to kiss it. More popish idolatry, as far as Williams was concerned, and he again refused.

The warrior then reached for his hatchet and brandished it menacingly, telling his captive that he would "dash out his brains" if he continued to refuse. Williams, inwardly praying for mercy, merely stood motionless. His master, discarding the weapon, threatened to bite off all the minister's fingernails. But Williams remained adamant—he offered his hand and proclaimed his willingness to endure suffering.

A man with a blunderbuss stands guard at a Puritan prayer meeting in Deerfield, Massachusetts, in 1675, to watch for signs of Amerindian attacks.

Philippe de Rigaud
M^s de Vaudreuil
gouverneur du Canada
1650·1725

The Abenaki made as if to chomp down on his opponent's thumb, then pushed it away. "No good minister, no love God, as bad as the Devil." And with that, John Williams's master strode angrily from his wigwam.

THE LONELINESS OF BELIEF

Relief from the hardships of Odanak would come from an unlikely source. In April of 1704, Philippe de Riguad de Vaudreuil, governor-general of New France, ordered that Williams be brought to him in Montreal. There, in quarters much more congenial to a man of Williams's experience, the minister healed his wounds and gradually, if painfully, reacclimated himself to the rich diet of a landed European.

The situation could not have been more ironic. Vaudreuil, like his predecessors, maintained the solvency of New France by using Indian allies to keep New England perpetually off balance. By his sanction had raiders blown through Deerfield, murdered two of the Williams children and both of their slaves, and dragged the surviving family members—and scores of others—through a long nightmare of murderous slavery.

And yet Williams, glad to be in the company of a white man of status, eagerly partook of his food, wine, and shelter. He also thanked the governor for placing him in touch with two of his children who happened to be in Montreal. This, understandably, was very important to the minister.

And still the religious tension seethed. His seven-year-old daughter, Eunice, remained with the Kahnawake Mohawks, and she was daily seduced by their Latin efforts. Against the wishes of the Jesuits, Vaudreuil managed to arrange two meetings between Williams and his youngest daughter, which proved to be more painful than the minister could bear. Seeing her lose her "true faith," he wrote to her, imploring her to memorize her catechism and reject the popish attacks on her belief. But to no avail. Eunice would remain among the northern Mohawks for the rest of her life.

Williams was a spiritual liability to his captors. In time, he was transferred to a château outside Quebec, there to be isolated from his fellow English captives and subjected to the finest conversion efforts that the Catholic orders could muster. He stubbornly held to his Puritan beliefs, and was finally released in 1706. Besides Eunice, all of the minister's children who were taken into captivity—Samuel, Esther, Stephen, and Warham—eventually returned to New England.

Philippe de Rigaud de Vaudreuil, governor-general of New France, 1703–1725. War required him to wear several faces: as commander-in-chief of his thinly populated province; as "French Father" to his Indian allies; and as a Christian gentleman who, during and after the war, negotiated with some New Englanders for the release of captives.

Immortalized in his memoir, *The Redeemed Captive Returning to Zion*, the experience of Williams comprises one of the central narratives of Queen Anne's War. His story, of course, is expressive of his personal bias toward an Anglo-Saxon, Puritan, agricultural dominion—precisely the environment that was even then gradually destroying the Amerindian world of the northeast.

In the Old World, Protestant England could take comfort in the distance from Catholic France that the English Channel afforded. But in America, Catholics and Protestants forever clashed in a wild frontier that gave their frenetic passions free reign—and that forced native peoples to choose between two alien worldviews. The result was a world that we would scarcely recognize today, but that shaped the world in which we now live.

chapter twelve

A Costly Colonial War Nearly Wipes South Carolina from the Map

1715-1716

The white men had come bearing promises. In the council house of Pocotaligo, northwest of the South Carolina town of Port Royal, they sat amid their Yamasee Indian hosts around the central fire and spoke of a new future—a fresh start for both peoples.

These English gentlemen were some of the colony's most prominent figures, including Samuel Warner and Thomas Bray, representatives of the Board of Commissioners. John Wright, a former Indian agent, was also there to lend his expertise. And Thomas Nairne—planter, trader, soldier—put his fellow ambassadors at ease, bringing to the council fire an abundance of wisdom that had made him the most respected frontiersman in South Carolina. Having sent such an esteemed group, the colony clearly viewed this mission to the Yamasee as one of grave significance.

In fact, they were attempting to head off disaster. Rumors had been flooding back to Charles Town that the Ochese, neighbors of the Yamasee, were plotting a war on South Carolina. The Board of Commissioners quickly sent delegates to Pocotaligo, largest of the Yamasee towns, to enlist their aid in working out some arrangement with the bellicose Ochese.

But since their arrival, Nairne and the others had sensed a growing unease among the Yamasee, who had long been allies of the South Carolinians. Many of the Yamasee headmen offered complaints over white encroachment on their lands and unfair trading practices.

Overleaf: Amerindians and English colonists fight on the Carolina frontier.

The white men, convinced that the Yamasee could be persuaded to the colony's side, promised redress for these issues. Indeed, they assured the stern-faced elders in the council house, Governor Charles Craven himself was on his way to personally guarantee his people's good faith. All would be settled to the Yamasee's satisfaction.

SLAUGHTER

Long after sundown the South Carolinians, weary from a day of travel and talk, retired to their bedrolls, confident that they had thwarted a calamity for their countrymen. It was the night of April 14, 1715—the night before Good Friday.

The council fire kept burning, however, and the Yamasees, now convening without the presence of the English, debated more freely. Divisions within the leadership showed themselves more clearly, and voices rose to the rafters as the argument grew intense.

The Ochese, they all knew, were planning war. But should the Yamasee thwart them—or join them? Could now be the time to settle all outstanding accounts with the acquisitive Carolinians? The appearance of these men in their midst was proof enough for some that the colony was preparing to attack them—they could be spies, rather than ambassadors. And was the governor coming by himself or at the head of his dreaded militia?

Hours after retiring, the white men were awakened by warriors daubed in red and black paint. Outside, drums beat a war dance, and some of the braves whooped provocatively. But was this a war against the Ochese—or against them?

The men were seized and stripped. One of them, Seymour Burroughs, broke free and ran for the swamp, taking two bullets in the back before collapsing out of sight of the town. He ultimately survived to raise the alarm back in Port Royal. The sixth South Carolinian, whose name has been lost to history, managed to escape without injury to a place of safety just outside of Pocotaligo. There, cowering in horror, he watched his fellows get butchered in the firelight. For Nairne, once a trusted friend of the Yamasee, death would come only after three days of slow burning.

Africans forced into slavery arrive at the Charleston, South Carolina, slave market in this twentieth-century painting.

THUGGERY AND MAYHEM
ON THE FRONTIER

News of the "Pocotaligo Massacre" struck South Carolina like a biblical curse. And little wonder: The colony had lost four valuable gentlemen in a night of despicable murder orchestrated by one of the largest native peoples of the southeast—a nation that was assumed to be friendly.

South Carolina's assumptions, however, were a fundamental part of the problem. Though originally part of the same colony since 1663, the northern and southern regions of Carolina had gradually diverged into separately governed provinces. Charles Town, the future Charleston, had become the heart of the southern province—the vast majority of South Carolina's African and European population lived within thirty miles of the town, creating a vulnerable, slave-based economic enclave surrounded by a vast arc of Indian settlements.

To secure this frontier, the colony relied more on trade than on organized defense: Merchants sold valuable European goods such as guns and clothing to neighboring Indian villages, fostering cultural exchange and treaties of friendship. The result was a string of "buffer" peoples that the government in Charles Town relied on to cultivate commercial growth and prevent the French and Spanish to the south from getting any expansionist ideas.

All well and good. But in a racist atmosphere like the one that prevailed in English Charles Town and its environs, it was easy for white officials to ignore signs that the whole frontier system was gradually falling apart—and at the expense of the Indians. From Port Royal, the settlement south of Charles Town that formed the other population center of South Carolina, merchants had been doing a brisk business with the Indians, particularly the Yamasee.

THE MAJORITY OF INDIANS IN THE BUFFER ZONE COULD HAVE BEEN FORGIVEN FOR LOOKING AT THEIR RELATIONSHIP WITH THE COLONY AS A KIND OF VAMPIRISM.

In exchange for all the extraordinary trade goods that they peddled in native villages throughout the frontier, these men had always accepted deer pelts, a commodity that managed to maintain a steady profitability throughout the seventeenth century.

The deer population, however, had begun to thin out by the first decade of the eighteenth century, not least because of the encroachment of white settlers, who tended to clear the land for livestock and planting. In the past, traders were instructed to extend credit to their Indian clients—after all, they were providing an invaluable

Indians of the Southeast, in disguise, hunt deer in the 1500s. Deer pelts were used in trade between native peoples and European settlers.

service as allies and guardians. But as the threat from Spain and France seemed more remote, traders started demanding that the Indians settle what had become a truly enormous debt—and most of them weren't exactly scrupulous about collecting.

If pelts or other goods weren't forthcoming, then a village's people would do nicely; many traders simply enslaved the relatives of Indian headmen who were powerless to reverse the flow of wealth that had resulted from their addiction to the white man's liquor, cloth, and firearms.

Other traders began to act like tyrants, demanding free labor from Indians, or even assuming control over villages like robber barons. And virtually every Englishman doing business on the frontier was sure to get his clients drunk before closing any deal—a practice that became accepted with alarming nonchalance. All of these practices were officially illegal, but enforcement was essentially a sham.

With their people disappearing, their land shrinking, their debt growing, and their English neighbors getting fatter and happier (not to mention more populous) by the month, the majority of Indians in the buffer zone could have been forgiven for looking at their relationship with the colony as a kind of vampirism. Indeed, one of the most striking facts about colonial South Carolina on the eve of its most devastating crisis is how clueless its leaders seem to have been regarding the Indian "allies" they were taking for granted.

The Ochese had certainly had enough, and the Yamasee dramatically made their choice early on the morning of April 15. Others would soon follow: Chickasaws, Catawbas, Apalachees, Apalachicolas, Yuchis, Shawnees, and Waxhaws, among others, would all take up the hatchet against South Carolinians.

They did not act in concert, nor were they in agreement over goals—some wanted only to humble the white traders; others wanted to overrun Port Royal and Charles Town and burn them to the ground. But the war whoop that shook the pines in spring 1715 looked to white South Carolina like an Indian conspiracy—and a nightmare from hell.

CLASH AT "SALTCATCHERS"

Charles Craven, thirty-three-year-old governor of South Carolina, steadied his horse and looked at his harried men. Since hearing of the massacre of Nairne and the others at Pocotaligo less than a week earlier, he wasted no time in gathering a force to strike a blow against the Yamasee. Now, at the head of some 240 members of the Colleton County militia, he hoped to do just that.

He shouted orders to his lieutenants, who struggled to get the men from column formation, used for marching, into linear ranks, employed when fighting. The enemy, ahead of them now in unknown numbers, would finally get a taste of his vengeance. He couldn't believe his luck.

It was a welcome shift in fortune. After slaughtering the four emissaries, the Yamasees divided their warriors into a pair of war parties that stabbed into South Carolina's underbelly like two prongs of a great fork. One struck into Saint Bartholomew's Parish, bagging huge numbers of captives and killing more than a hundred settlers and slaves. Columns of black smoke, roiling up from burning plantation houses, stood on the horizon like totems of disaster.

The other band moved on Port Royal, which—thanks to the wounded Seymour Burroughs—had been warned of its approach. Docked at the port by sheer chance, the vessel of a captured smuggler offered sanctuary from the advancing Indians. By the time Yamasee braves were torching structures on the outskirts of town, the ship groaned with the weight of several hundred refugees. They, along with countless others in hastily co-opted canoes, would escape the tide of violence. Much of their community, however, lay in ruins.

South Carolina reeled from the sudden onslaught. Horrified at the scale of his colony's plight, Craven struck southwest, into the teeth of the Yamasee attack, in the hope of forcing a confrontation to his advantage. That was a tall order: His militia, unpaid citizen-soldiers, was accustomed to drill and a wee bit of discipline. But there was precious little he could expect of them should the Indians stage an ambush or draw him into an endless guerilla conflict, as was their custom.

He made for the town of Salkehatchie, known to the English as "Saltcatchers." With much of South Carolina's military might (such as it was) bearing down on one of their larger settlements, the Yamasee felt forced to mass their warriors. And now, just a week after the Pocotaligo massacre on a plain outside of Salkehatchie, they barred the way forward for Craven's little army.

THE WAR WHOOP THAT SHOOK THE PINES IN SPRING 1715 LOOKED TO WHITE SOUTH CAROLINA LIKE AN INDIAN CONSPIRACY—AND A NIGHTMARE FROM HELL.

The governor hastened his men to deploy. This was a rare opportunity: It wasn't every day that an Indian force deigned to challenge colonials in a pitched battle on open terrain. Gone were the infuriating skirmishes in sylvan darkness, the fruitless chases into trackless bog land, the fluid defensive perimeters that defined nothing. The best forest fighters in the southeast were offering him a chance to lick them on European terms.

And they weren't wasting anyone's time. Drawn out into a broad crescent, the Yamasee—several hundred strong, the governor estimated—came on in a furious cacophony of war cries, their two wings spreading wide to enclose the colonials and crush them. Craven bellowed commands to bend the ranks, drawing his men inward to meet the onrushing pincers and deny them the flanking maneuver they clearly sought.

Though frightened and somewhat disorganized, the Carolinians stood firm and delivered against their attackers, protecting the flanks. The Yamasee reeled back, and then came on again, pressing one end of the line, then the other. But their attacks failed to break the colonial ranks.

Twenty-four of Craven's men lay dead, with perhaps an equal number on the other side. The Yamasee, however, had lost several of their captains, a greater price than they were willing to pay. They broke off the fight and scattered into the surrounding swamps.

Governor Craven had his revenge. But up north, new enemies were already opening another front.

DEFENDING SLAVERY

George Chicken blinked a drop of sweat off his eyelid and cursed the humidity under his breath. Removing his tricorne hat, he pushed a lock of soaked hair back over his head, and shifted his weight in an attempt to squat more comfortably. All around him in the waning, late-afternoon light of the forest, men muttered under their breath and swatted at flies. They were tense and, for the most part, silent. This was the uncomfortable art of ambush.

Some 120 strong, the men of his command were an accurate, if motley, representation of South Carolina society. Many of them were slaves, born in Africa and forced to defend the culture that kept them in bondage. The masters of these men paid for their property's martial service. The others, white militia, tended to be as wary of the black soldiers in their midst as they were of the Indians they hoped to catch in a trap on this stifling June evening.

We may never know whether they understood the greater absurdity of this moment: that Englishmen, thousands of miles from their homeland, found themselves defending a hostile wilderness they had taken from somebody else with soldiers they'd stolen from another continent—and led by a man named "Chicken."

Up to now the war had been indecisive. Down south, Governor Craven's victory at Salkehatchie had opened the way for further victories in Yamasee country, including the decisive destruction of several fortified towns. But the Yamasee had put the mistake of Salkehatchie behind them, concentrating instead on sending smaller war bands that were harder to detect deep into Carolina country to burn and take captives.

Despite the victories of their militia and veteran Indian fighters, the colony's white establishment continued to flee toward Charles Town, driven by rumors of raiders from every direction. The town soon showed the strains of overpopulation, running quickly out of stores and clean water. It wasn't long before the specter of starvation stalked the streets.

ENTER THE CATAWBA

More bad news came from the northern frontier. There, the Catawbas had added disdain for colonial squabbling to their complaints of white cruelty and perfidy. Dominating the Pee Dee and Santee river valleys, the Catawba had been the focus of attempts by traders from all three local colonies—Virginia, North Carolina, and South Carolina—to win their business.

The result was a distasteful decades-long display of greed and selfishness. As Catawba villagers watched in increasing disgust, colonial traders from the different colonies bickered and goaded each other, competing for financial scraps in an ongo-

Amerindians raid a South Carolina plantation.

ing melee that convinced the Catawba of the inescapable truth of colonial disunity. Such men, the Catawbas believed, would never come to each other's aid in time of war.

In the late spring of 1715, Catawba war parties flooded south toward Charles Town, further crippling a colony on the verge of collapse. Captain Thomas Barker, a young cavalier of the landed class, bolted north at the head of ninety fine cavalrymen, only to be ambushed. Barker and nearly a third of his men were killed.

The Catawbas went on to besiege the plantation of one Benjamin Schenkingh, which had been hastily converted by local authorities into a frontier fort.

After duping the defenders into allowing them inside the defenses for a parley, the Indians slaughtered most of the plantation's garrison and moved on. Virtually nothing now stood between them and the rich settlement of Goose Creek, north of Charles Town.

Nothing, that is, until Captain George Chicken and his hastily mustered militia unit struck north to fill the gap. Chicken, a veteran frontier planter and militia officer, hoped to take advantage of his enemy's confidence. After discovering the Catawbas' line of approach, he laid in wait for their advance scouting party on June 13, ordering his men to hunker down in the woods for a good, old-fashioned ambush. Nearby was a spot known as the Ponds, which would give its name to the fight that was about to unfold.

Evening had turned into night by the time Chicken's men spotted Catawba scouts making their way confidently through the woods. He waited until most of them had passed before ordering his anxious men to cut loose like coiled springs. They leapt into the fray, cutting down the surprised warriors with swords, hatchets, and bayonets. Finishing their grisly work, the men struggled with their officers to organize themselves for an even bigger fight—the main body of the Catawbas, after all, was moments away.

AFTER DUPING THE DEFENDERS INTO ALLOWING THEM INSIDE THE DEFENSES FOR A PARLEY, THE INDIANS SLAUGHTERED MOST OF THE PLANTATION'S GARRISON AND MOVED ON.

Sooner, in fact. The Indians were presently within musket range and growing alert to the mess they had walked into. Chicken struggled to get his men in order, then threw them forward in a howling mob. Gunshots ripped the darkness, illuminating faces of shock and rage, as the colonials swamped their enemies with a breaker of bayonets.

Fighting without quarter, the South Carolinians massacred all they could, claiming some fifty lives in the fight. The Indians, dazed and appalled at the slaughter, fell back into the woods and ultimately retreated. Like the Yamasees at Salkehatchie, they had not bargained on losing fifty irreplaceable braves for a campaign of shock and plunder.

George Chicken breathed a sigh of relief. But he would soon be embarking upon a mission of even greater importance—to engage the one nation of the southeast that had the power to end, or extend, what had become a struggle for South Carolina's survival.

INTO THE MOUNTAINS

Straddling the Appalachian Mountains from the Tennessee River to the upper waters of the Savannah, the great Cherokee nation had remained watchful and neutral since fighting began. Few things weighed more heavily on the minds of Charles Town's fretting leaders than the prospect of hostile Cherokees.

With their large numbers, a dedicated Cherokee war party would be enough to break South Carolina once and for all.

And yet, nothing stirred in that direction until October 1715. Since the outbreak of violence with the Yamasee and others, the vast majority of South Carolina's traders out on the

A slave sale ad taken from a Charleston, South Carolina, newspaper, 1766.

The Unwilling Newcomers

Africans outnumbered white settlers in South Carolina by 1708. Black slaves had first been brought to the region in the 1520s by Spanish traders, but it was English settlers from Barbados who established the first large-scale rice plantations.

Rice, like other area crops such as indigo and tobacco, fueled the slave trade because of its labor-intensive nature. It wasn't long before the white establishment of South Carolina was looking at a hostage population of Africans and enslaved Indians that was positively huge.

Faced with a disparity of racial demographics, the colony wasted little time passing laws to enforce its brutal control over nonwhites. According to the slave code of 1690, for instance, slaves—Indian, black, or mulatto—who were convicted a second time of attacking an Englishman could be subject to whipping, the slitting of the nose, or burning to the face.

Runaways in particular incurred severe punitive action. An act of 1712 provided that any slave who had escaped for a second time was branded on the cheek with an *R* for runaway; slave owners who refused to carry out the sentence were fined ten pounds.

✣

frontier—perhaps ninety men—had disappeared, almost certainly killed. But two of those who managed to return, Eleazar Wiggan and Robert Gilcrest, claimed that the Cherokee had sheltered them from hostile Indians, saving their lives. After making the shocking decision to go back across the frontier and into Cherokee country with goods for sale, the two men made a sensational return to Charles Town in October. And they brought company: around 120 Cherokee warriors, including twenty of the most senior men of the nation.

Governor Craven, beside himself with glee, welcomed the large party as honored guests and smoked the peace pipe. Rightfully interpreting the Cherokee mission as a powerful sign of support for the colony, Craven pressed his luck and asked whether the headmen would be willing to assemble a large army to fight alongside the South Carolinians against their enemies to the southwest. The Cherokees agreed, pledging to meet the colonials at Savannah Town (modern-day Savannah).

But they never showed. For three weeks the South Carolinians waited at Savannah Town's fort, until coming to the unnerving conclusion that they were waiting in vain.

Assuming that factionalism among the Cherokee had undermined the rendezvous, Craven assembled an army of three hundred men and charged it with helping the Cherokee make up their minds. In December the force entered the lands of the Cherokee and split up between the nation's three regions: Lower, Middle, and Overhill. They then settled in for the winter.

WITH THEIR LARGE NUMBERS, A DEDICATED CHEROKEE WAR PARTY WOULD BE ENOUGH TO BREAK SOUTH CAROLINA ONCE AND FOR ALL.

The plan was simple: As they dwelt in various Cherokee villages, the South Carolinian leaders—one of whom was George Chicken, now something of a legend on the frontier—would maintain contact with each other, reporting on the local sentiments for or against war as they conferred with village headmen. By the beginning of January 1716, they understood which towns and leaders favored which policy, allowing them to engage the Cherokee more effectively in negotiations.

But would this gain the English the allies they sorely needed? Chicken and his fellows were ruminating on this question when word reached them of a momentous Cherokee initiative: Intent on brokering a peace between South Carolina and the Ochese, the Cherokee peace faction had invited an Ochese delegation to Tugaloo, a Lower Cherokee town that lay close to the English frontier. Stunned by this bit of fortuitous news, the South Carolinians did an about-face, urging even the pro-war Cherokees to stop arguing for a fight. Peace, it seemed, was actually near at hand.

THREE ARMIES AT TUGALOO

George Chicken turned in the saddle and checked on the rest of the column. It was the end of January and the mountains, broad and majestic, loomed immediately behind them.

The men, still wrapped in their winter woolens to fight the highland winter, welcomed the relative warmth of the foothills as they made their way along the Indian trail. Returning his gaze to the direction in which his horse was taking him, Chicken saw the low country of South Carolina stretched out before him, its flat wilderness sliced by the shimmering Savannah River. The sun stood high in the sky, but they were making good time. Tugaloo lay just ahead.

Like the other leaders of the well-armed colonial army that had wintered in Cherokee country, Chicken thought the news from Tugaloo was promising indeed. South Carolina needed peace. Its outlying settlements were gutted or abandoned, skeletal ruins guarded by a belt of hasty fortifications that were powerless to stop stealthy encroachments by Yuchi, Apalachee, and Yamasee war bands. The economy was in shambles. And Charles Town, crowded and filthy, teetered on the edge of calamity. South Carolina had become a land of fear and suffering.

Chicken knew that this was his colony's best hope. Though celebrated as a frontier leader and fighter, he considered himself a planter first, and desired nothing so much as a return to the profitable days before April 15, 1715.

The trail descended more steeply now as it left the Appalachians behind. And there before him, Chicken spied the lodges of Tugaloo.

As they entered the Cherokee settlement, the English leaders dismounted and approached the headmen, while most of the South Carolinian force waited outside the town. Presently, the Cherokees spoke to them of great tidings, and as they listened, Chicken and his fellows blanched.

Nearby, explained the elders of Tugaloo, were eleven corpses—the leaders of the Ochese delegation. The Cherokee, it seemed, had fallen on them with weapons after a long and rather mysterious conversation. A twelfth Ochese captive remained alive and in custody, to be dispatched later at the Cherokee's leisure.

Confusion and no small amount of concern raced through the Carolinians until the men of Tugaloo explained further. According to them, the Ochese had shown up with an army several hundred strong, full of Yamasees, as well as their own warriors, ready to ambush and annihilate the South Carolinians. By murdering the leaders of the hostile force, the Cherokee had undone their plan.

Chicken and most of the other officers quickly organized a reconnaissance to locate the rest of the enemy host, but to no avail. They had retreated hastily, horrified by the assassination of their leadership. At a stroke, the Cherokee had not only abandoned their yearnings for peace in the southeast, but they had also thrown their lot in with the English, and very abruptly.

George Chicken scratched his head and wondered at the suddenness of it all. The war, it would seem, was still on. And the great untried masses of the Cherokee were now the only force that could bring it to an end.

THE LONG ENDGAME

No one will ever know for sure what happened at Tugaloo that late January day in 1716 when eleven (twelve) Ochese leaders were massacred. The Cherokee, perhaps seeing an opportunity to become South Carolina's primary trading partner, quickly resolved their divisions and jumped to the English side of the Yamasee War.

Certainly tempers had flown at their meeting with the Ochese, who clearly hoped for—indeed, had planned on—a union with the Cherokee to crush South Carolina. Whatever the details, they must have been dramatic. For, despite the efforts of the Cherokees' remaining peace faction, the whole nation was now at war, like it or not.

The event proved to be the deliverance of South Carolina. With the Cherokees bearing most of the burden of the fighting, tribes like the Yamasee were driven back to ancestral lands that lay farther away from South Carolina's borders. Many of the smaller tribes who took part in the war simply ceased to exist. Their members were captured into slavery, lost in combat, or absorbed by larger Indian nations when their numbers became too small to remain independent.

For the English, the war against their enemies on the frontier remained a sporadic, guerilla conflict well into 1717. Economic recovery would take decades. But the war had changed the history of South Carolina forever. Displeased with the proprietary, or private, government that had been in power and that had allowed the frontier chaos to progress out of control, South Carolina's elite welcomed an effort by England to replace it with a crown-appointed administration, responsible directly to the king. Expansion progressed apace: With the retreat of the Yamasee to lands farther south, the way was open for the founding of a new colony called Georgia.

chapter thirteen

Scalp Hunting in New Hampshire Spawns an Enduring American Legend

1725

The long column of hunters moved swiftly through a frozen wilderness. Weaving between ice-girded trees, they stepped over the deep snow with ease, their snowshoes tamping softly into the powder at a breathless rhythm. They had donned wool coats and caps as well as moccasins and leggings made of deerskin, making an eccentric, intimidating appearance even as they blended into the wilds through which they trotted. Attack dogs loped along beside them, throwing long gouts of white breath in the February air.

For three days the sixty-two rangers had been tracking Abenaki Indians through the forests of Maine and New Hampshire. They had covered twenty-two miles the day before alone. Now, after a five-mile run, they knew they were getting close to their quarry. It was February 20, 1725.

Captain John Lovewell, commanding, had originally intended to attack the Indian village of Pigwacket, farther to the north in central New Hampshire. That was the plan when his volunteers were mustered almost a month ago. But on February 16, the column (or what remained of it; Lovewell had had to send thirty-five of his men home for want of provisions) happened upon a clear track that led south. Knowing it had been left by Indians, the men left their packs and a contingent to guard them, and took off in pursuit.

That decision now paid off. As the tracks grew fresher, Lovewell and his men saw what appeared to be an encampment ahead. Cutting their vigorous pace and proceeding

Captain John Lovewell's scalp-hunting expeditions may well have looked like this.

cautiously, they soon discovered that the site had been abandoned—recently. They pressed on and, perhaps two miles farther, spied a thin plume of smoke rising over the trees before them.

Lovewell smelled the wood smoke and looked toward the midday sun. Night was far off, but they would have to wait. He ordered the men to muzzle the dogs and bed down, forbidding them to build fires that could give away their presence. It would be a long, cold vigil.

Hours later, at perhaps 2 a.m., Lovewell deployed his men in a tight circle around the Indian camp. In the firelight before them the rangers could see ten sleeping Abenakis, all of them oblivious to the fate that was about to befall them. By the time the New Englanders had carefully gotten themselves into position, not one of their muskets could possibly miss, so short was the range.

Lovewell fired first, shattering the quiet and killing two of the sleeping Indians. Several other volleys followed immediately, sweeping the campsite with smoke and lead. A lone Abenaki survivor jumped from the chaos into the night, but didn't get far. One of the rangers loosed a dog on him, cutting the chase brutally short amid a snarling ruckus in the darkness.

The rangers fell upon their wounded prey and dispatched them with hatchets and knives, cleanly scalping them in the process. They were now rich men: With the Massachusetts General Court offering £100 a scalp, the grisly prizes they took that night amounted to a small fortune. What's more, they had happened upon a war party from Canada, whose excellent muskets and other valuable accoutrements had clearly been procured from French authorities in Montreal or Quebec. The equipment only made Lovewell's haul even bigger.

LOVEWELL'S FIGHT

This was the famous captain's second scalp-hunting expedition in less than three months. When he was just a boy, his father's house had been the first English refuge for Hannah Dustan and her fellow fugitives after fleeing for their lives from their Indian captors. Lovewell would never forget the spectacle of those poor travelers, gaunt and tattered from their trials.

Now he and his "snowshoe men" were heroes in Massachusetts, Maine, and New Hampshire, where fighting the Indians and their French allies was a constant reality in war *and* in peace. Several years earlier William Dummer, acting governor of Massachusetts, had declared war on the Indians—especially the mighty Abenaki—who routinely harassed communities on the frontier with the backing of the French, who were alarmed at English encroachments along the Kennebec River in Maine.

In the summer of 1724, a party of Englishmen and Mohawks surprised the large Abenaki base at Norridgewock, killing many—including a French Jesuit named Sebastian Rale, infamous for inciting the Indians to war.

It was against this backdrop that John Lovewell came to prominence. A farmer with little to do in winter but fight off boredom, he decided to raise a company of volunteers, go off into the woods, and cash in on the government's offer of scalp money. A natural woodsman and Indian fighter, he buoyed English spirits in a time of dread. And soon, in the spring of 1725, he would do much more than that, giving his name to one of the most extraordinary events of the violent frontier.

Celebrated for generations afterward in song and myth for its length, ferocity, and the notoriety of those involved, Lovewell's Fight would show how entrenched the savagery of New England's frontier had become—and how far the English had come in their willingness and ability to claim the wilderness as their own.

THE CHAPLAIN AND THE WOODSMAN

The journey back home for Lovewell and his men was long but glorious. They marched through villages on their way to the coast, feted as heroes. By February 27, the party had boarded a sloop bound for Boston. There, amid cheering throngs of onlookers, the swaggering killers in buckskin made a barbaric procession through the streets, hoisting the stretched Abenaki scalps on poles for all to see. Boston reveled in the blood sport.

The captain and his men made a killing in other ways, as well, receiving £1,000— quite a tidy sum—from the General Court for their prizes. Lovewell sold the French muskets for an additional £70. For a month of frigid hardship in the New Hampshire wilds, they had scored a huge sum. Not surprisingly, as the captain made his way back to his home in Dunstable, he was already planning a third excursion.

Recruiting for volunteers began in earnest the following spring, and one of the most unusual of Lovewell's applicants was Jonathan Frye of Andover. A twenty-year-old graduate of Harvard Divinity School, Frye signed on as the chaplain of Lovewell's third expedition, and instantly became its most conspicuous member.

The others were hardened men of the soil from other Massachusetts frontier towns like Haverhill, Groton, Woburn, and Dunstable. Each knew how to fight the Indians in their own element—they understood the art and science of ambush; the practices of woodcraft and tracking; and how to handle a tomahawk, scalping knife, and musket at close quarters. Frye, on the other hand, though no slouch with a musket, was obviously more of a scholar than a fighter.

In fact, Frye had a very compelling reason to join the campaign—her name was Susanna Rogers. Born to a wealthy Andover family of influence, Frye had made the mistake of falling for a thirteen-year-old girl of lower station. Unimpressed with Susanna's dowry, Frye's parents forbade the match, driving the Harvard alumnus to find some means of severing his reliance on them. Scalps at £100 a piece would do that nicely. Lovewell, who wanted a chaplain along anyway, took a shine to the youthful, charismatic Frye. It wouldn't be long before everyone else in the company did as well.

This included Seth Wyman, a thirty-nine-year-old father of five from Woburn. Though older than most, he served as an ordinary ranger, rather than an officer. His relative experience, however, would prove invaluable in the hard days to come.

Aided by his veteran lieutenants, Josiah Farewell and Jonathan Robbins, Lovewell signed up forty-six men for the spring scalp hunt and set out from Dunstable in April. The weather was fine, the men in high spirits. They were with Lovewell, after all. What could go wrong?

French Jesuit Sebastian Rale, infamous for inciting Amerindians to war, died after a surprise attack by Englishmen and Mohawks in 1724.

HEMORRHAGING MANPOWER

Lovewell set his sights on the village of Pigwacket (near modern-day Fryeburg, Maine) and led his men into the bush. The usual attrition, however, set in early when Toby, the party's only Mohawk, succumbed to the pain of an old leg wound. Unable to keep up, he was forced to return to Dunstable. Farther down the trail, a ranger named Cummings also developed a limp from an old injury. Accompanied by a friend, he headed back. Three down.

Almost several weeks out of Dunstable, the column reached Lake Ossipee, in eastern New Hampshire. Another ranger was in trouble, however: Benjamin Kidder of Nutfield was far too ill to keep up, and Lovewell was only a day's march to his target. The captain made, under the circumstances, the only decision he could, directing the men to construct a small palisade with a sturdy blockhouse within. "Fort Ossipee," such as it was, would house poor Kidder and the company surgeon, along with seven rangers to secure the site.

On May 8, the remaining thirty-four men resumed their march north to Pigwacket, sans doctor and eleven other men who had started out in Dunstable. Though the Indians would no doubt outnumber them, perhaps drastically, Lovewell felt secure in his own luck and experience, as well as the resilience of his men. Besides, they were too close to the Pigwacket valley to turn back now.

The men wouldn't abide such a decision even if their leader could. Their futures were at stake; with the trees still bare of leaves, the open woods made it easier to spot Indian foes and avoid ambush. They wouldn't get another chance to hunt scalps in such conditions until the following winter.

The column marched all day along an ancient Indian trail that led them north to the Pigwacket valley, which they entered from the west by fording the Saco River in southeastern Maine. With daylight waning, Lovewell scouted the Indian village, a mile or so to the north, and then chose a spot to bed down for the night at the north end of nearby Saco Pond. No sign of Indian activity, either near the pond or from the direction of the village, could be observed by Lovewell or his scouts. After establishing a camp and posting sentries, the men enjoyed a quiet night at the water's edge.

THE PARSON'S BLOOD BAPTISM

Parson Jonathan Frye awoke early on May 9, the Sabbath, and called the men to morning prayers. As they gathered before him, the chaplain took in the beauty that lay all

A wounded Lieutenant Robbins asked that his fellow English leave him on the battlefield near the pond with a musket for one last shot, according to legend.

around him. Captain Lovewell had chosen to camp here, with the protection of the pond behind them, and the water now glittered with the bright spring sun.

The camp lay in a broad swathe of pitch pine barren, providing precious little cover to ambushers beneath the gnarled limbs and scraggly green canopy of the trees. Guarding access to the camp from the west was a marshy brook, gurgling away with snowmelt. Wild and stark, this peaceful place in the Pigwacket valley had a strange beauty all its own.

Not long into Frye's prayer meeting, the sharp report of a musket carried over the water from the northeast bank of the pond, snapping the men out of their pious reverie. Rushing to the water's edge, the rangers saw a lone Indian, perhaps a third of a mile across the north shoulder of the pond, apparently hunting ducks.

The rangers immediately gathered about their captain to discuss what to do next, the chaplain just as eager as anyone else to grapple with the Abenaki. Lovewell, however, urged caution; the Indian could be the bait for a trap. Some admitted to hearing noises out in the barren the night before, and it was possible that the Pigwacket villagers knew they were here. But after so many miles, the men were desperate to do what they had come to do in the first place, and they urged the captain to lead them into a fight.

Lovewell then made the most infamous decision of his life. To keep them light on their feet, he ordered the rangers to leave their blankets and packs behind at the camp, and then set off after the Indian.

NO ONE WAS LEFT TO GUARD THE FOOD AND BEDDING— AN ASTONISHING OVERSIGHT FOR A MAN LIKE LOVE-WELL...WHO NEVER LEFT ANYTHING UNGUARDED, MUCH LESS PACKS AND BLANKETS TO GIVE AWAY HIS PRESENCE IN HOSTILE TERRITORY.

No one was left to guard the food and bedding—an astonishing oversight for a man like Lovewell, who habitually sent out scouts both in front and behind his columns when marching through the woods, and who never left anything unguarded, much less packs and blankets, to give away his presence in hostile territory (and with the Pigwacket village just over a mile away to the northwest, this more than qualified as hostile territory).

After departing the pine barren, Lovewell and his men stalked cautiously through a stretch of swamp and thickets, going perhaps a mile and a half until they reached the eastern shore of the pond where the Indian was seen. And there, emerging suddenly from the bush with two muskets and a brace of ducks, was their Abenaki hunter.

The briefest moment passed as both parties stared at each other. In a flash, the Abenaki then dropped his ducks and the musket in his hand, swung his other piece

A contemporary print depicts an English officer with Abenaki Indians.

around and up to his shoulder, and fired at the rangers. Seth Wyman and the chaplain discharged their weapons an instant later, cutting down the Indian.

But in the awful quiet that followed, it became obvious to almost everyone left standing that the Indian's gun had been loaded with "swan shot," spraying the party with pellets. Two rangers lay bleeding, including a fellow named Whiting, whose wound was serious. The other, hit in the stomach, was Captain Lovewell.

Stunned but in good spirits, Lovewell insisted that the wound wasn't life threatening, and he turned the conversation to a more pressing matter: specifically, who should scalp the Pigwacket. To a man, the group elected young Frye, the company's unofficial mascot. Knowing the chaplain's family dilemma, they were glad to grant him the bounty.

Like an eager father figure, one of the veterans walked the Harvard graduate over to the corpse, held its head by the hair, and helped him make the long slice along the forehead with a scalping knife that would allow the skin to come free of the skull. The operation was over quickly, and Parson Frye sheepishly held up his dripping trophy for all to cheer.

Only then did the company give consideration to heading back to camp. Helping the two wounded men hobble through the underbrush, the rangers slowly made their way back to their belongings on the north end of Saco Pond. It was sometime shortly after ten in the morning when they returned.

THE IMMORTALS

The blankets and packs were gone. Most of the men understood what that meant, but they weren't allowed to act on it before howling braves ambushed them. From two directions—the brook, ahead and to the right, and the pond, to their left—spilled a storm of flashing musketry, raining sheets of ball and shot into the ranger column.

With many of their fellows dropping in the roiling smoke, the English returned fire at around fifty yards, reloaded, then cut loose with a second volley as their attackers did the same. At such short range, the two sides punched great holes in each other's ranks. Less than a minute had passed, and already the needle-covered floor of the pine barren seemed to writhe with the wounded.

One of them was Lovewell, who had just moments to live. In that time he would somehow get off two more shots before expiring. Just thirty-three years old, the captain's luck had run out. He would never know it, but he had been ambushed by the most famous Indian war leader in the northeast.

Paugus was a legend in his own time. A Mohawk by birth, he had acquired a dislike for the English after spending time in a Boston prison. Abandoned by his fellow Mohawks, he fled to the Pigwacket Abenakis and became their most effective warrior sachem, leading attacks all along the New England frontier.

AT SUCH SHORT RANGE, THE TWO SIDES PUNCHED GREAT HOLES IN EACH OTHER'S RANKS. LESS THAN A MINUTE HAD PASSED, AND ALREADY THE NEEDLE-COVERED FLOOR OF THE PINE BARREN SEEMED TO WRITHE WITH THE WOUNDED.

That day, as Lovewell and his men had watched Parson Frye cut the scalp from the head of his first kill, Paugus and a large band of his fellow Pigwackets were rowing their canoes back to the village from the south shore of Saco Pond. The sound of muskets caught their attention, and upon reaching the far side of the pond, they had struck east, only to find the rangers' unguarded baggage. Aware of the difficulty of hiding his braves in the scattered pines, the sachem had hidden them behind both the bank of the brook and a mud embankment on the water's shore. The plan had worked perfectly.

The combatants now dispersed to whatever cover they could find behind the pine trunks, spreading the firefight out to a wide perimeter of chaotic individual duels, many of them at close range. Pine boughs trapped much of the powder smoke, permeating the barren with a haze punctuated by musket flashes and shouts to comrades. Nine rangers lay dead, though English marksmanship had claimed at least that many Abenakis.

Incredibly, Paugus's numbers—he had begun the day with about eighty warriors—had failed to destroy the ranger unit outright.

Seth Wyman seized control of the situation and directed the men to fall back toward a sandy peninsula to the east and behind them. Jutting into the pond at an angle almost parallel to the shore, the bar was littered with fallen pines and brush—enough cover for the English to make a stand. Loading, firing, and sprinting, the men made a fighting retreat as best they could, pressed all the while by advancing Indians. More of them fell in the constant rattle of musketry, but Wyman managed to shepherd them onto the sandbar behind decent protection. But what now?

Paugus and his men now showed how far their rage had come. The English had ensconced themselves on a long strip of sand whose left was protected by the pond and whose right was guarded by a broad stretch of swampy ground at the mouth of another brook (eventually to be named "Fight Brook"). Reckless and furious, the Abenaki threw themselves screaming against Wyman's crude defenses, only to be slashed by patient, accurate musketry. Snipers moved around in search of targets, keeping up an intermittent curtain of fire. Both sides kept a wary eye on depleting stores of ammunition as the exhausting fight dragged on through the day.

The sun now began its descent, throwing longer and longer shadows over the scattered dead. Seth Wyman, calming and exhorting his men, looked out from his position behind a fallen tree trunk and saw—nobody. Off in the distance, the rhythm of Indian dance pounded away, signifying a powwow. The Abenakis were considering their options.

Wyman skulked forward from the sandbar, got on his knees, and crawled through the pine needles. As he approached the ring of Indians engrossed in their chanting, he spied Wahwah, the great medicine man, at the center of the group. Wyman took careful aim, and fired, dropping Wahwah and sending the Abenakis into a flurry of commotion. Sprinting back to the sandbar, the Englishman knew that he'd dealt a mortal blow to the Pigwackets by slaying their shaman.

The fight resumed with desperate intensity. As afternoon turned into early evening, the Pigwackets' ferocious, relentless attacks got them a foothold on the peninsula, just yards from the defiant English. Paugus, now within hailing distance of the English, began a dialogue with a Groton farmer named John Chamberlain, a long acquaintance of the famous sachem. According to legend, the constant firing had fouled both of their muskets, and they agreed to call a truce long enough for the two of them to meet at the swamp's edge, where they could clean their pieces and finish the duel.

As the story goes, Chamberlain proved the quicker, ramming his ball home by striking the butt of his musket on the ground, then firing at Paugus first. Whatever the

Overleaf: Chamberlain and Paugus face off at the height of Lovewell's fight.

"Song of Lovewell's Fight,"
1725

These rebels lay in ambush, this very place near by;

So that an English soldier did one of them espy,

And cried out, "Here's an Indian!" with that they started out

As fiercely as old lions, and hideously did shout.

With that our valiant English all gave a loud huzzah,

To show the rebel Indians they feared them not a straw;

So now the fight began as fiercely as could be;

The Indians ran up to them, but soon were forced to flee.

Then spake up Captain Lovewell when first the fight began:

"Fight on, my valiant heroes! You see they fall like rain."

For, as we are informed, the Indians were so thick,

A man could scarcely fire a gun, and not some of them hit …

✢

Amerindians perform a tribal group dance in this nineteenth-century lithograph.

truth, Paugus was dead by late afternoon, probably from a shot by John Chamberlain. By that time, young Parson Frye had also succumbed to wounds.

In the twilight of late evening, the Indians' intermittent fire tapered off until there was nothing but the noise of the swamp and its creatures. Wyman, wary of a trap, nevertheless allowed himself to believe the incredible: He and his fellows had survived the fight of a lifetime.

AN AMERICAN LEGEND

Twenty rangers survived the battle at Saco Pond, eleven of whom were wounded. In the days and weeks that followed, they trickled back to New England civilization, gradually sowing the seeds of a legend. Nobody knows for sure how many of the eighty Abenaki braves fell that day.

That both Paugus and Lovewell had perished in the daylong melee seemed proper and even divinely ordained. More important, the fight had broken the back—and certainly the leadership—of the Pigwacket Indians, a major French ally and tool with which to discomfit New Hampshire and Maine. The climax of Dummer's War, Lovewell's Fight proved how ruthless the English were willing to be in the quest for dominion in the northeast—and how accomplished they had become at beating the "savages" at their own game.

It also carved out a niche in the popular imagination. In the months following Lovewell's death, a commemorative poem appeared in print. According to at least one historian, the lyrics were penned by the elder Benjamin Franklin, the founding father's uncle. And that was just the beginning. Henry Wadsworth Longfellow was a teenager when he wrote "The Battle of Lovell's Pond" in 1820 and got it published. "Song of Lovewell's Fight," a ballad by the Reverend Thomas Cogswell, appeared in 1824, helping to keep the legend alive for the rest of the century and beyond.

chapter fourteen

America Strikes a Blow for Britannia—and Draws Further Away from the Empire

1745

The morning of May 11, 1745, was unusually warm and pleasant for the waters off Cape Breton, Canada. For the island's French-speaking inhabitants, however, the day's prospects were anything but sunny.

Gathering in the shelter of Gabarus Bay was a sight that sent a chill through all of them: a fleet of some ninety vessels—transports, fishing boats, gunboats, and men-of-war—that clearly marked the arrival of a New England invasion force. And there could be no doubt of the fleet's target: Louisbourg, fortress-guardian of the approaches to New France, just a few miles away from the gathering ships.

As church bells tolled the approach of danger throughout Louisbourg and its environs, Gabarus Bay came alive with frenzied action. A swarm of whaleboats made its way through choppy waters, converging clumsily on the beaches of Freshwater Cove. By late morning the craft had landed some 1,500 men beyond the surf, all of them grateful to make it without a hot reception from French soldiers.

That changed soon enough. Hastily marching along the shore road came a hostile welcome party. The New Englanders, having spied enemy activity on land, had made a feint to draw the French away. Though the ruse worked, the French had since caught on, racing back to Freshwater Cove in the hopes of stopping the main landing before it really started.

They were too late. Just eighty men strong, the French happened upon a force of New Englanders that, though disorganized and a little confused, outnumbered their

Gallic opponents by almost nineteen to one. The ensuing firefight went predictably the invader's way, sending Cape Breton's first line of defense scurrying frantically into the nearby woods.

The attack on Louisbourg—what one historian would later call "the most important military achievement of the American colonists prior to the War of the Revolution"—had begun in earnest. In just eleven weeks' time this disorganized rabble from New England would enter North America's greatest fortress as conquerors, completing a feat of the first order and delivering a stunning blow to the French empire.

Its triumph, however, would be fleeting. After the tremendous effort to subdue it, Louisbourg would be callously delivered back into the hands of its original owners by a treaty signed across the ocean and seemingly a world away from the chilly wastes of Cape Breton. In the end, the legacy of Louisbourg's siege would be an ironic one, driving New England from the British empire, which seemed increasingly ambivalent to its Yankee colonists and their sacrifices.

BEGINNER'S LUCK

The landings went better than anyone had expected, and by the end of May 12, the provincials had established a rudimentary encampment at a place called Flat Point Cove. Numbering some four thousand strong, the men came mostly from the royal colony of Massachusetts, though others hailed from New Hampshire and Connecticut. They were farmers, coopers, tinsmiths, shopkeepers, farmhands, and fishermen, virtually none of whom had martial experience beyond the occasional muster on the village green. And their leader was no exception.

William Pepperrell was a prosperous forty-nine-year-old merchant from Kittery, Maine, who got along with virtually everybody—a trait that, more than anything else, helped him get the job. He did not put much stock in military discipline, not least because the men entrusted to him wouldn't tolerate it.

William Pepperrell was a prosperous 49-year-old merchant from Kittery, Maine, who got along with virtually everybody—a trait that, more than anything else, helped him get the job of leading 4,000 New Englanders in invading Louisbourg.

Within hours of creating their little bridgehead, squads of Pepperrell's provincials advanced to the buildings at the northeast of Louisbourg's harbor and put them to the torch, setting an example for the campaign to come. In the ensuing weeks, New Englanders bent on plunder would plague the outlying communities of Cape Breton with fire and sword. They would take cattle, stores, souvenirs, and clothing, all of which they had been promised when signing on back in New England. Incredulous French *habitants* could only stare as their homesteads went up in flames.

Taking a stronghold like Louisbourg, however, was going to require a lot more than burning and rapine. This was a siege, after all. As Pennsylvania printer Benjamin Franklin warned his hawkish brother in Boston on the eve of the Louisbourg operation, "Fortified towns are hard nuts to crack, and your teeth are not accustomed to it." The future founding father may have been right. But if William Pepperrell's men were unaccustomed to the tough challenge, their luck more than made up for it.

A small scouting party led by William Vaughn took the abandoned Royal Battery north of Louisbourg on May 13, 1745. Lacking a flag to raise, Vaughn co-opted the red coat of one of his men, William Tufts, and had it run up the flagpole.

On the cool, windy morning of May 13, a small scouting party struck out from the Yankee camp on a wide arc that took them well north of Louisbourg in the direction of the Royal Battery—an outwork of the town itself that, in tandem with the massive Island Battery out in the water, dominated the harbor of Louisbourg with formidable, large-bore guns.

Leading the expedition was an ambitious Harvard graduate and entrepreneur named William Vaughn. One of the most outspoken firebrands for the mission to Louisbourg, Vaughn had once hoped to lead the whole expedition. Now, forced to be satisfied with a lesser command, he found himself on the verge of a tremendous coup.

Descending on a collection of storehouses, Vaughn and his group of twelve men set fire to everything in sight. Full of combustible naval stores, the burning structures threw up roiling pillars of black smoke.

But if Vaughn was looking to stir up a reaction from the nearby Royal Battery, he was sorely disappointed. From the grim bastion came nothing but silence. Upon closer inspection, Vaughn noticed a complete lack of activity behind the ramparts—most conspicuously, no smoke issued from the battery's chimneys. According to legend, Vaughn bribed one of his men, a Cape Cod Amerindian, with liquor to penetrate the defensive structure and discover whether anyone was there. Fortified with alcohol, the fellow went blithely to his task, making his way through the brush and into the French works. And there he found—nothing.

Signaled by the scout, Vaughn ordered his men forward. The Yankees crept like animals through the brush, still wary of a trap, and then crawled cautiously through the stonework embrasures. Within minutes, they had captured the impressive work without firing a shot—the French had apparently abandoned it.

Despite his good fortune, the proud Vaughn found himself without a standard to raise over his prize. He called over young William Tufts, one of his fellow assailants, co-opted his red coat, and ran it up the battery's flagpole like an ersatz Union Jack. "May it please your Honour to be informed," Vaughn wrote to Pepperrell as soon as he was able, "that by the grace of God and the courage of thirteen men, I entered the Royal Battery about nine o'clock, and am waiting for reinforcement and a flag."

GIBRALTAR OF THE NORTH

Vaughn's incredible success struck the camp at Flat Point Cove like a sign from Providence. To them, nothing else could explain it. This "army" of volunteers had ventured north to strike a blow for king and country—to do their part in the latest of a series of wars against the hated French. Known to history as the War of the Austrian Succession, it was dubbed King George's War by the English colonists in America. But to

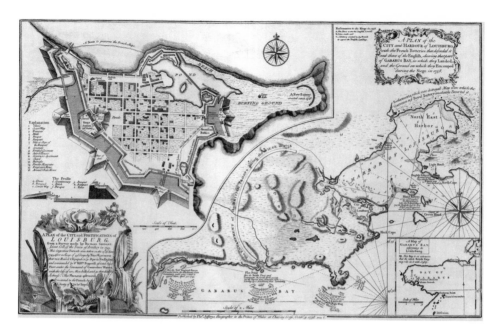

The construction began on the fortress at Louisbourg in 1719 by the French to protect their interests and harass British trade. The fort boasted state-of-the art stone works and was the most formidable stronghold in North America in its time.

the provincials of New England, swept up in a religious revival, the voyage to Louisbourg was nothing less than a crusade against Babylon.

Though hardly as great as that fabled city of biblical notoriety, Louisbourg was quite a marvel in its own right. Its origins lay in the Treaty of Utrecht of 1713, in which France lost nearly all of Nova Scotia to the British. Only Cape Breton Island remained French, turning it, in effect, into the sole guardian of Canada—an island bastion controlling the approaches to the St. Lawrence River and its vital settlements, Quebec and Montreal. Consequently, in 1719, construction began on Cape Breton of a port that would act as a naval base to defend French interests and harass British trade.

Christened Louisbourg, it would become the most formidable fortress in North America, incorporating state-of-the-art stoneworks unlike any that had ever been built in the New World. The barracks alone would be the longest structure on the continent. A twenty-year project, the site's construction followed designs originally laid down by the great Vauban, the most celebrated military engineer of his time. (According to legend, Louis XV, upon seeing the lavish expenses for Louisbourg's construction, blurted out that he ought to be able to see its spires from Versailles.)

When hostilities between France and England resumed in 1744, the new citadel hung above the American colonies like a Sword of Damocles. With its protected harbor and maritime resources, Louisbourg posed a direct threat to New England's trade routes

A House Divided

Louisbourg's French garrison consisted of around 1,500 men of the *Compagnies Franches de la Marine* (the "Independent Companies of the Navy"—essentially regulars raised and equipped by the French Navy to defend the colonies) and local militia, as well as soldiers from the Karrer regiment of Swiss mercenaries.

Though a somewhat diverse lot, they all had one thing in common: They had been miserable for months. As if coping with Nova Scotia's severe weather weren't enough, the defenders of Louisbourg also had to deal with "rapacious" officers who habitually made a profit by selling off food, firewood, and other supplies that were slated for the soldiers. By the final months of 1744, the garrison of North America's most formidable fortress had been driven into virtual squalor—and to the end of its tether.

The Swiss were the first to act. On December 27, three members of the regiment, sotted with brandy, roused their fellows into a mutiny. Before long the action spread to other units, and Louis du Pont du Chambon, governor of Isle Royale (as Cape Breton was known to the French), was forced, in wartime, to deal with every commandant's worst nightmare. Though the garrison's issues were ironed out to the satisfaction of most, a pall of gloom had settled over Louisbourg—a fact that made its way to New England.

William Shirley, royal governor of Massachusetts, heard of Louisbourg's situation from traders and recently paroled prisoners of war who had spent time there. Disaffection among the French played a major role in convincing Shirley that the time had come for a move against Louisbourg.

Interestingly, despite their previous uprising, du Chambon's troops fought tenaciously throughout the siege, galvanized by the threat from their Yankee enemies.

✛

as well as to its link with the invaluable Nova Scotia fisheries. Within weeks, privateers operating out of Louisbourg captured more than ten Massachusetts fishing vessels.

But all was not quite what it seemed. By the spring of 1745, Louisbourg had fallen on hard times, a fact that was not unknown to the enemy down in New England. The town's 1,500-man garrison had mutinied the previous December (see sidebar on p. 221), the storehouses weren't nearly full enough to withstand a proper siege, and some of the masonry defenses were crumbling from neglect.

Indeed, none of Louisbourg's defenses was in worse shape than the Royal Battery— which is why its French garrison had abandoned it. Before departing for the safety of Louisbourg, however, the Battery's soldiers had spiked the twenty-eight massive, forty-two-pounder guns they were leaving behind, hoping to deny their use to the Yankee invaders. It was just a day later that Vaughn and his party took possession of them.

BLOOD, SWEAT, AND TEARS

Almost as soon as the Royal Battery was taken, gunsmiths and armorers were summoned to undo the hasty French attempt to spike the guns. Within a day, one of the forty-two-pounders had been drilled out and made ready for action, and the provincials wasted no time in training it on the town.

Operating at the slow, methodical pace of amateurs, the gunners ladled the powder in, tamped it down with a rammer, repeated the procedure with the shot, charged the piece, stood clear for the recoil, and fired. Away in the town itself, though the gunners could not know it, the first shot crashed through the streets, killing fourteen people. It was the beginning of the end for Louisbourg.

In time the occupiers of the Royal Battery would give the French more than enough cause to regret its abandonment. But despite his great fortune so far, William Pepperrell frowned toward the town of Louisbourg like a man with a problem. If a proper breach were to be made in the town's defenses, the Yankees were going to have to start setting up new batteries of their own to complement the effort underway at the Royal Battery, some three miles away from camp.

The expedition had brought thirty-four guns and mortars along for just such a purpose, all of which had been laboriously unloaded onto the beach at Flat Point Cove. And an ideal location for a battery beckoned in the distance—a stretch of high ground called Green Hill that offered the perfect site from which to play on Louisbourg's bastions.

Getting the guns to Green Hill, however, posed a nasty problem. Scouting parties had brought only bad news to Pepperrell: Between here and there stretched a vast expanse of marshland. How were they going to get the guns through that?

Louisburg under attack. Note the royal battery at the bottom-center; Lighthouse Point, on the left, and the Island Battery just above it.

The Green Island

S
E — W
N

7	The Citadel ....
8	The Hospital ....
9	The West Gate of the City ....
10	The South Gate of the City ...
11	The Kings Gate of the City ....
12	The East Gate of the City ....

A Prospect of the City of Lewisbourg. Also the Harbours and Garrisons On the
Island of Gaspey or Cape-Breton in North America.
Surrendred to the New England Land Troops On the 17 June 1715 after a Siege of 48 Se-
Sier General Pepperril Esqr Commander of the Land Troops

Bereft of draft teams, the men had no choice but to drag the artillery themselves. At first the task went well: Harnessing the great weapons with anchor cables, grunting provincials hauled, shoved, and manhandled their burden through thickets and over rocky slopes. Ahead of them plunged teams of axmen who felled trees and laid down a corduroy road. Then came the hard part.

Not long into the effort, the ground gave way to a swampy, gelid morass. Boots came off in the sucking slop, artillery carriages sank up to their trunnions, and progress seemed impossible. Even worse, the struggling column had come within range of Louisbourg's guns. Along the French bastions in the distance, daggers of smoke and fire began stabbing out of the embrasures, sending shot and shell smacking into the muck. It looked like the end of the line, and the men—heaving and soaked from their exertions—began to despair. Pepperrell needed a miracle.

What he got instead was a good dose of Yankee ingenuity. Lieutenant Colonel Nathaniel Meserve of New Hampshire made a fortuitous suggestion. Back home, farmers clearing the notoriously rocky New England countryside for farmland made wooden sledges for transporting rocks once they'd been muscled out of the earth. Such sledges would be perfect here for carrying the guns over the bog.

For the rest of the day and most of the night, carpenters set about constructing a modest fleet of "stone boats." Slowly, inexorably, the column inched forward, braving the viscous mud and enemy fire. And on May 15, Yankee guns at last began firing from Green Hill. The siege had truly commenced.

DISASTER IN THE DARKNESS

Transport of the guns continued, and by the end of May, Pepperrell had four additional batteries pounding away at Louisbourg. French artillerists gave as good as they got, and they managed to shore up crumbling defenses even as Yankee shot played on the walls.

But the town itself, rather than the bastions that surrounded it, was taking the brunt of the damage. Cannonballs shattered roofs and went careening through the streets, mowing down hapless habitants. With their mortars, the Yankees were able to hurl exploding shells into the community, blowing structures to bits and filling the air with deadly shrapnel. And in June they began firing "hot shot": balls that had been heated in cauldrons, igniting combustible materials upon impact. Conditions in Louisbourg had become a living hell.

Life for some of the besiegers was hardly better. Disease, particularly dysentery, the bane of all military camps from time immemorial, raced through the ranks. And if the Yankees didn't have enough skilled artillery officers, they had too much of something else: rum. As Pepperrell himself remarked, "We are in great want of good gunners that have a disposition to be sober in daytime." The result was often catastrophic. Numerous gunners overloaded their pieces and were blown apart, accounting for almost as many casualties as those caused by French counterfire.

But Pepperrell had a bigger problem. After several weeks of hammering away at Louisbourg, plundering farmsteads, and skirmishing with guerrillas around the island, he had yet to see any indication that the town was on the verge of capitulating.

Moreover, the navy was beginning to give him almost as much heat as the French. Commodore Peter Warren, Pepperrell's colleague out at sea, had been blockading the harbor since the troops landed at Flat Point Cove. A professional officer of the Royal Navy, Warren had become doubtful of Pepperrell's provincial rabble.

CONDITIONS IN LOUISBOURG HAD BECOME A LIVING HELL.

While his ships had captured the *Vigilant*, a French ship hoping to bring aid to Louisbourg, Pepperrell's men were making a ham-handed attempt at the complex art of siege craft. Consequently, Warren and his officers had been pressing the Yankees to make an amphibious assault on the Island Battery in the harbor. Should that defensive work be taken, Warren would be able to sail his vessels into the harbor, train his enormous firepower directly on the town, and take credit himself for its capitulation. Pepperrell and his council of officers eventually relented.

On the night of June 6, some four hundred volunteers in whaleboats pushed off from the beach before the Royal Battery and rowed across the calm, fog-shrouded harbor toward their objective. Having made it to the island's northern point without incident, the men splashed ashore with their arms and scaling ladders.

Suddenly, from the ten-foot bastions that loomed ahead of them, voices began to holler in French. The alarm had been sounded. Within seconds, muskets chattered along the walls, dispersing the night with a cluster of flashes. Cannon and swivel guns soon joined them, blasting sheets of canister and chain shot down upon a crowd undone with panic and chaos.

Men ran for cover and found none, boats were holed and blown to slivers, and wounded soon littered the beach. With nowhere to go but back into the water, many New Englanders remained on the shore, putting up a valiant fight until sunup. But sixty of their comrades had been slaughtered. In the end, more than a hundred would be taken prisoner.

The nightmare of that night convinced Pepperrell—indeed, virtually everyone in the provincial camp—that battering the walls with cannon would have to be the main effort for now, at least until some extraordinary development.

In fact, that development had already happened. And, ultimately, it would prove the key to undoing the defense of Louisbourg.

THE NUT IS CRACKED

June 22 was King George II's birthday, and the weather graced his fighting subjects on Cape Breton with a sunny, pleasant day. They took advantage of the holiday to do two things at which they now excelled: firing guns and drinking rum.

Yankee batteries were now stretched in a three-mile arc that bowed around the circumference of Louisbourg and was anchored on the captured Royal Battery in the north, which had been blasting away since May 13. But another battery had recently joined them—and it would prove to be the most important.

Across the harbor from Louisbourg, on a great spit of land that came reaching out toward the unconquered Island Battery, was a prominence called Lighthouse Point. Dominated by—what else?—a lighthouse, it had been scouted some ten days before the disastrous June 6 assault on the Island Battery. In the slough of despond that followed, Lighthouse Point came under serious scrutiny. Indeed, it became obvious that it offered a commanding view of the whole harbor—and of the damnable Island Battery itself.

In another Herculean effort, stout Yankees wrestled artillery around the northern bend of the harbor and up to the point itself, creating the beginnings of a battery by June 13. As French fire from the Island Battery crashed about them, the provincials threw up defensive earthworks and prepared their position—strengthened, strangely enough, by old French guns that had been found abandoned in the nearby surf from some unknown accident.

JUNE 22 WAS KING GEORGE II'S BIRTHDAY, AND HIS FIGHTING SUBJECTS ON CAPE BRETON TOOK ADVANTAGE OF THE HOLIDAY TO DO TWO THINGS AT WHICH THEY NOW EXCELLED: FIRING GUNS AND DRINKING RUM.

Now, on the sovereign's birthday, those gunners celebrated in style by raining cannonballs onto the enemy position that had become the bane of their great crusade. The Island Battery shuddered beneath the bombardment, becoming shrouded in a cloud of blasted masonry.

Through the haze around the parapets came licks of flame in retaliation, but the French response was clearly desperate and wild—over on Lighthouse Point, rum-fortified provincials scoffed at the clatter and thud of incoming shot, and stood to their

Yankees wrestled artillery around the northern bend of the harbor on Lighthouse Point, creating a battery whose assault would ultimately undo the French defense of Louisbourg.

deadly work. They had learned their trade the hard way, having arrived on Cape Breton with scarcely an idea of how to aim and fire a cannon. Now, after countless hours of work under fire, after seeing careless comrades shattered and maimed, they went about their business like hardened professionals.

Across the harbor and beyond the town, in the camp at Flat Point Cove and in the batteries ringing Louisbourg, the drinking was heavier. With guns on Lighthouse Point, the French in the Island Battery had been rendered superfluous. It was only a matter of time for them. As a result, Pepperrell and Warren had agreed on a combined land-sea assault—Warren would force the entrance to the harbor and land his marines, while, simultaneously, Pepperrell's men would make a frontal assault on the landward defenses that they'd been shooting at for over a month now.

Preparations for the climactic operation were already underway—and ordinary men from Massachusetts, Connecticut, and New Hampshire wondered whether they had the sand to rush French guns. So on that day (and night) of celebration, the rum flowed liberally,

The French flew flags of truce on June 26, 1745, surrendering Louisbourg to the Yankees and British, who entered the town two days later as victors. Victory, however, was short-lived, as Great Britain returned Louisbourg to the French in exchange for possessions in India in 1748.

and between toasts to King George came prayer after prayer to the Almighty for safety in the coming fight.

They would not need it. On June 26, the day that Warren hoped to get a favorable wind for his warships, flags of truce appeared on the walls of Louisbourg. Talks the following day resulted in the town's surrender, and on the 28th—beneath a soaking rain—the victors, Yankee and British alike, occupied the great fortress that had once seemed impregnable.

THE PRICE OF VICTORY

The only appreciable British success during the War of the Austrian Succession, Louisbourg's fall was noisily celebrated on both sides of the Atlantic. But the event served to highlight the increasing divide between metropolitan England and her colonists in North America—between a culture of established, sanctified hierarchies and one of prideful egalitarianism. If the tensions between Pepperrell and Warren during the siege offered a taste of this growing schism, the months following Louisbourg's surrender made it painfully obvious.

For about a year following the port's conquest, New England was responsible for its garrisoning. It proved to be a much deadlier assignment than the siege itself. Some one hundred provincials died during the campaign against Louisbourg; its occupation claimed many times that number—from disease, malnutrition, and exposure. Moreover, these ordinary citizen-soldiers were ordered to guard the French households they were led to believe would be theirs for the plundering. The experience proved as humiliating to them as it was deadly—especially since the Royal Navy loudly proclaimed sole credit for Louisbourg's fall.

The ultimate insult, however, came with the war's official conclusion in 1748. In the Treaty of Aix-la-Chapelle, Great Britain returned Louisbourg to the French in exchange for possessions in India. To many New Englanders, it appeared as if their extraordinary and courageous sacrifice had been squandered for the callous motives of empire.

Although only a few saw it at the time, a new reality had emerged. New England had proven itself as a vital, dynamic society in its own right, capable of projecting power on a scale that was normally the province of sovereign states. And with the feelings of betrayal and mistrust that came as a result of that projection, they found themselves on the road toward a new destiny—one that would put them in direct conflict with the empire on whose behalf they had willingly laid down their lives.

chapter fifteen

A Novice Named Washington Helps Spark a World War

1754

As the smoking chimneys of Williamsburg beckoned at last in the distance, George Washington took heart and spurred his horse to a canter. He and his small party had come a long way through the frigid wilderness, and a warm Madeira by the fire sounded very inviting indeed.

On that cold January day in 1754, the young major carried news for Robert Dinwiddie, lieutenant governor of Virginia. And none of it was good.

Washington had been out west, at the governor's request, to reconnoiter the Ohio country and deliver a message to the French, who apparently believed they had a greater right to the Ohio valley than the English did. Worse, they had backed up their claim with a string of fortresses extending from Lake Erie down the Allegheny River toward its confluence with the Ohio River. Washington had stayed briefly at one of them in December, Fort LeBoeuf in northwest Pennsylvania, where he delivered Governor Dinwiddie's blunt message: Depart "the King of Great Britain's territories," or suffer the consequences.

Major Washington entered Williamsburg and made straight for the governor's residence. The gravity of the information he carried brooked no delay, even for the briefest rest from his long journey.

The French officer with whom Washington had met, Captain Jacques Legardeur de Saint-Pierre, was as firm in his reply as the Virginia governor was in his warning: "As

Twenty-one-year-old George Washington surveys territory in Virginia.

to the summons you send me to retire," the captain wrote to Dinwiddie, "I do not think myself obliged to obey it." Washington, impressed by the manners and cordiality of his Gallic hosts at Fort LeBoeuf, had nevertheless departed for Virginia with a rebuff and a heavy heart.

"The Forks," where the Monongahela and Allegheny rivers joined to create the Ohio River, had become the focal point of a regional controversy that was already several years old by the time the young Virginia major strolled brashly into Fort LeBoeuf. Two English colonies, Pennsylvania and Virginia, had been vying with each other for control of the Ohio River valley, sending streams of traders and speculators to establish ties with the Indians and prepare the way for settlers.

THERE'S NOTHING LIKE THE PROSPECT OF FINANCIAL DISASTER TO GET A MAN MOVING. AND DINWIDDIE–NORMALLY DELIBERATE AND SOMEWHAT CIRCUMSPECT–NOW MOVED WITH IMPRESSIVE CELERITY.

But if the competition between Philadelphia and Williamsburg was intense, the friction that their contest was causing with New France was downright combustible. With claims on the region going back to the last century, the French looked upon the flood of Englishmen into the Ohio country with grave consternation. And they were only too happy to send Washington packing with a message of defiance.

Warming himself by the governor's fire, a mud-spattered Washington felt the blood return to his cheeks and listened as Dinwiddie inveighed against the French in his Scottish burr. *Something would have to be done,* urged the governor, *before all of this got out of hand.* He already had orders from London to stand firm against French trespassing in the west. But Washington knew that Dinwiddie's concern came from more than an obligation to defend His Majesty's interest in America. In fact, the governor of Virginia was also a shareholder in the Ohio Company; to him, a French takeover of the Forks was tantamount to a mugging.

There's nothing like the prospect of financial disaster to get a man moving. And Dinwiddie—normally deliberate and somewhat circumspect—now moved with impressive celerity. He ordered that the building of a fort at the Forks be hastened, even in the daunting winter weather; brought the Company men out in the Ohio country under official control by giving them officers' commissions; pestered the Virginia legislature for funds (no small ordeal, given the longstanding enmity between him and the House of Burgesses over earlier clashes); called for two hundred volunteer soldiers; and chose George Washington to lead them (after promoting him to lieutenant colonel, of course).

The theater of operations in the French and Indian War, 1754–55, is depicted in this nineteenth-century drawing.

Dinwiddie's choice of commander was perhaps a little naive. A twenty-one-year-old surveyor whose social aspirations had earned him connections in Virginia's elite as well as in the Ohio Company, Washington had no firsthand knowledge of combat and no understanding of the tricky business of forceful diplomacy. He didn't think much of Indians, and he didn't speak French. Nevertheless, he was heading into Indian territory to deal with the French. His instructions emphasized the defensive—nobody wanted a war, after all.

But war is what they got. It didn't have to happen that way; that it did was the result of bad timing, bad luck, miscommunication, and a callow provincial officer named George Washington.

THE BEST-LAID PLANS ...

Great Meadows, in southwest Pennsylvania, must have been a very pretty place under normal circumstances. It probably still was—but Lieutenant Colonel Washington was too dour to notice.

It was late May and the grasses were lush, offering plenty of fodder for his horses and wagon teams. A creek wound conveniently right through the middle of the broad marshy ground, bringing more than enough fresh water to his men from the mountains that loomed to the east. Nestled between two hills, the area seemed ideal for building a fortified base to which the unit could retire if need be after forging ahead.

The men were hauling in trees from which to fashion a stockade. Sawing, chopping, digging, they slowly gave shape to a simple fort, some fifty feet in diameter, surrounded by a circuit of trenches. Soon to be dubbed "Fort Necessity," it wasn't much to look at.

And neither were his men, a fact that gave Lieutenant Colonel Washington such agita. He looked at them and tried not to despair. Although he was commissioned to raise 200 soldiers, Washington had managed to scrape up only 160 before setting out through the Allegheny Mountains. They were untrained, poorly clothed, inexperienced, and terribly paid. Not far into the trip, he had learned that the men building a fort up at the Forks—the party to whose support he was trying to march with this rabble—had surrendered to an unknown number of Frenchmen. The site at the Forks did indeed now have a fort. But it was French, named for the governor-general up in Canada: Fort Duquesne.

Washington had pressed on, determined to continue his advance. But the going had been dreadfully slow. With wagons in tow, Washington's meager column had had to hack a road out of the wilderness as they went, proceeding at a snail's pace. Then, after pressing for weeks through the mountains, they arrived at Great Meadows, some fifty miles southeast of the Forks.

All Washington knew now was that the French were at the Forks in unknown strength, a plan was in the offing back in Williamsburg to send him reinforcements as soon as possible, and his men had become experts at chopping down trees but little else. All of this, combined with an admonition against starting a war, would've been a

Washington and his company retreat from their defeat at Great Meadows, 1754.

lot for a man with twice his experience. Washington turned to his toiling soldiers and realized that this pathetic ring of split logs rising before him comprised the most impressive accomplishment of his command since starting out from Williamsburg.

Then a horseman appeared—it was Christopher Gist, an acquaintance of the colonel's who ran a trading post a dozen miles north of Great Meadows. Washington was pleased to see his old guide (Gist had ridden with Washington to Fort LeBoeuf) but alarmed by the intelligence he brought. Just yesterday, claimed the trader, he had spotted a group of French soldiers headed this way.

Washington scratched the stubble on his jaw. It was time to rise to the occasion.

ON THE KNIFE'S EDGE

That night was a miserable one for a march. Drenched by a steady downpour and chilled to the bone, Colonel Washington struggled to see the rest of his column in the tenebrous wild, worried that the men would lose touch with each other and wander off. He wondered whether the French, wherever they were, struggled like this to maintain a semblance of order and cohesion.

He also tried to banish from his mind the idea that this shot in the dark was a fool's errand. Much had happened since Gist had ridden into camp with information about the French. Later that day, not long after sundown, another messenger paid Washington a visit. A Mingo Indian, the fellow had come with a message from his leader, an Iroquois named Tanaghrisson. And at the mention of that name, the colonel's ears pricked up.

Like Gist, Tanaghrisson had been with Washington on the wintry sojourn to Fort LeBoeuf. Not an Iroquois

Though not an Iroquois by birth, Tanaghrisson—the "Half-King"—was adopted by the Seneca, a member of the Iroquois Confederacy of tribes.

by birth, he had been adopted by the Seneca and now served as a representative of Iroquois power over the Indians of the Ohio valley—a sort of governor, in his own right, who regulated the relationship between the Iroquois Confederacy and its client peoples in the region.

All of this was known to Washington, who looked upon the "Half-King," as he was known, as a friend of the English. What the colonel did *not* know, however, was how precarious Tanaghrisson's situation had become of late. With throngs of English settlers coming into the area, most of the Indians of the Ohio valley had thrown their allegiance to the French, who seemed more inclined to trade rather than settle on Indian land. Consequently, Iroquois dominance over the region—and Tanaghrisson's authority, so far from Onondaga—had waned significantly. The Half-King had become a virtual figurehead. And the only thing that could restore his pivotal role as a powerbroker on the Forks, he reckoned, was a war between the Europeans.

That evening, the Mingo told Washington that Tanaghrisson, whose camp was not far from Washington's little fort, knew the precise whereabouts of the French party Gist had spoken of. Washington, who had earlier sent out seventy-five men in search of the French (in the wrong direction, according to the Mingo warrior), was loath to split his men up further. But he decided that the Half-King's invitation to join him for a joint raid was impossible to ignore. Taking half his remaining force, he set out with the Mingo in the soaking night to find Tanaghrisson's camp.

Now, trudging through the woods as the rain began to abate, Washington saw the dull glow of dawn in the east and remembered how tired he was. The Mingo spoke up and pointed ahead: They had arrived.

WHEN EMPIRES BUMP INTO EACH OTHER

The white men, now in the presence of a band of Indian warriors greased and painted for battle, forgot their fatigue in the anticipation of a fight. As the forest came to life in the morning light, Colonel Washington and his officers conferred briefly with the Half-King and agreed on a joint raid of the French. Presently the column was off, following Tanaghrisson and his swift Mingo associates into a collision with destiny.

It wasn't long before the Iroquois leader halted the column. Not far ahead, he explained to Washington, was the hollow in which the French party was camped. Tanaghrisson sent two braves to scout the position. When they returned with confirmation that the French were indeed still there, it was agreed that Washington and his provincials would advance on the hollow while the Indians went around to the rear to catch the hapless French in a pincer.

Overleaf: Washington and his Virginia regiment spy the French at what has come to be known as Jumonville Glen.

Directing his men forward through the brush and trees, Washington soon spied the glen within which the French and Canadians were beginning to awaken, their bedrolls lying at the foot of a great rock face. The provincials, stalking as quietly as they could, spread out along a broad crescent in the trees, looking down upon the French as they rose and ate in the sun-dappled bowl beneath. The Indians were somewhere almost opposite Washington's men by now, though the colonel could not see them, so stealthy was their advance.

Then several of the French looked up in the direction of the colonel's men, alarmed by some noise, and seized their muskets. With the alacrity of veterans, they discharged their guns into the woods just a moment before Washington ordered his own men to fire, loosing a volley whose deafening rumble careened around the walls of the vale. The forest became a smoke-smothered battleground.

IN A BLINDING FLASH OF REALITY, IT OCCURRED TO WASHINGTON THAT HE WAS IN COMMAND OF NOTH-ING—AND COMPLETELY OUT OF CONTROL.

One of the French, clearly an officer, was shouting into the woods for the melee to stop, but Washington's men rammed their shot home and let fly with another blistering fusillade. Many of the French toppled bleeding into the dirt. The officer, stanching a wound and holding his other hand aloft in a gesture of supplication, boldly stepped out from behind some cover and caught the attention of Washington, who called a cease-fire.

The battle could not have lasted more than a couple of minutes. Nevertheless, many French lay wounded on the ground, the Indians having prevented their escape. Washington, seeing to his men, found that three lay wounded while one had been killed outright. His first firefight had truly been a lopsided one.

Fourteen French casualties lay at the bottom of the hollow out of a total force of thirty-five. As the English advanced upon them and secured the position, Washington discovered that their leader, the officer who had tried to stop the violence, was one Joseph Coulon de Villiers de Jumonville. Now reclining on the ground, wounded and clearly in pain, the thirty-five-year-old ensign insisted that his mission was a peaceful one. (A fact born out by the small size of his party.) Jumonville produced a letter from his superior that, he was sure, a translator could read for Colonel Washington.

After listening a while to Jumonville's translator get through the letter, Washington, perhaps frustrated at the strange impasse he had come to with these damnable Gallic fellows, took the letter over to his own translator, an old friend and Dutchman named Jacob Van Braam. There, surrounded by his men, the colonel listened carefully and tried to gauge what his next move should be. The gist of Jumonville's letter, it seemed, was that its bearer was an emissary of His Most Christian Majesty, Louis XV, and that his mission—a diplomatic one— was to urge any English trespassers on French territory to immediately depart in peace.

The Indians appeared, walking into the hollow from their position in the woods. Three groups—English, French, and Indians—now milled about uneasily, the English happy to keep their guns pointed at the French until their colonel could suss out the situation. Tanaghrisson, gripping his hatchet, stepped over to Jumonville and said something. Then he sank his weapon into the Frenchman's skull.

The tense quiet of the glen suddenly vanished with the noise of slaughter. As his warriors set upon the wounded French and began scalping them, the Iroquois Half-King reached into Jumonville's yawning cranium and ritually washed his hands in the gray matter. With awesome quickness, as the English stood frozen and agape, all but one of the wounded French were murdered.

By that time, Washington, white with revulsion, had resumed his composure and ordered the Indians to stop. In a blinding flash of reality, it occurred to him that he was in command of nothing—and completely out of control.

THE HORNETS ARE STIRRED

Washington had stepped into the no-man's-land between empires. Tanaghrisson may have been the one who dispatched Jumonville and twelve of his countrymen, but it was Washington who had made all the decisions—and it was he who would have to answer for the debacle that was now unfolding in the Ohio country.

His greatest concerns, however, were more immediate. After returning to his fort at Great Meadows, Washington decided to advance on Fort Duquesne. But after failing to coax local Indians to his side, Washington received intelligence that a large French force was headed his way. Time to assume the defensive.

He had no idea. The "large French force" in question was led by Captain Louis Coulon de Villiers, older brother of the late Ensign Jumonville. Having received word at Fort Duquesne of his brother's massacre, the captain begged to be loosed on Washington like an avenging angel. And he had some seven hundred men at his disposal—regulars, militia, and Indians.

Washington, having given up on his drive to Fort Duquesne, now led his fatigued army back to Fort Necessity, where it collapsed in a state of complete exhaustion. Despite the sorry state of his men, the colonel's situation had improved since the firefight with Jumonville. By the first week of July he had four hundred men, including a

More Disaster in the Bush

In the wake of his 1754 misadventure, Washington seemed to have gotten in touch with his limitations: The next time he went into the Ohio country, he insisted on doing so strictly as an advisor rather than at the head of a unit of troops. Nevertheless, he would once again encounter disaster—and on a much greater scale.

Once war with the French became a reality, the English sent reinforcements to America under the command of General Edward Braddock. In the summer of 1755, Braddock resolved to take Fort Duquesne and seize control of the Forks. Washington demurred at the suggestion of a field command and opted to join the general's staff as a voluntary aide-de-camp.

With a long siege train in tow, the large English force—around 1,800 strong, including two regiments of regulars—struck out from Fort Cumberland, Maryland, at the end of May. Pioneers at the head of the column cleared the way and laid down a road for the wagons and heavy artillery that followed, cutting

English General Edward Braddock makes his exit at the Battle of Monongahela, 1755.

through 110 miles of dense forest. It was an interminable, backbreaking trek.

Indian scouts eventually alerted the French commander at Fort Duquesne of the approaching English. With just 250 regular troops at his command, along with 650 Indian allies, Captain Claude-Pierre Pécaudy de Contrecoeur had no hope of enduring a siege. Consequently, on July 9, he sent out a raiding party to ambush the enemy in the hopes of hobbling his advance. More than 800 strong, the force included all of de Contrecoeur's Indian allies— Wyandots, Ottawas, Mississaugas, and Potawatomis.

Later that day, in the early afternoon, the two armies essentially bumped into each other near the Monongahela River. Although the advance parties of both sides were surprised, the French responded, naturally, in the fashion that suited their woodland combatants: fanning out to flank the long English column on its ersatz road, relying on trees and brush for cover. Washington, already suffering horribly from hemorrhoids that compelled him to cushion his saddle, spent the afternoon by

Braddock's side and watched, increasingly helpless, as the regimented redcoats tried to respond to their elusive assailants with parade-ground discipline.

Without proper light infantry, guerrillas, or flankers, the English force found itself surrounded and decimated over a grueling three hours of hellish fighting. By the time the English began to retreat, some two-thirds of their number had been either killed or wounded. Braddock himself had a musket ball in his chest, and would not live to see home again. The French and their Indian colleagues suffered fewer than fifty casualties.

The Battle of the Monongahela was the first of many British disasters in the French and Indian War. And though many observers would insist that it confirmed the superiority of Indian-style warfare over European discipline in the American wilderness, it would be a combination of both that ultimately brought the British empire victory.

✠

hundred British regulars of a South Carolina independent company. Huddling within the beggarly walls of Fort Necessity, the English—those who weren't too sick—prepared themselves for of the French assault they knew was coming.

THE AGONIZING DEATH OF FORT NECESSITY

July 3 broke wet and miserable. Having rained the previous day, the fort wallowed in a morass of pools and puddles. Late that morning, as the troops labored to dry their valuables and ordnance, the first shots came zinging in from French muskets. The siege of Fort Necessity had begun.

Under a drenching rain, the English huddled behind the walls and within the encircling trenches, struggling to find dry powder while ducking incoming shot. Coulon de Villiers' men, settling into the high ground that surrounded Washington's stockade, contented themselves with pouring lead into the English position from the vantage of the wooded slopes. Under the trees, they were able to thwart the rain and maintain a steady fire, gradually subjecting the cowering Virginians to a nightmarish suppression.

It was a long, long day for the English. With so many of their weapons rendered useless from the water and weather, the men, surrounded in an all but worthless fort, broke into the rum and drank themselves silly. So it went. French lead kept thumping into the trenches and over the stockade, claiming the occasional victim. By sundown, roughly a third of the English were casualties.

Washington was running out of options when a voice in lilting French hailed him from the woods. The Virginia colonel grasped at the olive branch he was being offered and sent Van Braam out to the tree line to negotiate.

The Dutchman later returned with a sopping document in his hand and a look of hope in his eyes. As Van Braam explained to Washington, Coulon de Villiers was satisfied that he'd humbled his brother's killers, and he was willing to let the Virginians retreat in good order and with honor. With thirty corpses and seventy wounded, the tall Virginia colonel was beside himself with relief at the leniency of the French terms. All Washington had to do, explained Van Braam, was sign the drooping surrender document he held in his hand.

Washington looked it over with his officers and conferred with his Dutch friend over its meaning. In the saturated darkness, with the promise of life hanging in the balance, none of those present gave the water-smudged letter a thorough reading. Washington signed.

Even as the pitiable defenders of Fort Necessity marched out the following morning to begin their long retreat back across the mountains, none of them—least of all Washington himself—realized that the twenty-two-year-old colonel had signed an admission of guilt in the assassination of Jumonville.

GLOBAL WAR

Having fixed his signature to the wanton butchery of Jumonville, scion of a prominent military family and ambassador of New France, George Washington made his entrance upon the world stage with a pratfall. His long, arduous mission in the Ohio country produced no successes—indeed, it served only to animate the courts of Europe toward a war that would ultimately decide the fate of empires.

Although there can be little doubt that a clash over the American interior between England and France was inevitable, Washington's stumbling in the wilderness—with the eager help of Tanaghrisson—pushed the schedule up considerably.

The Seven Years' War, whose North American theater would come to be known as the French and Indian War, would ultimately involve nations as diverse as Prussia, Austria, Sweden, Russia, and Spain. And the two principle combatants, England and France, would clash wherever their far-flung empires chafed against each other, from the sun-baked islands of the Caribbean to the teeming cities of the Indian subcontinent. Nowhere, however, would France's worldwide defeat be as spectacular as it would be in North America—a defeat made possible by the British government's willingness to spend itself into virtual bankruptcy in pursuit of victory.

Interestingly, the British would attempt to allay much of that debt after the war by taxing its American colonies, gradually driving them into a state of open revolt. And leading the nascent American army to victory and national independence would be the very man who, it can be argued, got the whole process rolling back in 1754.

LOUIS-JOSEPH. MARQUIS DE MONTCALM. LIEUTENANT GÉNÉRAL DES ARMÉES DE FRANCE.

Non Sibi,
Sed Patriæ vixit.

chapter sixteen

Victory Against All Odds Marks the Swan Song of New France

1758

On July 5, 1758, the surface of Lake George in what is today New York State became a stage for one of colonial America's most breathtaking spectacles. Those standing on the upper slopes along its thirty-mile length were treated to a truly unforgettable sight: the emergence, from the lake's far southern neck, of a great creeping tide, moving slowly over the glassy waters like spilled port from a giant glass.

In the brightness of morning, tiny flashes twinkled throughout, belying their menacing origins—guns, buckles, and sword hilts, all of them catching the sun on that summer day. Sails, little white squares beyond number, eventually gave the truth away: This was a mighty army, borne over the shimmering surface by barges that seemed to continue without end.

More than one thousand bateaux and canoes, arranged with near-geometric precision, came majestically north, their crowded decks forming a carpet of humanity that nearly spanned the mile-wide lake from shore to shore. Nothing like it had ever been seen before in North America.

This was the army of Major General James Abercromby, commander in chief of British forces on the continent. For weeks this huge force, more than 17,000 strong,

The Marquis de Montcalm was a dynamic leader of the forces in New France from 1756 until his death in 1759.

had been massing around Albany and the ruins of Fort William Henry, preparing for the greatest concentrated military strike yet attempted by any power in North America. And most of those who bore witness to its stately advance up Lake George tarried only briefly to gawk.

That's because most of them were French, and it was for their destruction that Abercromby's awesome host was sailing serenely north. What was unfolding along this beautiful stretch of watery wilderness was a showdown between empires that had, until now, merely sparred for control of a vast frontier that demanded a title fight to win.

METHODICAL AND RESOURCEFUL, THE FORTY-SIX-YEAR-OLD MARQUIS DE MONTCALM HAD MADE THE MOST OF HIS LIMITED RESOURCES BY DEALING THE ENGLISH A SERIES OF STUNNING BLOWS.

England meant to force that fight now on her Gallic enemies, and push them all the way back to Montreal, where they could be crushed in a conclusive denouement. One of the most crucial stepping-stones to that ultimate goal was the destruction of Fort Carillon, whose bastions, overlooking the strategic wilderness between Lake George and Lake Champlain, had been holding a dagger to the throats of New York and New England since 1755.

But if Abercromby, confident in his might, predicted a walkover, he was in for an awful shock. This was to be one of the greatest upsets in the history of North American arms—and one of the final, most spectacular victories of an empire that very nearly decided the fate of America.

DAVID AND GOLIATH

Since George Washington's disastrous mission in the Ohio country had hastened the commencement of the French and Indian War (see chapter 15), France and England—which officially declared war on one another in 1756—had performed in North America in inverse proportion to their sizes. New France, with a population of around 70,000, had dominated events in its struggle with an English colonial presence of 1.5 million, mostly through crafty and resourceful leadership.

But the British empire had more than just population to bring to the contest. In the enormous conflict that now spanned the globe, known to history as the Seven Years' War, the French assigned primary importance to Europe, concentrating their considerable military might there. England, by contrast, relied on allies—Hanover and Prussia—

to fight in Europe while turning its own attentions overseas, especially to North America. In time, this difference of opinion on the significance of the New World would pay off for the English.

With the hard-driving William Pitt leading Britannia's wartime government by 1757, redcoats began turning up on American shores in unprecedented numbers, backed up by large contingents of provincials raised by the various colonies.

Abercromby envisioned a three-pronged invasion of New France—up the St. Lawrence, along the Lake George–Lake Champlain corridor, and through the Ohio country along the Great Lakes—that would converge ultimately on Montreal. In overall command of the roughly 40,000 troops in North America, Abercromby would personally lead the central thrust through the Champlain valley with 17,000 men. Fort Carillon—known to the British by its Indian name, Ticonderoga—was the commander in chief's first obstacle.

Waiting for him there was a man whose name would remain forever linked to the French and Indian War: Major General Louis-Joseph, Marquis de Montcalm. Methodical and resourceful, the forty-six-year-old Marquis de Montcalm had made the most of his limited resources by dealing the English a series of stunning blows.

In 1756 he had captured Fort Oswego on the south shore of Lake Ontario, employing conventional siege tactics that most Europeans thought impracticable in the American interior. The following year he descended on Fort William Henry and forced its surrender—a triumph that inadvertently led to a massacre of English

General James Abercromby was a symbol of British frustration in the French and Indian War.

soldiers and civilians by Montcalm's Indian allies that later became immortalized in James Fenimore Cooper's *The Last of the Mohicans*. Bereft of enough men to garrison his prize, he razed the fort and retired to Fort Carillon, preparing to meet the English onslaught he knew was coming.

When the campaigning season opened in 1758, Montcalm could have been forgiven for considering himself a tragic figure. At Fort Carillon he had some four thousand men to meet the storm of Anglo-American fury that was about to break upon him. Perhaps two hundred of them were members of the *Campagnies Franches de la Marine*, blue-clad soldiers raised by the Ministry of Marine to defend France's colonies. Another four hundred to five hundred were militiamen.

The remainder were Montcalm's best and favorite troops: metropolitan infantry, the white-coated professionals of the king's army brought over from France to form the true heart of Canada's defense. If he were to perform any miracles at Carillon, it would be with these men.

And miracles, it soon turned out, were all Montcalm could hope for.

ABERCROMBY MAKES HIS MOVE

All around the commander in chief, nearly as far as his eye could see, stretched his colorful insurance policy. These were the men who were going to guarantee his future. James Abercromby, fifty-two and feeling at the height of his powers, allowed himself a moment of fulsome pride: *My God, I almost feel sorry for Montcalm.*

The size of the force that accompanied him that day up the narrow valley of Lake George was intended to obliterate the possibility of defeat. Two men had preceded Abercromby as commander in chief, and both had been dismissed for failure. When it came to the Champlain corridor, the English were no longer taking chances.

The general had an extraordinary force at his disposal. Nearly 6,000 red-coated regulars formed the backbone of his command, including the 1,100 Scots of the famous Black Watch regiment. There were other celebrated infantry regiments, such as the 60th "Royal Americans," recruited mostly from the colonies, and 125 men of the Royal Artillery, with forty-four guns to pulverize Carillon into submission.

Additionally, Abercromby could count on some 11,775 provincials and auxiliaries—men from the colonies, both in uniform and without, who did everything from man the bateaux to fight alongside the regulars in line of battle. All of them, having moved from points throughout the northeast to the general's vast encampment alongside the burned hulk of Fort William Henry, took pride in filling out a host of historic proportions. As any of them could see, great things were afoot.

"The Fight in the Forest," a color lithograph for the 1920 edition of The Last of the Mohicans. *The novel immortalizes the English surrender of Fort William Henry to French forces led by Montcalm.*

By late afternoon, according to plan, the enormous armada made landfall some twenty-five miles north of William Henry at a place on the western side of the lake called Sabbath Day Point. There, assuming control of the land like a colony of giant ants, the army settled in to camp and covered the landscape with cooking fires. The French, watching from a safe distance as they retreated north to Fort Carillon, took notice and made preparations.

THE DEATH OF A HERO

The English army's stop at Sabbath Day Point had been a ruse. That night, Abercromby ordered his troops to board their barges again in strict silence for a journey farther north. By the time the sun was rising over the eastern shoulder of the valley, the great army was approaching the northern reaches of the lake, having bypassed many of Montcalm's units that had been posted as sentries. The French had been caught unawares.

After getting his army ashore, Abercromby could pat himself on the back for getting within two miles of Fort Carillon with no resistance to speak of. Now what?

His second-in-command had an idea. George Augustus, Viscount Howe, was beloved throughout the army for his dashing charisma. If Abercromby was deliberate, thorough, and detailed, Howe—nineteen years younger—was brave and innovative. It was Howe who had promoted the special outfitting of light infantry units for the North American wilderness, complete with shorter coats, shorter hair, loose formation, and skill in woodcraft. Charismatic and popular with the men, Lord Howe was an excellent and canny choice by Abercromby to be his right hand.

On the morning of July 6, Howe led the army forward on its march through the wilderness toward Carillon. His plan was simple, if far from easy. Having landed on the northwest coast of Lake George, the army now had to march overland to Carillon along the left bank of the La Chute River, whose twisting course covered several unnavigable stretches of rapids. In fact, there was a shorter route that followed a portage road, bypassing a huge bend in the river. But Howe, knowing that path to be defended, took the longer route so as to bring his army around and eventually behind the portage road, outflanking its defenders.

Four columns marched ahead through the woods and thickets. One of them, commanded by Howe himself, consisted of light infantry and provincials whose task was to guard the right flank of the other columns along the river. Not long after four in the afternoon, the forest erupted in musket fire. Howe's column had run into a French unit that was trying to find its way back to Fort Carillon after being bypassed by the English army's surprise early morning landing.

Fort Ticonderoga, pictured here, was known as Fort Carillon to the French.

Upon hearing the gunfire echoing through the woods, Howe instinctively rushed to its source, determined to lead a sweep of these Frenchmen to clear the way for the rest of the army's advance. Once there, he soon fell to enemy fire, struck by a ball through the heart and lungs. He died almost immediately.

AN ARMY IN CONFUSION

General Abercromby removed his hat and wiped the sweat from his forehead with a handkerchief. He couldn't believe his eyes. The army seemed to be in a rout.

Soldiers ran past him and his staff, their red coats streaming through the trees like blood trough a sieve. Officers called out angrily to their men, but they were powerless to stanch the flow. Feeling the blood rush to his head, the general steadied his horse and strained to listen for bits of information that could tell him what was going on. Up ahead, a firefight had been raging, and was only now beginning to peter out. Had Montcalm brought his army out and struck a blow?

Then officers and men approached with reports and rumors, and Abercromby couldn't believe his ears. General Howe was dead. Panic at the front had spread through the ranks.

Many suspected an ambush. Others heard the wailing of Indians and ran to save their scalps. *Howe was dead.*

Abercromby felt his stomach lurch. This was all wrong, all wrong. He knew that he outnumbered the French drastically. Could reinforcements have come from Montreal without his knowing about it?

Oh, Howe. He'd lost Howe!

This was a mob. Abercromby understood the mentality of an army better than most. A soldier since 1717, he had fought in France and in Flanders, had felt the hot punishment of battle wounds, and had mastered his terror of it. He had warmed to the challenge of leadership, and discovered that he liked it. As second-in-command to his predecessor in North America, the Earl of Loudoun, he had thrown himself into administrative tasks, becoming intimate with the vast logistical apparatus that bound the individuals to their purpose, making of them something enormous and irresistible—and, ironically, vulnerable as no individual could be. For the numbers that amplified the volley of their fire also inflated the scale of their panic—and the dread of thousands was a thing unmanageable.

ABERCROMBY COULDN'T BELIEVE HIS EARS. GENERAL HOWE WAS DEAD. PANIC AT THE FRONT HAD SPREAD THROUGH THE RANKS.

Nevertheless, he would have to manage it. Sending his aides-de-camp riding off in all directions to seize control, the general scanned the woods for his senior line officers, and cursed the gallantry of his late second-in-command. This was what came of heroes: The only thing greater than the spirit they gave an army was the devastation of their loss.

But Abercromby had more than Howe's death to deal with. As his men swirled about him and slowly began to rally, he took in the wilderness and winced. The trees, ancient and mute, were as devastating as any battery of guns. His soldiers, hailing from the towns and windswept landscapes of Europe, were in awe of them. Even the provincials, going back generations in this huge and wild land, looked with distress at the limitless green kingdoms that surrounded their sea-bound strip of civilization.

No one that day marched into the forest gloom without thinking of the Monongahela and the slaughter of General Braddock. Montcalm, in fact, didn't even have any real Indian presence under his command at Carillon. But the fear of scalping, pervasive and entrenched in the Anglo-American world, stalked the redcoats that day like their own shadows—a reality the French had always been happy to exploit. And as shouts of "Howe's dead!" and "Ambush!" echoed through the leaves, a great imaginary scalping knife cut through Abercromby's army.

It was a long evening. Some of the units fell back onto the landing sight with the dipping sun, coming to their senses more out of shame and exhaustion than from the efforts of General Abercromby. By nightfall their broad camp once again flickered with firelight along the banks of Lake George, as if the long nightmare of July 6 had never happened.

And that's precisely how Abercromby and his officers wanted it.

PLAN OF ATTACK

It was a hot and humid July 8th morning when General Abercromby presided over the most fateful meeting of his career. Around him were the officers of his regular units, a large circle of nobles in scarlet. The provincials, dismissed as nonprofessionals, were not invited.

The previous day had gone well. After the horrors of the 6th, Abercromby had agreed to forego trying Howe's route again, and decided to force the portage road. Expecting to find it well defended, the British were relieved to encounter no resistance. At the end of the route, they found abandoned sawmills and a partially destroyed bridge over the La Chute, which they set about repairing immediately. By the end of the day, the rest of the army was brought up, securing a bridgehead on the north bank of the river.

His officers, already feeling the heat, grew slick with perspiration under the trees. He put it to them: How should the army proceed against the defenses of Fort Carillon?

Guarding the confluence of the La Chute River (which flows roughly northeast from Lake George) with the southern neck of Lake Champlain, Fort Carillon's only real landward approach from Abercromby's bridgehead was over a broad swathe of ground that rose, sometimes rather steeply, toward a plateau—"Ticonderoga Heights"—that crested perhaps a thousand yards northwest of the fort itself. In addition to denuding this ground of trees to deny attackers any cover, the French had constructed defenses to guard the western slopes of the heights. The relative strength and sophistication of these defensive works, which were some seven hundred yards or so east of the English bridgehead, were the central issues.

And on that topic Abercromby had some telling reports. The previous afternoon, the army's chief engineer, Lieutenant Matthew Clerk, had ascended Rattlesnake Mountain, a wooded hill whose peak offered an excellent view of Ticonderoga Heights and Fort Carillon from across the river. In addition to judging the hill ideal for mounting cannon with which to command the French positions, his expert's eye judged the works along Ticonderoga Heights minimal and unfinished.

The French fight defiantly on Ticonderoga Heights in this famous illustration by Canadian artist C.W. Jefferys.

That wasn't all. That morning, another party had sneaked up to the very tree line at the edge of the cleared ground and viewed the defenses themselves, confirming Clerk's report. The French were still working to improve their trenches and earthworks, but they had a long way to go.

These points figured prominently in the conversation as, one by one, Abercromby's officers presented their opinions. Rather than going through the trouble of hauling cannon up Rattlesnake Mountain, why not launch an all-out assault on the weak defenses before they were allowed to get any stronger? Such a move seemed timely, even prudent—especially since French deserters had brought news that some three thousand additional troops were on their way to reinforce Montcalm. Better to act decisively before they showed up. After taking the works along the top of Ticonderoga Heights, the army would be in an ideal position from which to threaten the fort itself with bombardment.

The conference concluded, its leader happy to have settled on a direct and simple plan of action. Abercromby gave final instructions for the assault itself. Four lines, one behind the other, would break upon the French positions like waves. The first, made up of rangers, light infantry, and bateauxmen, would skirmish with French pickets and drive them back. Behind them would come two provincial regiments from New York and Massachusetts to begin pouring fire on the enemy works, and then a line of regulars, which would deliver the main attack that would take the French positions themselves. Bringing up the rear would be the New Jersey and Connecticut regiments.

The plan, a classic frontal assault, was intended to smash the defenders with withering fire and overwhelm them with superior numbers.

But that's not what happened.

A LONG AND BRUTAL DAY

By one o'clock in the afternoon, General Abercromby was standing near the edge of the woods, looking up toward Ticonderoga Heights upon a scene of bedlam.

Barely visible through the great pall of powder smoke were throngs of men wrestling with the very ground over which they were trying to move, as if tentacles had reached up from the soil to hinder their progress. Beyond them, along the top of the crest, a long row of earthworks crested with logs marked the French positions, from which came an incessant, otherworldly rumble of musketry, dropping the hapless Anglo-Americans by the score. The general, for all intents and purposes, had lost control of his dying army.

Since ten o'clock that morning, chilling reports filtered steadily to the rear: The French, it seemed, had brilliantly camouflaged their defenses with fir trees and shrubbery. What Clerk had failed to see from Rattlesnake Mountain was a broad *abatis* in front of the French positions—a great carpet of felled trees whose branches, sharpened to deadly points, impeded the progress of the army to a pitiful crawl. It was this tangled morass of wood that Abercromby now saw his soldiers struggling to get through, only to get cut down by the terrific fire from above.

As shock, confusion, and smoke conspired to make a mess of things, Abercromby lost the ability to communicate with his officers out in the field. He was all but impotent.

The French, by contrast, were in complete control of events. Initially stunned to learn of the total success of the previous day's camouflaging efforts, they settled down to take advantage of the situation and methodically turned the abatis into a vast killing ground. Montcalm and his officers had ordered each brigade of regulars to put their best shots at the wall. Behind them were their fellows, responsible for keeping a constant rotation of loaded muskets, which were regularly handed up to the front.

The result was a devastating rate of fire—as much as eight aimed rounds a minute, compared with the three that could be fired by the best veterans reloading themselves. Indeed, so fast and furious were the volleys that several fires broke out in the abatis throughout the day, requiring French soldiers to bravely venture forward and put them out to restore a clean line of fire.

The ground before them had become a genuine hell for the British. Focusing on the right and center of the French line, the redcoats and their provincial comrades—parched by thirst and hammered by the July sun—attempted to force their way through the deadly thicket, but to no avail. Even an attempt to set up a battery at the foot of Rattlesnake Mountain was repulsed. Not long after two o'clock, an English flotilla of barges laden with cannon made its way down the river, but it was spotted by gunners in the fort. Accurate French fire began plunging into the water, and several of the craft were sunk. So much for the battery.

Abercromby now began to despair, knowing that news of a breakthrough was increasingly unlikely as the afternoon marched on. By mid-afternoon elements from all four waves mingled in front of and in the abatis, desperate to find a way in or to flank the enemy positions. But all of their thrusts had been repulsed. Not one had even reached the French, so ferocious was the scything fire throughout the broad thicket. Truly the day seemed lost.

ATTACK OF THE HIGHLANDERS

By five o'clock there was one unit of the battered British army that hadn't had enough yet. For the Highlanders of the 42nd Regiment of Foot, known as the "Black Watch," the day's horrific sacrifices could not be borne without a breakthrough.

With their bonnets and kilts, they made a colorful image, and every one of them carried a broadsword and pistol in addition to musket and bayonet. On the far left of the British line, they formed up with the army's surviving grenadiers (a type of elite infantry) and went into the abatis with a fury that nobody who saw it that day would forget.

Hacking at the wood, bellowing themselves hoarse, they waded through the awful defenses, then withered before a welcoming volley from the French. Witnesses saw Scotsmen hacking at the wooden barriers in a kind of rage, desperate to clear a way forward. But it was not to be.

At least, not yet. Repulsed, they measured their losses, mustered their courage once more, and threw themselves at the center of the line.

They found themselves in a nightmare. Wreathed in smoke, the gory landscape, where so many stubborn attacks had failed, was a charred tangle of flesh and wood. The desperate Highlanders pressed on and on, forcing themselves forward into the teeth of Montcalm's musketry. Falling in alarming numbers, the wounded merely screamed for their comrades to keep going. Ahead, over the ramparts, they could see the enemy's regimental colors snapping in the breeze, and they fixed upon them as a goal. And then,

The Black Watch

The origins of the Highland regiment that fought so remarkably at Ticonderoga were exceptional. In the wake of the 1715 Jacobite Rebellion, in which much of Scotland rose up against the new Hanoverian dynasty of King George I, the crown authorized the raising of independent companies throughout Scotland from clans who had been loyal to the king, primarily those of Munro, Campbell, Grant, and Fraser. These companies were charged with keeping the peace in the Scottish Highlands—to thwart cattle raids, enforce settlements between feuding clans, and generally present an armed manifestation of royal authority.

In 1739, with the raising of several more companies, King Charles II ordered all the independent units to be formed into a regiment of the line, its ranks filled entirely by Scottish recruits. Their uniform, which included a blue bonnet, dirk (a kind of dagger), and kilt, was to feature a tartan that would become famous throughout the world as the "Black Watch" for its dark coloring and its association with a unit that once "watched" the glens of Scotland.

At Ticonderoga, the regiment, officially numbered the 42nd, comprised the largest of General Abercromby's regiments, with 1,100 men—647 of whom were killed, wounded, or missing when the army retreated on July 9.

✛

incredibly, a small group of them made it to the French, scaled the ramparts, and began slashing wildly with their broadswords, only to be bayoneted or shot.

It was hopeless. Demoralized and incredulous, the Scotsmen—having lost more than half their number—limped back to the rear.

AN ARMY DEFEATED

It wasn't until seven in the evening, after three more futile assaults, that the broken British army faded back into the woods, resigned to its failure. Abercromby, stunned at the completeness of his repulse, gave up on Fort Carillon altogether. He ordered a retreat back to the camp at William Henry.

The Fort Carillon campaign had been a major British disaster. Although the figures are inexact, it is safe to say that Abercromby's men had suffered around 2,500 casualties, of which nearly 1,000 were killed. The French, by contrast, had lost perhaps 500 killed, wounded, and missing.

If the Battle of Fort Carillon has any lasting significance, it is in the stunning blow that New France was once able to deal, in New York, to the largest army the continent had ever seen at that time—a reminder of the enormous challenge Britain faced in purging what it considered its own territory of an empire that helped shape the course of North American history. The final Gallic triumph of the French and Indian War in what is now the United States, July 8, 1758, is a reminder of what could have been.

Sadly, Abercromby's 17,000 men had been no insurance policy at all. He was replaced in 1759 by Sir Jeffery Amherst, who presided over the defeat of New France. Needed along the St. Lawrence, Montcalm retreated north, where he would ultimately meet his death during the conquest of Quebec. Fort Carillon was razed in 1759 to deny its use to the British.

chapter seventeen

America's Founding Ranger Makes History with a Dubious Enterprise

1759

It was well after dark on September 13, 1759, when seventeen whaleboats rowed quietly into the waters off Crown Point on Lake Champlain. Laden with men and equipment, the convoy rode low in the water, heading north under a starlit sky. The hour of their departure was an indication of the nature of their mission. Around two hundred strong, these buckskin-clad warriors were going into harm's way, intent on using the night to shield their approach. Stealth was a hallmark of the rangers.

Their leader, Major Robert Rogers, was emblematic of the changes that war in this colossal wilderness wrought in men. Born in 1731 to Ulster-Scotch settlers in northern Massachusetts, he had been a soldier during King George's War (1740–1748), a scout, and a thief. The outbreak of the French and Indian War spared him the consequences of a conviction for counterfeiting—the English, it seemed, needed every able-bodied frontiersman they could get.

He became a well-known recruiter and trainer of scouts skilled in ambush, a type of soldier the English called rangers. Generals learned to scorn and depend on him, usually at once, and his men came both to view him as a rogue and to respect him as a natural leader. Obsessed with mastering the Indians' own woodcraft to use against them, he accorded Native Americans an almost reverential respect that could change to blind revulsion as quickly as the weather over Lake Ontario. He was ambitious, indomitable, and often drunk, and in time the scale of his considerable reputation would be matched by the respect for his writings throughout the English-speaking

world. By the end of the French and Indian War he would scratch up more defeats than victories, but he would also become a kind of legend.

As the men rowed, parting the dark plain of the lake, Rogers recalled his orders from General Jeffery Amherst:

Proceed ... to Misisquey Bay, from whence you will march and attack the enemy's settlements on the south side of the river St. Lawrence, in such a manner as you shall judge most effectual to disgrace the enemy, and for the success and honour of his Majesty's arms.

"The south side of the river St. Lawrence"—the general was casting a wide net with these orders. For Rogers, the true prize was more specific: the Abenaki village of St. Francis, between fifty and sixty miles down the St. Lawrence from Montreal, whence so many of New England's ills had originated for generations going back.

Remember the barbarities that have been committed by the enemy's Indian scoundrels on every occasion ... Take your revenge, but don't forget that tho' those villains have dastardly and promiscuously murdered the women and children of all ages, it is my orders that no women or children are killed or hurt.

The document was a neat reflection of the quandaries facing soldiers in these parts who believed themselves gentlemen in a chivalrous tradition. Amherst wanted to have his cake and eat it, too. But the frontier between New France and New England was also a frontier between reality and perception—between the circumstances that compelled men to act like animals and the civilized delusions that allowed them to stop noticing. Because he wore a scarlet coat and held a king's commission, General Amherst was constrained to use men like Rogers carefully, framing orders as far as possible in notional language. But in their hearts both men were in agreement: The Abenaki must be made to pay dearly for being the bogeymen of New England. And Robert Rogers was just the man to collect.

In fact, the sheer ambitiousness of Rogers's plan bore grim testament to the vengeful spirit that had come to dominate the war between empires and races in North America. Rogers was a creature of this pitiless world of snow, swamp, ice, and woods, where guerrillas, white and red, measured success by gathering scalps and dreaded capture for fear of slow death.

It was a war in and around the greater, more thunderous struggle between linear formations of infantry and artillery. And the two types of warfare were as different as the codes of conduct that each demanded.

It was Rogers's comfort with the hatreds he stored up like wood for the winter that allowed him to plan a well-equipped lunge in and out of Canada involving epic distances, all to butcher as many Abenakis as he could get his hands on. This, more than

Frontier terrorist: A rare portrait of Robert Rogers, from 1778, is shown here.

any of their other exploits, would become the most famous achievement of Rogers's rangers. It is hardly surprising that it would get so many of them killed.

THE WAY NORTH

Lake Champlain was as dangerous a place as any the rangers were likely to encounter on their trek to Canada. The reason they kept to the shallows along the banks and moved only at night was simple: The French also plied these waters. And they did so in sloops and schooners, any one of which mounted enough cannon and swivel guns to rake Rogers's whaleboats into kindling. The English goal, Missisquoi (Misisquey) Bay, was eighty or so miles from Crown Point. To make that distance in one piece, the men would have to be alert, careful, and quiet. Rogers had no doubts about their ability to do so, even though only half of them were actually rangers.

Through death and desertion, the war had been hard on the rangers. The major had had to turn to the other branches of the Anglo-American military to fill the ranks for his St. Francis operation. Owing to the nature of the French and Indian War itself, he had little trouble. The British regulars, having long adopted light infantry units for the open-order fighting of the forests, were full of men who yearned for action beyond the garrisons or the strictly regimented line units. And provincials, routinely relegated to the backbreaking boredom of rear-area tasks, leapt at the chance to serve with the great Rogers. The major found interested volunteers among the Highland regiments, including the Black Watch. And twenty-five Amerindians, Mahicans and Mohegans, formed a kind of cadre for the operation. The result was a fascinating microcosm of the Anglo-American world, with heads donning a variety of blue bonnets, trimmed-down tricornes, feathers, furs, and leather ranger caps.

Their weapons were equally eclectic, though nearly all bore the ubiquitous hatchet and scalping knife. Some stowed fusils ("fuzees"), a smaller kind of officer carbine, while others brought standard-issue British "Brown Bess" muskets, sawed off and blackened for use in the bush. Most, however, were armed with rifled hunting muskets, long and deadly accurate. On more than a few of them, a sword pommel or the wooden grip of a pistol showed itself in the folds of their deerskin, a leather "hammercap" slipped over the frizzen—the steel plate against which the hammer would strike to produce a spark—to prevent an accidental discharge. Despite all the waistcoats and calico shirts, the army's most common feature was leather, a practical arrangement of moccasins, leggings ("Indian stockings"), haversacks, and bandoliers.

The bane of officers: Rangers, like this frontier marksman, were excellent shots and skilled in ambush.

General James Wolfe would take Quebec in 1759 but die in the process.

By September 18, Rogers and his men were holed up somewhere on the eastern shore of Lake Champlain, perhaps twelve miles from Crown Point. Waiting for favorable weather and a dark night to elude the French vessels, he faced the bane of every eighteenth-century commander: attrition. Something like a fifth of his force had already been forced to turn back, owing to everything from disease to the accidental discharge of firearms. Before long half of the Indians were back at Crown Point from sickness. In such circumstances, the numbers quickly multiplied, as every injured or ill member of the party had to be escorted by fellows to ensure his safe return.

Such misfortunes were to be expected. Rogers pressed on, eventually getting the favorable conditions he'd hoped for. In the earliest hours of September 23, under a steady downpour, the rangers rowed safely into Missisquoi Bay at the northeast extremity of Lake Champlain. They pulled their boats onto the stony shore in the soaking darkness hoping nobody had seen them. There they hid them in the nearby woods with the supplies for the return journey, putting a two-man guard on them. This was to be their tiny, vulnerable bridgehead in hostile territory. From there, without the water-road of the lake, the going would truly be rough.

THE PLOT THICKENS

Robert Rogers sloshed through the water and peered ahead, straining to see an end to the swamp. Clouds of mosquitoes filled the dead air, feasting on English faces and fore-arms, and the morass—no matter where the major looked—extended to the horizon, a great wet thicket of croaking, buzzing greenery. He hid his disappointment and forced his legs forward, ignoring the soaking chill that had been eating at his legs and feet for two days now.

Since leaving the shore of Missisquoi Bay on September 23, the rangers had rarely made a step without wading through at least a foot of brown water. They moved during the day now, from before sunup till after dusk, cutting boughs of fir trees at night to build makeshift rafts on which to sleep. The water world in which they lived was getting cold, a sharp reminder of autumn's approach, and the mosquitoes made tireless companions.

Although St. Francis, called Odanak by the Indians, lay northeast of them, Rogers was leading the party due east. His intention was to take a course that bowed signifi-cantly, forming the front of a great *D*, at the top of which waited their target. Although this added some twenty-five miles to their hike through hostile territory, it was vital if they were to have any chance of getting to St. Francis alive.

The reason for that lay in the inspiration for the mission itself. The previous August a party of British officers and Indians led by one Quinton Kennedy had attempt-ed to deliver orders from General Amherst to James Wolfe, commanding British forces on the St. Lawrence. Traveling without uniforms to disguise their intent, they had attempted to cross Canada but were captured on the Yamaska River by Abenakis hunt-ing out of St. Francis. After failing to bribe the Abenakis to let them go, they were turned over to the French authorities.

French General Montcalm, in a subsequent communication with Amherst, was pleased to inform his opposite that Kennedy and his fellow officers, though technically spies because they were out of uniform and therefore subject to hanging, would instead be treated like the gentlemen they were. The rest of the party, however, was clapped in irons. Amherst, as embarrassed at being bested by an opponent's chivalry as he was infuriated at having been caught sending men to skulk across enemy territory, fumed.

The incident gave birth to the St. Francis operation; Amherst, stung and vengeful, approached Rogers, who had been seeking approval to hit Odanak for years. Now, as the major led his men on that very operation, he was eager indeed to avoid the area around Yamaska where Kennedy had been caught—an area that lay directly on the path between Missisquoi Bay and St. Francis. The French would no doubt have increased their vigi-lance there. As a result of this decision, however, around one hundred miles had to be traversed before reaching Odanak. And in two days, they'd gone only eighteen miles—all of it through swamp.

The major uncorked a canteen and filled his mouth with rum, feeling its warmth go all the way down. There had to be an end to this godforsaken swamp. And he was going to find it.

The sound of heavy sloshing to the rear drew his attention and he turned to see what the commotion was about. Soon two figures made their way up the column. And when Rogers recognized them, his heart sank.

It was the two men, Mahicans, whom he had left to guard the boats and supplies at Missisquoi Bay. Rogers took another long draught of rum and prepared himself for the bad news he assumed was coming.

The Indians, breathless from catching up with the column, told Rogers what he desperately did not want to hear: A French force of about four hundred men had discovered the landing place on Missisquoi Bay. Before abandoning their post to the enemy, the Indians had holed the boats and destroyed the supplies. But the French were no doubt tracking them even now through the swamp, keen on discovering the raiders in their backyard.

The rangers now faced enemies in front of *and* behind them. And worse, the supplies intended to sustain them on the return journey, including food, ammunition, and extra clothing-as well as the boats with which to make that journey—were lost.

A SOLUTION TO MATCH THE PROBLEM

Somewhere in the waterlogged wastes east of Missisquoi Bay, Rogers and his officers conferred over their dire situation. There was always the option of turning on their pursuers and attempting to destroy them. But while the rangers were a relatively small force behind enemy lines, their foes could reinforce themselves almost at will. That seemed suicidal.

It soon became clear that most of the men were keen to accomplish their mission. They had come this far; they might as well finish what they'd come to do. Home was a long way away in any event. They might as well get there via St. Francis and victory.

There, amid the mosquitoes, the raw, bitten faces concealed an awareness of sorrow that lurked within. The decision they were making condemned some of them to death then and there. It remained only to be seen which ones would stagger back to New England when this murderous odyssey was finally over.

And the major was determined to allow as many of them to do that as was conceivably possible. Putting their heads together, he and his officers conjured a plan as daring as any in the annals of North America.

Lieutenant Andrew McMullen was given a mission of grave importance. Returning to Crown Point, he was to report the rangers' situation to Amherst, and then request that the general send provisions under guard to the junction of the Ammonoosuc, Wells, and Connecticut rivers, a well-known and conspicuous landmark around seventy miles from Crown Point as the crow flies. Rogers meant the great confluence to become an ersatz depot for his men, who, returning from St. Francis after a grueling march south, would reprovision themselves for the final sixty miles to Fort Number Four, the closest English settlement. It was a profoundly risky proposition, involving an overland retreat south from St. Francis through some two hundred miles of dangerous territory—all while being pursued by enemies hell-bent on avenging the fight at St. Francis.

And nobody knew whether Amherst would even get word, or be able to comply in time. Circumstances had certainly taken a desperate turn.

Lieutenant McMullen was sent on his way with five others as escort. And not a few of the men who saw him head back through the swamp mumbled a prayer to themselves.

A WOLF AMONG THE SHEEP

It was an hour before midnight on October 3, and the sky was clear and brilliant with stars. In the village of St. Francis, fires and dancing marked a wedding celebration. And Major Rogers, smiling and watchful, was there to see it all.

To those who thought him a curious sight, his replies to their inquiries were always in impeccable French, which he had spoken since childhood. But most took his presence in stride—after all, St. Francis was a well-known location along the St. Lawrence valley, accustomed to the presence of transient scouts or trappers. And if Robert Rogers was well known throughout New France and the villages of its Indian allies, his face was not. Having decided to reconnoiter the settlement upon reaching its outskirts, the major left his makeshift camp and did just that—by striding right into town, as was his wont. Brave to the point of foolhardy, he was always on the lookout for stories to boast about. And this was going to be a doozy.

Twenty days had passed since he and his men had first set out from Crown Point, and just over 142 of them remained. Not until that morning had they found a way out of the seemingly endless bog land. Their rations now exhausted, they emerged a gaunt and ragged troop, like ghouls from a swampy grave. From there, just a day's quick march to St. Francis, they forded a narrow stretch of the St. Francis River by forming a human chain through the five-foot current. Once across, they sped north and made camp just six miles outside of St. Francis. Then Rogers, accompanied by a few of his men, went to see the people he meant to slaughter.

It was not what he had expected to see. St. Francis, or Odanak, long an Abenaki settlement, had become a focus of Jesuit conversion efforts in the previous century, creating a town that now looked as European as it did Amerindian. French-style houses lined the main street, at the end of which stood a large white church with a handsome steeple.

The people, joyous in their wedding celebration that night, were in fact a composite of many different native peoples, refugees from the French and Indian Wars who had found a home there within the sheltering presence of the Society of Jesus. The language of the Abenaki, most numerous of the settlement's peoples, had become predominant.

But the Jesuits—teachers, confessors, and builders—had also been fomenters of war over the decades, using the hatred of English encroachment on lands farther south to generate a stream of reliable bush warriors to fight for France. The loyalty of St. Francis had become almost as legendary as the far-ranging, stealthy raids by its warriors. Both would now cost the town dearly.

ANGELS OF DEATH

At 2 a.m. Rogers reappeared among his men to report what he had seen, the mouthwatering aroma of fresh meat still in his nostrils. No time was wasted in the assembling of an assault. Within an hour, their lean and filthy ranks were assembled just outside of town.

The Indians among them, slick with animal grease, smeared what colors they had on their weather-beaten faces. Brits hailing from Scotland, New Jersey, and a dozen other exotic places straightened their headgear and dropped their packs, lightening the load for the melee to come. Leggings were tightened, muskets loaded, knives sharpened, and cartridges counted. And then the lot of them set off in the dark with the easy gait of coyotes.

The town upon which they descended was almost entirely undefended, and only partly because of the night's revelry. War with England had sent St. Francis's warriors to far-flung battlefields, especially near Quebec. The rest, ironically, were out helping the French look for Rogers and his men.

Per the major's orders, the rangers skulked into position at the entrances to the town's houses and waited for the signal from Rogers—a gunshot—to commence their destruction. Once started, however, the plan quickly degenerated into reckless butchery.

It is hard to know whether Rogers or any of his men recalled their general's injunction against targeting women and children. But in the emotionally charged maelstrom that morning, with so few young warriors to offer resistance, the corpses of scalped women and children soon proliferated. After so many hardships, Rogers's rangers were going to make this count.

Eventually the structures of St. Francis themselves were consigned to destruction, erupting in great gouts of flame. From the attics of many houses, where Abenakis had hidden themselves, the blood-curdling cries of the immolated carried over the town.

The Jesuits had long been a formidable presence among the Native Americans of Canada, and they succeeded in converting many of them to Catholicism.

The sun rose over a scene of smoking desolation. In the broad mud streets, old men, women, and a scattering of youth lay motionless, the blood from their corpses gathering in great pools. Overhead fluttered some of St. Francis's legacies: the scalps taken in numberless raids of old, their desiccated hair-banners flying away with the flames.

Rogers exerted control over his raiders, preparing them for a withdrawal before the smoke of their deeds brought retribution with the noonday sun. Wild-eyed, they had fallen on the town's plunder with slavering delight, including silver-girt tapestries and candleholders from the church, which had been ravaged and set to the torch. The men continued to sort the loot as the major interrogated survivors for any information on the enemy's whereabouts. He soon learned that many of the villagers had fled before the raid, warned by someone, probably one of Rogers's Indian rangers, that the English were coming. Those who remained—who now lay dead in the street—had done so either out of disbelief of the warning or from exhaustion after the previous night's revelry. It hardly mattered now, however. St. Francis was all but destroyed; the mission had been accomplished.

ACCORDING TO AT LEAST ONE ACCOUNT, THE MAJOR HAD EVEN SLAUGHTERED ONE OF THEIR CAPTIVES, A SQUAW, FOR CONSUMPTION.

Abenaki casualties remain contested to this day. Rogers's official report would claim around two hundred, while French accounts agree on thirty. What is known for sure is that the town was razed and that a sizeable proportion of those killed were women and children. The raiders departed that morning with a handful of captives. For all this, only one of the raiders who made it to St. Francis was killed.

The safety of Fort Number Four, however, was still two hundred miles away. And the French, already hot on their heels, would soon be fired up with vengeance.

TO CROSS A MAMMOTH WILDERNESS

Wan and sickly, draped in tatters, Major Rogers steadied himself by remaining in motion, one foot after the other. The Wells River, to his right, made a pleasant rush and gurgle that he had long since stopped hearing. Behind him staggered a clutch of skeletons in rags, silent and sunken-eyed. *This was going to be easy*, thought the major to himself. They were on the last leg-ahead waited the junction of the river with its two sisters, the Ammonoosuc and the Connecticut. *And there* ... he could not think of it without tearing up.

In his hunger-addled mind he reckoned the date to be October 20, seventeen days since setting out from the smoldering ruins of St. Francis. The men, those who hadn't stowed too much plunder, had filled their sacks with the village's corn before setting out into the wilds. But the corn hadn't gone far without beating or cooking, two activities that didn't make the fleeing raiders' "to do" list. By the time the column made it to Lake Memphremagog, seventy miles south of Odanak, they were staring hunger in the face. Already eight days into their journey, the men were still less than halfway home. Rogers made a bold decision.

By splitting the army up into smaller groups of various sizes, he hoped to better everyone's chances of survival. The odds of finding scarce game would be multiplied and the trail would scatter to throw off pursuers. Some made for Crown Point to the southwest, others kept on the trail ahead toward the supplies and Fort Number Four. Rogers continued south, toward the junction of the three rivers, where, he knew, relief waited from General Amherst. Most of the others fanned out around his group, coming up behind him and flanking him, all of them like streams flowing to the same pond.

Rogers came to a halt and turned around. The frail shapes coming up behind him owed almost everything to him, he knew. He had showed them which mushrooms to look for, which roots to boil, and how long to rest before heading out again, exhausted and dizzy with deprivation. Captain Amos Ogden, wounded from bullets at St. Francis, had ridden on the major's shoulders across rivers and up slopes. Thanks to Rogers, he was healing nicely, despite the lack of real sustenance. According to at least one account, the major had even slaughtered one of their captives, a squaw, for consumption. Over the nine days since departing the others near Lake Memphremagog, he had done all that was humanly possible to sustain their chances of going on—including, when all else failed, reminding them of the supplies that awaited them at the designated rendezvous point.

Now that succor lay just ahead, and Rogers tried to keep from thinking about it until he was actually upon it. He resumed his awkward gait, seeing now the great conjunction of the rivers. Soon, its pace quickening now from anticipation, the party reached the chosen place and saw a fire. Amherst had not let them down.

But no one was in sight. And though the spot had clearly seen a great deal of activity, it had been abandoned—recently.

Rogers could not fathom the scale of his own disappointment. Hearing gunshots from farther down the Connecticut, the men fired their muskets in response. But as the moments passed in agony, it became clear that nobody was coming back. The supplies were gone.

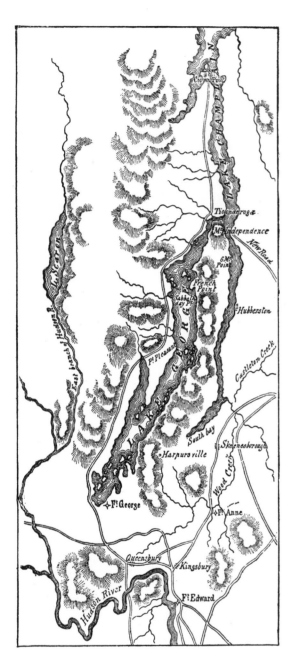

Lake Champlain was a dangerous place in colonial times as both the French and English—and their respective Indian allies—plied its waters.

FORT NUMBER FOUR

As devastated by the letdown on the Connecticut as his men were, Rogers seemed utterly defeated by it. For a week he tarried at the location before leaving his men and, with three others that included Captain Ogden, continued down the Connecticut with a promise to send help once he had reached the fort sixty miles distant. After stumbling into Fort Number Four on October 31, by all accounts nearly incapable of standing, the first thing he did was arrange for a canoe full of supplies to be sent back up the river to the men he had left behind.

The mishap at the junction of the three rivers owed more to dreadful misfortune than anything else. A party had in fact been sent with provisions to the rendezvous point from Number Four, only to wait for days without any sign of Rogers. They left just hours before his arrival. The desperate men's gunshots were interpreted as evidence of an enemy war band, and only hastened the expedition's return to the fort—a disaster not only for Rogers and the men in his group, but for all those who were aiming for the river junction.

From Lake Memphremagog onward, their going had been hellacious. Some of Rogers's men were ambushed by French and Indians, either killed outright or brought back to St. Francis for retribution. Most of those who never made it, however, succumbed to the enormous, unforgiving territory—almost all of which now lies in Vermont and New Hampshire—that seemed only to swallow them deeper with every step. They died of exposure or starvation after fortifying themselves against the advance of autumn with

The Old Soldier Fades Away

Life for Robert Rogers after the French and Indian War was anything but glorious. Having been forced, due to materiel shortages, to equip many of his men out of his own pocket, he emerged from the conflict a debtor. Like so many impecunious heroes before and since, he attempted to exploit his fame with a memoir, which he published in 1765 in England. Received there as a celebrity, Rogers had an audience with King George III, who appointed the ranger governor of Michilimackinac.

But America had become almost as hostile for Rogers as the banks of Lake George had been back in the 1750s. Sir Thomas Gage, now commander in chief of British forces in North America, dismissed Rogers as a dangerous yokel who owed his elevated station to a convenient friendship with Jeffery Amherst. While Governor Rogers sent parties of explorers after his dream of finding the Northwest Passage to the Pacific Ocean, Gage did everything he could to dredge up compromising information about his colorful subordinate. He seems to have found it: In 1767 Rogers was arrested for treason, charged with offering the territory of his governorship in Michigan to the French.

Whether there is any truth to this rather immense charge will probably never be known. But Rogers, who had become something of a royal favorite, escaped conviction in any case. Would that the rest of his days were as full of good fortune.

During the Revolution, Rogers, like many American-born Englishmen of the time, suffered an identity crisis and constantly toyed with the idea of serving the Patriot cause. But the only service he actually performed was on behalf of the crown, including participation in the capture of famed revolutionary Nathan Hale. An alcoholic and plagued with financial troubles, Rogers was a military has-been of the first order. After the war he retired to Britain, where he died, indebted and sickly, in 1795.

Overleaf: Sir Thomas Gage, who became commander in chief of British forces in America, dismissed Rogers as a dangerous yokel and sought to have him removed and discredited.

the most horrid of meals, from boiled cartridge boxes and leather belts to clusters of leaves and worse. Of the 140 or so men who set out from St. Francis, forty-nine were lost. The rest trickled in from the wilderness in November, both at Crown Point and at Number Four, bringing with them vague and dreadful tales of flight, hunger, barbarity, and cannibalism.

In a crucible of such searing force, it is hardly surprising that Rogers's name echoes down the ages as one of the progenitors of today's special forces. But more than anything, he stands as a symbol of the brutality that dominated the struggle to decide the fate of North America. In a place and time in which the sowing of fear through savage deeds could expand the borders of an empire, Major Rogers—for good or ill—excelled as few in the English-speaking world did.

The St. Francis raid itself stood out more as a daring act of viciousness than a great victory for British arms. Though it caused a stir along the St. Lawrence at a time when New France was pressed on all fronts, it hardly undermined Canadian military deployments for 1759 and 1760—hence the triumph of French forces in the Battle of Sainte-Foy, a forlorn attempt to retake Quebec before overwhelming British forces finally brought an end to the war. St. Francis lives on primarily as yet another incendiary moment between Amerindians and Europeans—a vision of America's bloody saga in microcosm.

chapter eighteen

British Victory in the French and Indian War Incites a Vast and Ugly Conflict

1763

It was June 2, 1763, and Ojibwa Indians outside Fort Michilimackinac thought it was a fine day for stickball. A forerunner of lacrosse, the game, also known as "toli," revolved around a leather ball, or *towa*, which players hurled with rackets at a tall pole to score points. As the players weaved around and slammed into each other to get at the ball, the English garrison stood about watching the full-contact affair with fascination. The stockade, built by the French, who surrendered it in the late Seven Years' War, looked out upon the broad blue strait connecting lakes Michigan and Huron, its front gate swung wide for traders and Indians to pass while the redcoats enjoyed the toli.

The action was constant and absorbing—almost anything was legal in this ancient pastime, and the soldiers loved to watch the Ojibwas grapple and trip in what some Indians called "war's little brother" for all its hard knocks. Presently, the ball made its way up to the front gate, the amused guards stepping aside to let the players chase after it, and the game continued apace inside the fort.

Suddenly the Ojibwas dispersed, running for every redcoat they could see and attacking with their long wooden rackets. Some soon had hatchets, obviously secreted in by unknown accomplices, and the butchery began in earnest. Slack-jawed soldiers were bayoneted with their own muskets, and soldiers on the wall were shot from behind, tumbling into the fort. The battle continued, but clearly the British had already lost. Many of them simply threw up their hands in surrender. Fifteen of them, almost half of the small garrison, were slaughtered.

Known to many as "war's little brother," lacrosse was a game shared by numerous Indian nations.

A WORLD TURNED UPSIDE DOWN

Without apparent provocation, Fort Michilimackinac had been captured by Indians the British were trying to consider new allies—a development that would have been disquieting all by itself. But what happened that day in far northern Michigan was hardly an isolated incident. In fact, virtually the whole frontier from the Great Lakes to the Ohio country was in violent chaos.

What had happened to bring about such a disaster? In a word, *victory*. Since the conquest of Montreal in 1760 by Jeffery Amherst, commander in chief of Anglo-American forces, the British were masters of North America. At long last, the French and Indian War was over. Seemingly overnight, the relationships that had endured throughout Canada and the *pays d'en haut*, or "high country" around the Great Lakes, was abolished.

Since the early seventeenth century, the French on the St. Lawrence had maintained close ties with the native peoples of those regions, cementing their loyalty over the generations by accepting native ways of life, offering generous and regular gifts, and constantly trading. The Indians had relied on French help to keep the expanding English agriculturalists off their lands. Now "Onontio," the French Father, was gone.

Filling the vacuum was the very power that France's Indian allies had been wary of for so long. And the British, far more interested in land and much more dismissive of native culture in general, made poor partners indeed. As the war was winding down, English promises to abandon the forts out west and leave native lands alone had helped convince many of France's Indian allies to lay down the hatchet or even switch sides.

But now that victory had been assured, the British seemed to have developed short-term memory loss, posting red-coated garrisons in nearly all of the far-flung forts that had been turned over to them. And unlike the French, the English cleared and settled the area around their forts, turning them into enclaves of European farmland that in turn attracted more settlers from the east.

Overseeing Britannia's moment of triumph during and after 1760 was Jeffery Amherst, who, by his very way of thinking, posed a direct threat to the health of his empire's new "friends." Contemptuous of Indians in general, Amherst forbade the venerable custom of gift giving, certain that it rewarded bad behavior rather than won the hearts of potential allies. And the sale of gunpowder to the Indians was drastically cut back. Looking at the vast, multicultured native presence beyond the mountains with bigoted oversimplification, he chose to deal with the Indians like a schoolmaster would his unruly children. It was a recipe for disaster.

THE FUTURE REJECTED

Some Indians found none of these ominous developments surprising. Already an old tradition by the end of the war, nativism sought to make a return to the way things were before the white man showed up with his rum, his firearms, his perfidious diplomacy, and his diseases. For nativists, turning back was the only way forward—and anyone who doubted that, they insisted, need only look around. The lying, expanding, red-coated menace in their midst was slowly destroying them.

The latest of the celebrated nativist prophets to emerge was Neolin, a western Delaware Indian of the Ohio country. By 1760 his radical vision espoused complete separation from the Europeans—from then on, he said, children must be reared in the old ways, from hunting with bow and arrow to rejecting the white man's cloth. But he did more than teach; he also prophesied. According to Neolin, the approach of a new and terrible war in the west would be preceded by the encroachment of whites on Indian lands, the precipitous decline of game populations, and other signs that soon proved all too true. His fellow Delawares took notice, as did other peoples.

The nativists ended up inspiring new dreams of Pan-Indian cooperation. Alarmed by the turn events had taken since the British victory, and incredulous of the negotiations being conducted across the Atlantic that may decide their fate, pro-French Indians believed that only the return of Onontio could save them from calamity. They found inspiration in Neolin's call to arms against the English, whose ways seemed entirely at odds with the way the French had run things. Indeed, one pro-French war leader in the coming struggle would give his name to a war that, though viewed by English eyes as a massive conspiracy, would in fact be something far less unified but just as formidable. His name was Pontiac.

Pontiac. His attack on Detroit was merely part of a war that spanned the entire frontier.

BLOODY RUN

It was 3:30 in the morning of July 31, 1763, and Pontiac peered from behind a tree to see whether the redcoats were coming. Scouts had sent word that a column was headed that way, and he had set an ambush. There would be blood that night.

Events had favored his cause for almost three months now. Indeed, he was getting used to victory. In the final days of April he had found his voice as never before, reaching huge audiences of his fellow Ottawa Indians as he preached the words of Neolin. His was a grand vision: that Potawatomies and Wyandots join with his Ottawa people to form a council of three nations that would topple the English in the central Great Lakes and beyond. Just ten miles away, the British garrison at Fort Detroit made a target too tempting to pass up.

Gathering a great host from all three nations, he had pounced on May 7 with a surprise attack that couldn't fail. But somebody had warned the English, probably another Indian. No matter. Pontiac besieged the fort with a tight cordon of warriors, waylaying all who approached the fort unawares. By the end of July, with some nine hundred braves under his leadership, Pontiac had taken scores of captives, both soldiers and civilians, and killed scores more. He had even captured boats on the Detroit River with their supplies, strengthening his camp even as the 125 redcoats under Major Henry Gladwin slowly starved within the fort.

Even better, his bold strike had sparked fire in the hearts of Indians right across the frontier. Fort Sandusky at the west end of Lake Erie, Fort St. Joseph in Michigan, and Fort Miami in the Indiana territory all fell to attacking Indians in May. The following month forts Ouiatenon, Michilimackinac, Edward Augustus, Venango, LeBoeuf, and Presque Isle were captured. Miamis and Kickapoos, Mascouten and Weas, Chippewa and Seneca, all sensed the arrival of a moment on the long border with the English. Messengers had raced from town to village, valley to shore, bringing the hopeful news of natives on the warpath. Pontiac couldn't help wondering as he scanned the ground ahead whether the Master of Life himself were directing this great, unprecedented drama.

Fort Detroit still defied his efforts to capture it. But a large relief convoy had reached the fort's anchorage, bringing soldiers—soldiers who, it seemed, now foolishly sought battle with Pontiac's men.

His own camp, some two miles from the fort, was clearly the target of the 250 redcoats who had marched out an hour ago. Although Pontiac needed to leave the majority of his warriors strung out along the perimeter to maintain the siege, he had more than enough to spare for an ambush. Behind him gurgled a creek, whose shallow, tree-lined banks hid several hundred of his best men. The creek, which flowed into the Detroit River off to the left, was known to the French as Parent River. Although Pontiac couldn't know it now as the British began to creep into view, it would soon be renamed Bloody Run.

Native Americans burn a schooner in the Detroit River during Pontiac's siege in this nineteenth-century hand-colored woodcut.

Major Henry Gladwin, commander of Detroit's garrison, meets with a party of Indian leaders headed by Pontiac.

Robert Rogers and his rangers, in fact, led the forward elements of the British column, scanning ahead and moving from brush to tree, maintaining cover as best they could. But Pontiac had positioned his men well; and the rangers were still oblivious to them when the redcoats started moving forward under Captain James Dalyell.

The darkness flashed with musketry as hundreds of war whoops announced disaster for the English, caught while crossing the creek. After several volleys, the Indians fell on their victims from all around, dealing grievous wounds to soldiers who still hadn't fired a shot. The column lurched backward almost as one, instinctively recoiling from the horror unfolding around it, and then tried to order itself for a counterattack. But Pontiac had caught the redcoats, and they knew it. The British made a fighting retreat back to Fort Detroit, returning after sunup with 120 fewer men than when they'd set out—one of whom was the captain.

Dalyell's head, in fact, would make an appearance in the coming days on the top of a stick in Pontiac's camp.

The Paxton Boys

In 1764 the governor of Pennsylvania, John Penn, approved an act by the colony's assembly to reinstate the bounty offered for the scalps of enemy Indians aged ten or older. Such was the state of hysteria and desperation in the midst of Pontiac's War. But plenty of British on the frontier didn't think such measures were enough, and simply took matters into their own hands.

Of these, the Paxton Boys were some of the most notorious. Naming themselves after the Scotch-Irish community on Paxton Creek, whence most of them hailed, these vigilantes were typical of groups who acted out of frustration with what they considered the inadequate prosecution of the war.

Convinced that even friendly Indians were covertly aiding war bands throughout Pennsylvania, they took violent initiatives based on an overtly racist agenda. In December 1763, they descended on the Christian Indians at Conestoga Creek, leaving twenty corpses in their wake. That same month, they forced the entrance of the jail in Lancaster to slaughter fourteen Conestogas being held in protective custody. Governor Penn issued warrants for the arrest of all those involved, but, ominously, the countryside remained mute as to their identities and whereabouts.

Indeed, the Boys' brazen acts had increased their popularity among the terrified populace, inspiring them to take on their boldest caper yet.

The following February the Paxton Boys, five hundred strong, headed east to Philadelphia with the express purpose of forcing the colonial government to their will. Met by an embassy of prominent Pennsylvanians that included Benjamin Franklin, they bluntly stated their intentions, which included the murder of all the Christian Indians then taking refuge within the capital. Fortunately for all parties involved, the vigilantes were talked out of it with assurances that nobody would be prosecuted for the murders already committed.

✦

SAVAGERY AT FORT PITT

Captain Simeon Ecuyer, commandant of Fort Pitt, had had a long summer. Built at the Ohio Forks, where it gave birth to Pittsburgh, his post was the strongest on the western frontier, with more than 250 soldiers and militiamen to defend it. But that hadn't made him feel any safer when, at the end of May, a war band of Mingos and Delawares showed up at a small settlement twenty-five miles away and burned it to the ground. On the day after that, two of his men were slaughtered at the fort's sawmill.

An officer of the Royal Americans, Ecuyer was smart enough to know that something was afoot in the Ohio country. Soon word had reached him that confirmed his worst fears. All the forts between his and Fort Niagara, between lakes Ontario and Erie, had been either destroyed or captured. Rumors of Detroit's siege raced through the valley. Throughout June parties of refugees streamed into Fort Pitt, crowding the structure and bringing smallpox. Nevertheless, the captain was convinced that he could hold out. The Indians finally showed up in great numbers and put the fort and its settlement under siege.

On June 24, two Delaware headmen had requested a parley. Surrounded by hundreds of hostile braves, Ecuyer was instructed to surrender all of Pittsburgh or face dreadful consequences. What he did next made history.

Confident that his numbers and remaining supplies would get him through until relief came, Ecuyer refused to surrender. He then disarmed the brooding Delawares with a formal presentation of gifts, including the ever-popular rum and a few blankets—which had been deliberately infected with smallpox from the hospital.

As August 4 dawned over the besieged fort, Ecuyer ascended the bastions and looked out, as he had done nearly every day since the cordon of Indians had severed his contact with the outside world, and thought about that fateful exchange weeks ago. Only that morning, something was different.

No signs of the siege were present. The Indians had left. Ecuyer, perplexed, considered the possibility that his injection of pox had taken a month to work its way through the warriors. Whatever the case, he was glad of the development, to say the least. Just yesterday, the Indian line had gotten into the outer defensive ditch itself, offering deadly fire to those British unlucky enough to be on the bastions.

Ecuyer's act of naked brutality, in fact, had probably not worked. At worst, it merely added to the smallpox that was already sweeping many of the Indian bands that were wreaking havoc with the British. The captain wouldn't know it for at least another day, but the besiegers of Fort Pitt had been drawn away to confront a British force trying to come to his relief.

Henry Bouquet negotiated peace with Amerindians toward the end of Pontiac's war.

TURNING POINT AT BUSHY RUN

Simeon Ecuyer wasn't the only officer willing to try severe measures to break the Indians. Colonel Henry Bouquet, a Swiss in British employ, claimed to be willing to "extirpate that vermin from a country they have forfeited, and with it all claim to the rights of humanity." Indeed, Bouquet was on his way to do just that by coming to the relief of Fort Pitt.

On August 5, he rode with his little army, now four hundred strong, and relished the opportunity to grapple with the hated savages who had made such a mockery of British security on the frontier. Just the previous day, he and his men had departed Fort Ligonier, near modern Ligonier, Pennsylvania, for the last forty miles to Pittsburgh. The operation had been a travesty from the start, a drama of mishaps that, taken together, put the vast dilemmas of the British empire in the wake of its great victory in bold relief.

To begin with, there had been the problem of finding soldiers. Although there were still plenty of them in North America, so many were laid up with tropical illnesses from the recent siege of Havana, Cuba, that Amherst's command looked more like a vast hospital than anything else. The intrepid and resourceful Bouquet scrounged up some 460 regulars and a complement of rangers, many of whom, though better than their dying fellows, were still sick from the Caribbean.

Things went from bad to worse once the column reached eastern Pennsylvania. With rumors of Indian attack sweeping through the panicked countryside like a winter gale, settlements had been depopulated, depriving Bouquet and his men of the support they needed along their supply route. By shedding groups of redcoats along the way to guard depots and secure his line of advance, he ended up with only four hundred left by the time he reached Ligonier. There he decided to leave his wagon train, replacing it with more than three hundred horses, their flanks heavy with bags of flour for the poor folks of Pittsburgh. By the afternoon of the 5th, making good time in the hilly backcountry, the force was within twenty-five miles of Fort Pitt near a creek called Bushy Run.

Bouquet worried about those last twenty-five miles, knowing that Indians would be trailing his column, if they weren't already. Looking at his watch, he saw it was just around one o'clock in the afternoon. His eyes then fell upon a hill that stood straight ahead. And there, to his horror, rose a throng of Indians, painted for war and yelling like devils. He was still trying to shout commands when the first volley came whizzing into his hapless redcoats.

Caught on exposed high ground that in turn was dominated by the rise, called Edge Hill, from which the ambushers now poured fire on them, the British deployed into a defensive posture, quickly realizing that they were nearly surrounded. Bouquet, forcing calm on his weakened men under the withering August sun, formed his unit into a perimeter with the animals and supplies in the center.

Although the Indians were probably outnumbered, their advantage in ground and cover soon took its toll. Hidden behind trees and fallen timbers on the crest, they maintained a terrifying tempo of aimed shots into the huddled, increasingly exasperated redcoats. By late afternoon the wounded had become numerous enough for Bouquet to order the construction of a defensive rampart out of the flour sacks, behind which the injured could be seen to. The British, physically and emotionally exhausted, began to sense the helplessness of their situation.

By sundown, the men were relieved for the cover of darkness. Moreover, Bouquet had been turning an idea over in his mind. And when the sun came up the following morning, he gave it a try.

Firing started in earnest with the coming of light, giving the redcoats a rude awakening. The colonel then set his plan in motion, sending two companies of light infantry streaming back to take shelter behind the breastwork of flour. Soon Bouquet saw what

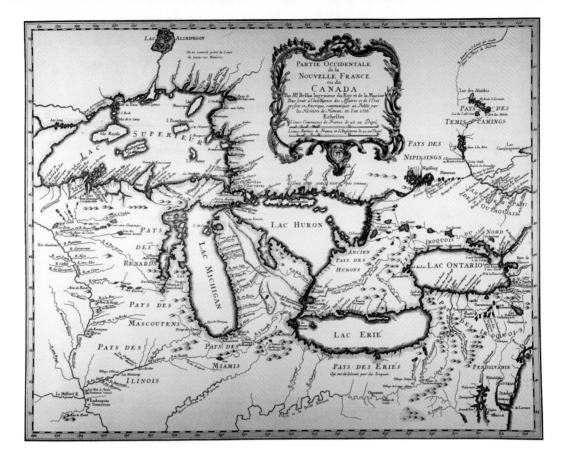

Map of the Great Lakes, 1755. In 1763, the British faced hostile Indians throughout the entire region.

he'd hoped would happen. The Indians, sensing a crumbling of the British line, charged into the redcoats to take advantage of the failing morale and finish them off.

But the men who had appeared to fall back to the breastwork had kept going into the covered ground beyond, and then swept around to outflank the oncoming Indians. Now, as the onslaught fell upon the main British position, those men opened up on the Indian attackers, sending a devastating volley into their exposed flank. As the Indians reeled in confusion, the flankers finished the chaos they'd started by charging with bayonets, sending the Indians fleeing back into the woods.

Colonel Bouquet had averted disaster, but not by much. Having lost a quarter of his strength, he was forced to destroy the flour and use the pack animals to carry the wounded. By the time the column filed into Fort Pitt three days later, they were in no position to do more than reinforce the garrison.

Nevertheless, the large force of Delawares, Shawnees, Mingos, Ottawas, and others who had put Pittsburgh under such a close siege had been dispersed, their powder stores running thinner after Bushy Run.

THE TIDE RECEDES

Not all of the raiders along the frontier, however, were experiencing such a dearth of supplies. Indeed, the Seneca, having broken with their pro-English brothers in the Iroquois League during Pontiac's War, found the bottleneck in the long, tenuous supply line that brought sustenance to Britain's western forts. And in September they struck the mother lode.

For all those supplies in Albany and Montreal destined for the western forts, a journey awaited that spanned Lake Ontario to the port of Little Niagara. From there, everything going west—*everything*—had to be portaged over a nine-mile trail along the rapids of the Niagara River to Lake Erie, where the trek to distant outposts commenced.

On September 14, 1763, a large band of Senecas with Chippewa and Ottawa allies hit the supply train along the most vulnerable section of the Niagara portage road, killing nearly all the teamsters and even routing two companies of nearby soldiers who came to chase them away. The raiders not only plundered the rich haul of food and ammunition but also rendered the road useless for a time, holding up the whole western supply system.

Although triumphs like this displayed the enormous range of Indian cooperation while simultaneously highlighting the fragility of their opponent's far-flung network of outposts, the high watermark of this "War of Indian Independence," as it has often been called, had already been reached. Raids against English settlements in Pennsylvania and Virginia continued at an alarming rate into 1764, but were mostly small in scale and aimed at vulnerable civilian communities where women and children captives could be taken. The British, by contrast, would make great strides in 1764—and they would do so through a change in strategy that would say much about the realities of America's interior.

DESPERATE MEASURES

Blamed for the unprecedented disaster of 1763, Amherst was replaced by Major General Thomas Gage. In 1764, Gage launched two armies into the mess that had become the British frontier. Colonel Henry Bouquet struck into the Ohio country in October from Fort Pitt with 1,500 regulars and provincials.

What ensued was a mirror image of the previous year's bloody chaos. Bouquet's column, well supplied and served by supply wagons, made a steady and deliberate thrust into the territory of hostile Delawares, Shawnees, and Mingos, encountering no resistance and filling the countryside with the dread of destruction. With so little powder left for a serious fight, the Indians of the Ohio country were turning away from their fire-breathing war leaders.

The second of Gage's two punitive expeditions met with less success. Roughly as large as Bouquet's, the column, led by Colonel John Bradstreet, was charged with subduing the heart of the pays d'en haut in the Great Lakes. But after reaching Detroit and dispatching men to garrison the outlying forts in the region that had been captured or abandoned during the Indian insurrection, Bradstreet held a peace conference with local Indians in which he destroyed a wampum belt sent by Pontiac, who could not attend. Wampum belts were sacrosanct under such circumstances, making Bradstreet's hatchet job a diplomatic faux pas of the first order.

Having disappointed the Indian headmen, he went on to disappoint his superiors by refusing to campaign down the Scioto River, in the heart of modern-day Ohio, for want of sufficient supplies. He ended up staggering back to Niagara in November, his reputation in tatters. Nevertheless, his mission had restored a kind of British presence in the Great Lakes region. Those Indians who wished to continue the fight—and there were increasingly fewer of them—fled farther into the interior toward the Mississippi.

WITH SO LITTLE POWDER LEFT FOR A SERIOUS FIGHT, THE INDIANS OF THE OHIO COUNTRY WERE TURNING AWAY FROM THEIR FIRE-BREATHING WAR LEADERS.

That these two military expeditions achieved some success owed a lot to another British effort that preceded both of them. Sir William Johnson, superintendent of Northern Indian Affairs, had been chomping at the bit under Amherst to open negotiations with the Indians, but Amherst had refused to treat with the Indians until they had been all but crushed through force. Once Gage took command, Johnson pressed the issue again and was granted permission. In July 1764, Johnson presided over a massive congregation of Indians from the pays d'en haut who were tired of war and willing, begrudgingly, to look upon Britannia as the new "Father" of American affairs.

Johnson's methods, however, marked a complete reversal of British policy. In addition to distributing thousands of pounds sterling worth of gifts to the attendees at Niagara, he promised a resumption of the liquor trade that had been halted under the uncompromising Amherst. The Niagara conference set the pattern for future negotiations. In exchange for a complete cessation of hostilities, the return of all white-skinned captives, severing of ties with those nations who remained hostile, and kind treatment of British traders, Bradstreet and Bouquet paved the way for the resumption of gunpowder sales and gift giving to ensure Amerindian goodwill.

In other words, the numerous Indian peoples who had taken up the hatchet against the British had won—though the British would never be another "Onontio," they had been compelled by force to acquiesce to demands that the Indians of the pays d'en haut and elsewhere had come to expect from their white "Father." But to Indians who had been fighting to rid their people of the white man's pervasive influence, the conclusion of hostilities had been a defeat, merely confirming native America's reliance on the eternally conniving European and his endless hunger for more land, wealth, and power.

As for Pontiac, the great Ottawa leader whose boldness had made him a legend, he had given up Detroit back in the autumn of 1763 for lack of progress. He spent the years after his Detroit gambit trying to leverage his notoriety into more influence, primarily as a peacemaker whose reputation could bring both Indians and whites to the bargaining table, but to little avail. In time he would be derided as a has-been who had brought down the wrath of the British empire.

That the long, bloody conflict that followed his impulsive move still bears his name seems strange, especially since no single leader or nation directed the great outbreak of violence. Rather, the seeds of discontent among so many peoples had born bloody fruit in 1763. The British, fighting in the French and Indian War for a way of life that could not exist in harmony with natives in the west, had kidded themselves into thinking that they could appropriate the relationships forged by the vanquished French.

The result had been dreadful. An estimated two thousand British settlers were killed or wounded, along with an indeterminate number of Amerindians. In 1763 and 1764, the peoples of the huge frontier had become divided inalterably into Europeans and Indians, devoid of inconvenient distinctions—British, provincial, Ojibwa, Shawnee, Delaware, Mingo, Ottawa—that got in the way of sanguinary goals. The long hardship of the Seven Years' War had made America thus, and the fight waged by both sides during Pontiac's War, from Michigan to Virginia, had been rife with atrocities.

In the end, the British, though forcing an end to the nativist attacks through conquest, were compelled to recognize their Indian neighbors not as subjects but as sovereign peoples—partners in the increasingly crowded American backcountry. But a barrier had been created between white and red that would never again be significantly bridged. As they had fought in Pontiac's War, so they would live from now on: separate, suspicious, and all but irreconcilable.

Select Bibliography

Anderson, Fred. *Crucible of War: The Seven Years' War and the Fate of Empire in British North America, 1754–1766*. New York: Alfred A. Knopf, 2000.

Baker, Raymond F. *A Campaign of Amateurs: The Siege of Louisbourg, 1745*. Ottawa, Canada: Department of Canadian Heritage, 1995.

Brumwell, Stephen. *White Devil: A True Story of War, Savagery, and Vengeance in Colonial America*. Cambridge, MA: Da Capo Press, 2006.

Cave, Alfred. *The Pequot War*. Amherst, MA: University of Massachusetts Press, 1996.

Chartrand, René. *French Fortresses in North America 1535–1763*. New York: Osprey Publishing, 2005.

Chartrand, René. *Ticonderoga 1758: Montcalm's Victory Against All Odds*. New York: Osprey Publishing, 2000.

Chet, Guy. *Conquering the American Wilderness: The Triumph of European Warfare in the Colonial Northeast*. Amherst, MA: University of Massachusetts Press, 2003.

Crane, Verner W. *The Southern Frontier, 1670–1732*. New York: W. W. Norton & Company, 1981.

DeForest, Louis Effingham. *Louisbourg Journals 1745*. New York: The Society of Colonial Wars in the State of New York, 1932.

Downey, Fairfax. *Louisbourg: Key to a Continent*. Englewood Cliffs, NJ: Prentice Hall, 1965.

Duncan, David Ewing. *Hernando de Soto: A Savage Quest in the Americas*. New York: Crown Publishing Group, 1995.

Favata, Martin A. *The Account: Álvar Núñez Cabeza de Vaca's Relación*. Translated by Jose B. Fernandez. Houston, TX: Arte Publico Press, University of Houston, 1993.

Findling, John E., and Frank W. Thackeray, eds. *Events That Changed America through the Seventeenth Century*. Westport, CT: Greenwood Press, 2000.

Haefeli, Evan, and Kevin Sweeney. *Captors and Captives: The 1704 French and Indian Raid on Deerfield*. Amherst, MA: University of Massachusetts Press, 2003.

Hawke, David Freeman. *Everyday Life in Early America*. New York: Harper & Row, 1988.

Hoxie, Frederick E. *Encyclopedia of North American Indians*. Boston: Houghton Mifflin, 1996.

Jennings, Francis. *The Ambiguous Iroquois Empire: The Covenant Chain Confederation of Indian Tribes with English Colonies*. New York: W. W. Norton, 1984.

Kamen, Henry. *Empire: How Spain Became a World Power, 1492–1763*. New York: HarperCollins, 2003.

Kayworth, Alfred E., and Raymond G. Potvin. *The Scalp Hunters: Abenaki Ambush at Lovewell Pond, 1725*. Wellesley, MA: Branden Books, 2002.

Konstam, Angus. *Historical Atlas of Exploration, 1492–1600*. New York: Facts on File, 2000.

LaPlante, Eve. *American Jezebel: The Uncommon Life of Anne Hutchinson, the Woman Who Defied the Puritans*. San Francisco: HarperSanFrancisco, 2004.

Lustig, Mary Lou. *The Imperial Executive in America: Sir Edmund Andros, 1637–1714*. Cranbury, New Jersey: Associated University Presses, 2002.

Lyon, Eugene. *The Enterprise of Florida: Pedro Menéndez de Avilés and the Spanish Conquest of 1565–1568*. Gainesville, FL: The University Press of Florida, 1976.

Malone, Patrick M. *The Skulking Way of War: Technology and Tactics among the New England Indians*. Plymouth, MA: Plimoth Plantation, 1991.

McLynn, Frank. *1759: The Year Britain Became Master of the World*. New York: Grove Press, 2004.

Milton, Giles. *Nathaniel's Nutmeg: The True and Incredible Adventures of the Spice Trader Who Changed the Course of History*. New York: Farrar, Straus and Giroux, 1999.

Moore, Christopher. *Louisbourg Portraits: Five Dramatic, True Tales of People Who Lived in an Eighteenth-Century Garrison Town*. Toronto: Macmillan Canada, 1982.

Morison, Samuel Eliot. *The European Discovery of America: The Northern Voyages*. New York: Oxford University Press, 1971.

Morison, Samuel Eliot. *The European Discovery of America: The Southern Voyages*. New York: Oxford University Press, 1974.

Oatis, Steven J. *A Colonial Complex: South Carolina's Frontiers in the Era of the Yamasee War, 1680–1730*. Lincoln, NE: University of Nebraska Press, 2004.

Oliphant, John. *Peace and War on the Anglo-Cherokee Frontier, 1756–63*. Baton Rouge, LA: Louisiana State University Press, 2001.

Philbrick, Nathaniel. *Mayflower: A Story of Courage, Community, and War*. New York: Viking, 2006.

Rawlyk, George A. *Yankees at Louisbourg: The Story of the First Siege, 1745*. Wreck Cove, Nova Scotia, Canada: Breton Books, 1999.

Salvucci, Claudio R., and Anthony P. Schiavo Jr., eds. *Iroquois Wars II: Extracts from the Jesuit Relations from 1650 to 1675*. Bristol, PA: Evolution Publishing, 2003.

Schneider, Paul. *Brutal Journey: The Epic Story of the First Crossing of North America*. New York: Henry Holt and Company, 2006.

Schultz, Eric B., and Michael Tougias. *King Philip's War: The History and Legacy of America's Forgotten Conflict*. Woodstock, VT: Countryman Press, 1999.

Shomette, Donald G., and Robert D. Haslach. *Raid on America: The Dutch Naval Campaign of 1672–1674*. Columbia, SC: University of South Carolina Press, 1988.

Shorto, Russell. *The Island at the Center of the World: The Epic Story of Dutch Manhattan and the Forgotten Colony That Shaped America*. New York: Doubleday, 2004.

Steele, Ian K. *Warpaths: Invasions of North America*. New York: Oxford University Press, 1994.

Washburn, Wilcomb E. *The Governor and the Rebel: A History of Bacon's Rebellion in Virginia*. Chapel Hill, NC: University of North Carolina Press, 1957.

Webb, Stephen Saunders. *1676: The End of American Independence*. New York: Alfred A. Knopf, 1984.

Weber, David J. *The Spanish Frontier in North America*. New Haven, CT: Yale University Press, 1992.

Winship, Michael P. *The Times and Trials of Anne Hutchinson: Puritans Divided*. Lawrence, KS: University Press of Kansas, 2005.

Zaboly, Gary. *American Colonial Ranger: The Northern Colonies, 1724–64*. New York: Osprey Publishing, 2004.

Art Credits

The pictures in this book are used with permission and courtesy of:

Alamy: p. 36, 52, 62, 65, 70, 93, 113, 120, 140, 149, 174, 202, 281, North Wind Picture Archives; p. 90-91, 116-117, 195, Stock Montage, Inc.; p. 135, Mary Evans Picture Gallery; p. 212-213, The Print Collector

Bridgeman Art Library International: p. 6, 38, 124-125, 146, 151, 155, 235 private collection; p. 14-15, Palacio Nacional, Mexico City, Mexico; p. 17, American Antiquarian Society, Worcester, MA, USA; p. 28, Museo Nacional de Historia, Mexico City, Mexico; p. 34, National Museum of Bogota, Colombia, Giraudon; p. 40, Service Historique de la Marine, Vincennes, France, Lauros / Giraudon; p. 43, 68, The Stapleton Collection; p. 66, 157, Massachusetts Historical Society, Boston, MA, USA; p. 78, 86-87, Bibliotheque Nationale, Paris, France, Lauros / Giraudon; p. 84, 197, 230, 280, Peter Newark American Pictures; p. 96, Collection of the New York Historical Society, USA; p. 99, 158, Philip Mould Ltd, London; p. 100, Museum of the City of New York, USA; p.108-109, Musee des Beaux-Arts, Angers, France, Giraudon; p. 145, Cadogan Gallery, London, UK; p. 163, The Crown Estate; p. 165, Florence Griswold Museum, Old Lyme, Connecticut, USA, Gift of the Hartford Steam Boiler Inspection & Insurance Co.; p. 214, Newberry Library, Chicago, Illinois, USA; p. 251, Archives Charmet; p. 259, Malcolm Innes Gallery, London, UK

Getty Images: p. 81, 111, 171, 181, Hulton Archive

The Granger Collection: p. 12, 18, 22, 75, 104-105, 133, 233, 249, 256, 287

Harper's Ferry Art Commission: p. 238-239

Library of Congress: p. 30, 61, 129, 130, 143, 189, 209, 262, 278, Library of Congress Prints and Photographs Division

National Park Service: p. 236

New York Public Library: p. 101, 220, 227, The Picture Collection of the New York Public Library

North Wind Picture Archives: p. 46, 49, 57, 58, 123, 126, 137, 186-187, 191, 223, 265, 271, 282, 285

ABOUT THE AUTHOR

CORMAC O'BRIEN is the author of several books, including *Secret Lives of the U.S. Presidents* and *Secret Lives of the Civil War*. He has been a featured speaker at the Jimmy Carter Presidential Library and a guest on many radio programs, including three appearances on National Public Radio. He lives in New Jersey with his wife and daughter.

ACKNOWLEDGMENTS

Many thanks go out to Fair Winds Press publisher Will Kiester, who was gracious enough to receive the idea for this book with enthusiasm. I would also like to thank Cara Connors, whose wisdom and inexhaustible patience (not to mention editing skills) have been greatly appreciated. And to Lauren Beck goes my eternal gratitude for too many things to mention.

Index